A Lady of Lunenburg

Nova Scotia 1752

Other books by Laurel Pardy

Life on a Carousel

A Lady of Lunenburg

Nova Scotia 1752

The Cauldron That Shaped a Nation and Tempered a Woman's Spirit

Laurel Pardy

ISBN: 978-1-4269-2874-1 (sc)
ISBN: 978-1-4269-3052-2 (e-b)

Our mission is to efficiently provide the world's finest, most comprehensive book publishing service, enabling every author to experience success. To find out how to publish your book, your way, and have it available worldwide, visit us online at www.trafford.com

Trafford rev. 03/22/2010

www.trafford.com

North America & international
toll-free: 1 888 232 4444 (USA & Canada)
phone: 250 383 6864 ♦ fax: 812 355 4082

In Memoriam

Harry Robbins Balsor

1919–1944

My brother Harry was born in Centreville, Kings County, Nova Scotia. He spent his summers at the family cottage at Hall's Harbour on the Bay of Fundy, reveling in the freedom and joy of being young.

By 1939 freedom, joy, and youth were forfeit to the reality of the Second World War. He volunteered for the fight and joined the West Nova Scotia Regiment. In 1944, after nearly two years waiting in England, he went with the West Novies to fight the Axis armies in the final push up through Italy.

He made it as far as Ravenna. Harry was killed in action on December 15, 1944, less than a month before he was due to ship home. He is buried with his comrades in the Commonwealth War Graves Cemetery in Ravenna.

To those who made the journey;
To those who made the journey possible;
To those who journeyed but never reached their goal.

Author's Fore Words

In September, 1752, Anna Elisabeth Baltzer, her husband and five children arrived in Halifax. They were among the Protestant German and Swiss families recruited by the London Board of Trade and Plantations to settle in the English colony of Nova Scotia. Nova Scotia was the gateway for timber and fur from the northern forests of the new world, commodities coveted by both England and France. These settlers were desirable because, being Protestant, they were loyal to England, a perfect counterbalance to the Nova Scotia population of French Catholic Acadians and their Indian allies who were continually harassing their English overlords. The settlers were moved a day's sail west of Halifax, to the vacated Acadian-Mi'kmaq village of Merlegueche that the English renamed Lunenburg.

Within three years England and France were at war over the domination of North American trade, the Protestants and Catholics were at odds over which religion would shape the new country and both the Acadians and the Indians were paying the price. The Protestant settlers kept neutral, worked hard and built new lives. Two and a half centuries later Lunenburg continues to flourish, and the German and French heritage still flavours much of the region.

Elisabeth is my grandmother, five generations removed. Her travails are deduction and speculation based on the few facts available. Records are scarce. Many have been lost or were never made, but shadows of a trail exist for those who believe that the apple doesn't fall far from the tree.

I admire these courageous, hardy ancestors who cleared land, survived cold and drought, fought disease and deprivation, built houses and planted gardens and made a life in a new land. Especially, I feel a debt to the women, many of whom are unknown, who laboured as hard as the men. Women who married for survival, who took up the burden whenever their partner faltered, who fed a family for the winter on a slaughtered pig and a barrel of sauerkraut, who sewed rags into quilts, who bore children and watched them die and who died themselves. Women who "did their duty" because it was theirs to do.

This story is written with respect for their courage and tenacity. It is based on fact where possible, inspired guesses where not. It is a story. It may be true. If it isn't, it could have been.

Ottawa, 2009

Rosenthal, Hesse,
The Germanies
October 13, 1751

"*Lieber Gott, dear God, enough rain already. How I long for the sun,*" thought Elisabeth as a gust of wind flicked the corners of her apron. A drop of rain plopped carelessly on her cheek. She pulled her cloak closer around her shoulders and continued to walk resolutely along the cobbled lane with her market basket in one hand and the fluttering ends of her bonnet ribbons in the other. The worrisome thoughts that churned in her mind did not show in her steps.

A whirl of grit and garbage twisted into the air, causing something to flutter to the ground. It was a sheet of parchment, wet and stained from the recent rain, but clearly covered with writing. Intrigued, she picked it up. Hearing footsteps approaching, she quickly folded it and shoved it under the onions in her market basket.

"Guten Tag, Frau Baltzer," a deep voice intoned from behind her. "I see you have taken one of Herr Dick's handbills."

She recognized the over-familiar tone of Herr Metzger, the new pastor recently come to the Lutheran church where she and her family worshipped. Herr Metzger had moved to Rosenthal from Bracht where many of her relatives lived and he assumed a familiarity that was not warranted. She took a small step back but greeted him politely.

"Good day to you, Herr Metzger. What is this handbill you speak of? I do not know of it," she answered, hoping uselessly to prevent further prying questions.

"The parchment you just hid among your onions is a recruiting handbill. An agent of the British government, John Dick by name, was in the alehouse last evening regaling us with stories of the free land, homesteads and the riches to be made in the colonies across the Atlantic. Apparently the English are seeking Protestant families to go as settlers to the New World, to one of the English colonies called Nova Scotia. He tacked this handbill to the door; the wind must have blown it loose."

"I do not understand. Recruiting? For the Hessian regiments? The mercenary soldiers?"

She pretended misunderstanding. Elisabeth could read the Bible and do her husband's accounts, but she had not had time to decipher more than a few words on the parchment. Her curiosity had been aroused; she wanted to peruse it more carefully, in privacy.

"No, no. Not recruiting for soldiers, for settlers, for people to go and start farms and businesses in their colony. To move there and establish permanent homes. To live there."

"I was not hiding it," she clarified. "It is an unlikely thing to find in the street; I was merely curious."

"Perhaps I could tack it up again," Herr Metzger offered, holding out his hand. His fingers were long and thin, rather like the rest of him. They seemed to hover over her basket like a spider dangling at the end of a web.

She opened her mouth to agree.

Startled, she heard herself say, "No." Recovering, she added, "I will take it to Stoffel, he can take it back this evening." After his supper, her husband liked to take a cup of ale with the other merchants who also lived along the Marktstrasse, the market street.

The Lutheran pastor raised his unruly eyebrows at her.

"So, you and Herr Baltzer would consider following in the footsteps of those who left for the American colonies," he said, referring to the German emigrants from the Palatinate who went to the American colonies earlier in the century.

"Oh, no, we are most settled here," she said. "Please excuse me, I must be getting home, there is the meal to get." She stepped firmly around him. He had a habit of slightly blocking your way and standing too close. "Good day to you, Herr Metzger."

Elisabeth continued along the winding alley, passing the open window of the baker's shop with its fragrant fresh bread and the tiny cubicle of the cripple who mended boots. The familiar smells brought no comfort as her mind wrestled with newly sprung thoughts, thoughts that held tantalizing possibilities, tantalizing solutions to her growing anxieties.

The roughly cobbled street was narrow; its centre gutter dotted with garbage, horse droppings and worse. The village of Rosenthal was a small market centre in a rolling valley divided by a lazy little river and surrounded by deeply wooded hills. Some of the streets were so narrow that old women could sit on opposing balconies and gossip with each other while old men dozed in the doorways until it was time to go to the alehouse.

Elisabeth was a sturdy woman who held herself erect, her feet neatly and firmly carrying her on her way. Her heavy wool cloak was dark grey, unadorned save for a hammered silver clasp. Her black boots were leather, designed for durability rather than for fashion, but softened with beeswax so that they fit comfortably. The cuffs of her green wool gloves, embroidered with coloured silk threads, were her only display of vanity. Underneath her cloak, she wore a dark blue skirt and jacket with a white apron and neck shawl. A black hat covered her thick braid of slightly graying blond hair sedately coiled on top of her head and held with bone pins. Her eyes reflected the colour of the sky and missed very little. She looked like the respectable wife she was. Only the square chin and strong jaw warned people that she might not be as pliable as one would wish in a woman.

Her husband was a respected butcher, working for his Uncle Konrad for more than thirteen years. They were not wealthy, but her Stoffel was a skilled merchant and they had money enough for their needs. She considered herself fortunate.

"—but I wonder. Do I trust that it will continue?"

She was no longer certain that her family's future was secure. Uncle Konrad had recently married a widow much younger than he, and was already strutting like a rooster at her growing belly. If Gisela carried a boy, he would become the heir because Uncle Konrad had no other children, his first wife having died in childbirth along with the child some thirty years ago. What with the increasing taxes, the continuous wars that surged back and forth across the Germanies, and the Hessians—thoughts of her sons being called up into the mercenary regiments chilled her blood. It was very possible that she and Stoffel could end up with nothing for their years of work. Their future looked less secure with every month that passed. First she must think and then she would talk with Stoffel.

It lacked only an hour of suppertime when she reached home. The house was narrow, but deep, with a second floor and a garden at the back. The only entrance was through the butchery which ran the full width of the dwelling. Meat was displayed on the Schirn, a narrow table with high sides that sat out in the street. In the hot weather, chunks of ice could be bought at a price and kept in the bottom of the table. The smell of the blood mingled with the savory smell of the herbs and dried sausages. Sawdust covered the floor.

She, Stoffel and their two youngest daughters shared the one bedroom off the main room behind the butchery which also served as the kitchen and sitting room for both families. Her oldest daughter had a sleeping bench here while her two sons slept in the storeroom. Uncle Konrad and his wife now occupied the two rooms upstairs.

"Imagine," she said to herself, "two rooms for only two people. What nonsense."

For reasons she didn't want to explore, she hid John Dick's handbill inside her bodice before hastily tying on her working apron and covering her braid with a house cap.

Elisabeth began preparations for their Wednesday meal of sauerkraut, Fleischwurst and potatoes by chopping onions at one end of the sturdy table that filled most of the room. Today they were having fresh sausage; there would be enough of the dried ones in the winter. There was a soup simmering in the iron kettle hanging on the hook in the hearth. Gisela must have started it. Elisabeth said a prayer of thanks, pleased at the woman's unusual show of helpfulness. Her happy mood dimmed as Gisela herself made her way into the kitchen and demanded petulantly to know what Elisabeth was doing.

"What I always do on Wednesday, preparing the sauerkraut and sausage for our meal," she answered. Before she could stop it, an uncharitable thought entered her mind. "Why can't she simply enter a room like other people instead of making such a drama of it, one hand to her head and the other supporting her belly? She is not the first woman to have a baby."

"*God, forgive me,*" she thought automatically.

Having babies was something Elisabeth knew about, having had seven herself, as well as having delivered several hundred since learning midwife and healer skills at her mother's side.

"*God, help me to be patient. It is her first child,*" she added silently.

"What are you muttering about now," demanded Gisela querulously. "You are always muttering to yourself. It's annoying."

"I'm sorry if it annoys you. I was just thinking to myself. I was unaware I was doing it out loud."

"Well, think quietly. I have a headache."

Talking to God was a habit of Elisabeth's. Words of thanks, prayers of blessing, requests for guidance and tales of the day were all sent heavenward. She believed that God watched over his children and, for her part, it was a duty to keep Him informed so that He could guide her wisely. If one were patient, his wisdom would finally be understood.

She was sure Reverend Herr Metzger would not approve of her bothering God so often, but she long ago had learned to ignore that particular prick of conscience. She was not sure Stoffel approved but he didn't say anything.

Gisela resumed her complaining.

"We don't want it. It is too fatty and too spicy. It will upset my husband's stomach." She went to the hearth and lifted the cover on the iron kettle. "I made some soup for us. You can bring it to us upstairs. And some black bread."

"There is only enough bread for breakfast," the older woman reminded her, thinking to herself about all the wood wasted in making soup for only two people. "And Uncle Konrad and Stoffel like to discuss the day's business in the evening, over their supper."

"My husband is not your uncle; it is a courtesy by your marriage to Stoffel. You should call him Herr Baltzer," Gisela said, her mouth pursing into a pucker which reminded Elisabeth of a pig's snout. "Anyway, now that he will have a child, we have important things to talk over privately. Plans for our future." Then she smiled slyly and, gently stroking her protruding belly, cast a sideways glance at Elisabeth, repeated, "About the future of Konrad and me and our baby."

Elisabeth methodically chopped an onion into little squares. Then she said, "If Uncle wishes to eat soup upstairs, you may carry up the tray yourself. If Uncle wishes to eat sauerkraut and sausage with the family, it will be served in the kitchen as usual."

"*Father in Heaven,*" she entreated God, "*forgive my uncharitable thoughts, but I cannot always find the good in her, she is lazy and selfish. She is turning Uncle's head. What am I to do?*"

In the pre-dawn darkness, Elisabeth slid out from under the warm quilts, careful not to wake her sleeping husband. The wind was making the old courtyard gate creak on its hinges. The rain had stopped, but rivulets still dripped from the roof into the puncheon that collected the rainwater for washing. When she listened intently, she could hear the shop sign swinging on its iron hooks over the display table in the street.

She put her hand to her bodice; the parchment was still there. Eva, her youngest daughter stirred on her cot and moaned in her dreams. Elisabeth settled her with a stroke of her hand and tucked in her bedcovers. Quietly, she inched up the latch, opened the door and entered the kitchen.

Silently closing the door behind her, she snuggled her shawl around her shoulders. With her hand she stroked the fine warm wool; it had been woven by her mother as a wedding present and was still good despite twenty years of wear. Her mother was a weaver of such quality that her cloth commanded top prices. She had woven the blankets that covered their bed and the fine wool cloth from which Elisabeth made Stoffel's winter shirts. Her own loom sat in the corner of the kitchen. On it was a length of flax cloth waiting a day when the sun shone brightly enough for her to see, and a spare hour in which to work.

"I should be making bread," she thought as she lit the oil lamp with a glowing taper from the banked grate. "There is not enough left for the nine of us to break our fast."

After a moment she decided on barley cakes and sweet syrup, maybe some sausage. She could do those quickly on a griddle iron in the hearth. Carefully, so as not to wake Maria, she laid out the supplies she needed to prepare breakfast and then sat down at the wooden table. She had not risen to make bread, but to think.

For Elisabeth, thinking meant discussing her problems with God. This helped her to order her thoughts and see more clearly what she should do. Her mother had taught her not to bother God with too many requests, to decide carefully ahead of time exactly what it was you needed from Him and then ask. However, He didn't seem to mind if she discussed it with Him first, before she prayed for his help.

She spread the carefully folded handbill on the table. Placing the lantern so the dim light fell on the writing, she folded her hands on it.

In the yellow glow of the oil lamp, the words were difficult to decipher, "... passage from Rotterdam in exchange for... family men with wife and children... 300 acres of land... tools... materials and utensils for husbandman... trees for lumber... garden lots... Halifax in the colony of Nova Scotia."

The parchment was stained with the mud of the street and the rings of the ale cups. One corner was torn off the wrinkled handbill.

"A match for my hands," she thought ruefully as she used them to smooth the tattered parchment.

The lantern revealed two wide square hands with strong fingers and short nails. The knuckles were slightly swollen and the skin marked with the signs of cooking, washing, chopping, dyeing, sewing and tending her herb garden. One nail had split as she was making supper and she had torn it off roughly, too busy to take time to smooth it. She rubbed at the first finger of her left hand where nicks from the chopping knife had made it permanently rough. It was stained with juice from the beetroots she had preserved in vinegar yesterday. She was always surprised at the coarseness of her hands and smiled at her own vanity.

Her hand fell to her stomach, soft and rounded under her chemise, sagging a little from bearing seven children. Automatically, she said a short blessing for the two that lay in the churchyard.

"A woman of forty years should not expect to have the hands of a maid," she reprimanded herself, "nor the waist of a virgin."

Aware she was avoiding the main reason for her early rising, she laid her problem before God.

"O, Heavenly Father," she prayed. "It is Anna Elisabeth, your servant. Thank You for what You have given me, for my husband Stoffel, for our warm house, our healthy children."

She always remembered to be grateful for her blessings. Her gratitude was real; there were many women who weren't as blessed as she.

"What had seemed clear and sure is now uncertain. If Uncle Konrad has an heir, Stoffel will have to start his own business again; this is not the time. War and taxes have seen to that."

Surely God understood the concerns of a mother's heart that wanted her daughters to marry well, her sons to be prosperous, and her grandchildren to be many. Elisabeth was not unduly superstitious, but it did not do to ignore any signs that God sent one's way and, so, she came to the heart of her present worry.

"Father in Heaven, did You put the wind in the air and cause the handbill to fly in my face? Not any scrap of parchment, that particular one. You know my worries. Are You trying to tell me we should give up our home, our family and sail to the New World? Are You warning me that our future here is uncertain? Please, dear Lord, what should I do?"

God never answered quickly, sometimes it took years to understand his intent. However, there was some urgency this time, as people wanting to go as settlers to Nova Scotia had to notify Herr Dick before the end of the year, three months away.

"Dear Lord, I will trust in your guidance and wisdom. Amen."

Trust in God and work hard. She decided to talk with Stoffel.

Overnight the rain stopped and the sun shone for the first time in over a week. At breakfast, Elisabeth said to Stoffel, "I've been thinking—"

"Oh, no," he answered, grabbing for the money purse that lay under his shirt. "Every time you start thinking, I become a poor man. What is it this time? A new baby to join our table?" He smiled to show he was jesting.

"No, not another baby. Not today. Perhaps we could talk after our mid-day meal?"

"Ja, we will talk after the mid-day meal, instead of resting," he agreed.

True to his word, Stoffel joined his wife in their room after lunch. He closed the door. It was the only way to have privacy in a small house.

Maria, who was in the kitchen teaching her sister, Gertrud, to twist wool into yarn on a drop spindle, heard her father exclaim, "Leave our home?" followed by his feet hitting the floor as he jumped up from his chair. She heard her mother hush him and nothing more. She knew better than to eavesdrop.

Stoffel ran his hands through his thinning hair. "I confess that I have had some of these thoughts myself; it is possible that an heir of his own could change Uncle Konrad's mind and our expectations—but to leave our home. For the colonies! They are full of savages that would cut off our scalps as quickly as I skin a rabbit. Some of father's relatives went to the American colonies and we never heard of them again."

"You have relatives in America?"

"Ja, but not close ones. I don't even know their names."

He resumed his seat and she knelt at his feet in silence.

"We might starve to death. We might die on the ship before we even get there," he said.

"The English soldiers will protect us from the Indian savages and give us provisions until we can feed ourselves. God will watch over us on the voyage."

He leaned forward and kissed the top of her head. "If we survive, God will have plenty of help from you, my dearest wife."

HM *Sally*,
Mid-Atlantic
August 1, 1752

Elisabeth's hands grip the ship's rail as she draws fresh air into her lungs. It is the first time in two weeks she has been allowed on deck. She is thin with lack of food and exhausted from lack of sleep. For the first time in her life, she feels that God has deserted her.

She hates the *Sally* and the claustrophobic hold to which they are confined; she hates the ceaseless movement, the snap of the canvas and the moaning of the wooden hull. Above all, she hates the sea. She hates the sea for it capriciousness, for being too still, or too violent; she hates the sea for taking her away from her home and causing her so much pain. Above all, she hates the sea for rendering her healing skills useless, for rendering her useless.

"*God, help me. I don't know what to do. Everything I know is useless,*" she whispers into the wind. "*So many of us are dying.*"

Even the ship's captain is dead and they are sailing on under the first mate. It isn't the sailors' fault; they suffer as badly as the passengers. The first mate has allowed her on deck only to see to the burying of two more little bodies, children who had died in the night from water fever, from too much sickness in the air, from too many night buckets spilled onto the boards.

"*Vater im Himmel, look down at your servants and take pity on them. We are suffering horribly, and dying needlessly. Take pity on us, please.*" Remembering her own good fortune she adds a prayer of gratitude. "*Thank You for looking after my little family amid all the suffering. Thank You for my patient Stoffel; for the lives of my sons, Christof and Peter; for the health of my daughters, Maria, Gertrud and Eva. Thank You for my own continued survival. For that I am grateful.*"

She turns from the rail in response to the gesture of a sailor sent to return her below deck.

"*Gott helf uns!*" she cries to the world at large
"Amen. May God help us all," the sailor answers.

1

HALIFAX WINTER

September, 1752–November, 1752

Elisabeth pulls the quilt over her ears and holds her head in her hands, partly to stifle the moans and cries from the other people on the beach, partly to quell the nausea threatening to engulf her. The hard stones hurt her legs, yet she cannot move. She is finally off the pitiless ship, but the rocky beach mimics the heave and roll of the waves and, even with her eyes closed, the horizon tilts with sickening rhythm.

The screech of the gulls and the endless slap of the waves mingle with the shouts of men and soldiers, soldiers who wave rifles and sticks at her and shout at her in English, a language she does not understand. For two weeks she has stared at this shore with desire and longing, willing anything to be off the stinking ship. Now she feels they have merely left one hell for another.

Nova Scotia. Destination of hope and promise. Where is the English welcome? Had they not come at their request? Where is the fertile farmland? The fields and pastures? The City of Halifax is part frontier town, part military camp. The town is a chaotic maze of buildings and streets; the waterfront is a muddle of docks and warehouses which sprawl at the foot of a forested hillside crowned with a brick and stone fort. A palisade of rounded timber marches across the headland. All else is dark forest and rocky shore shrouded in roiling fog. She fears these rocks and trees and the ceaseless ocean will dog her steps until the end of her days.

"Mama, I feel sick," whimpers her youngest daughter.

"Shhh, Evie. Close your eyes, it will stop soon."

Elisabeth lays her daughter's head on her lap and strokes her hair.

"It will stop soon," she repeats.

She feels her younger children cluster closely around her; Eva is five, Gertrud is nine, and Peter, older, but also nine. Her oldest daughter, Maria, 13, and her older son, Christof, 15, sit beside their father. They had been aboard their ship, the *Sally*, for nearly 17 weeks, 119 days of incessant rocking in stifling darkness permeated with the smell of urine, feces, vomit and unwashed bodies. Forty of the 258 settlers would remain forever in the ocean behind them, tossed overboard when their souls fled their bodies.

"What have we done? Give me strength, O Lord," she prays weakly.

In a few minutes, or an hour, she hears a voice shouting nearby. It grows more peremptory. As she lifts her head and gingerly opens her eyes, she sees a man pushing at her husband's shoulder and gesturing at the woods behind them.

"Leave him. He is tired. Was sagen Sie?" she calls out. "What are you saying?"

Stoffel had made the whole voyage without falling ill, but three days ago, within a hundred yards of the shore, he developed a flux and refused to eat or drink any of the remaining foul water from the ship's barrels. When the soldiers had brought some fresh water aboard he accepted a cup, but still could not eat bread.

The man looks blankly at her, not understanding her German words. He points at the water and then at the woods, gesturing vigourously for them to move. Elisabeth looks and finally understands. The water is coming closer on its daily cycle of rise and fall.

"Ja, ja," she answers. "Wir stehen auf, we're getting up."

"Christof," she calls to her son, "help your father into the woods. Peter," she turns to her younger son, "sit on the trunks while Maria and I find a place for us to shelter. Christof will come back and help you carry them."

The two trunks they had been allowed to bring aboard ship contain everything they own. How many times had she packed and repacked them? Ten? Twenty? Her Stoffel had wanted to bring his butcher tools, certain he would be able to set up shop again and build a business as he had at home. And his father's woodsman's axe and smoothing adze. She had wanted her pots and skillets, her platters and her jars of herbs, her loom.

"No need," the recruiter's agent had assured them. "Everything you need will be provided when you arrive. Tools, seeds, lumber. See, here in the handbill, 'will provide all the necessities for the husbandman....'"

The German translation was awkward but that was what it said. Elisabeth had read and reread it many times. Stoffel believed that the agent spoke truly and so must she. In the end, they had brought only a cleaver, a few of his best knives, the finest axe, one cooking kettle and an open iron skillet, a pewter platter, tin plates for the voyage and a few linen bags of flax and buckwheat seed. Elisabeth had included some seeds of healing herbs wrapped in linen and oiled silk, a handful of savory herbs for cooking and dried simples for healing—dill and sage and caraway, feverfew and heal-all.

She had also packed thick woolen cloth, thread and needles for vests and cloaks, a pair of carding brushes and her drop spindle. She had taken out her soft leather house shoes and replaced them with extra vials of her homely simples. The trunks also included their Sunday clothes and newly quilted winter petticoats for the girls and vests for the men. They had rolled all their bedding into bundles, donned all except their Sunday clothes and pulled their heaviest shoes on their feet.

Aboard ship they had longed to get away from each other for a time, tempers had grown short and they became sick of the smell of each other. Now they are afraid to be separated. She looks back at Peter. He is sitting on his father's trunk with his feet on hers; he never takes his eyes off her. She feels anxious; he looks so small and forlorn amid the scattered groups of immigrants. She gives him an encouraging smile.

As soon as they reach the edge of the trees, she stops and sends Christof back.

"We will rest for a minute, go and fetch Peter."

She sits so that Stoffel can lean against her.

"Stoffel," she says in encouragement, "we are here. Soon we will begin our new life. We are all here while so many did not make it. Tonight we will thank God."

As they wait for Peter and Christof to arrive with the trunks, she watches a man pace slowly past with a leather bound trunk on his shoulder and disappear into the trees. Four young girls and a weeping woman follow him. One of the girls is helping the woman and dragging a wooden trunk by its leather straps; the others have smaller canvas sacks with handles and are lamenting among themselves. She does not recognize them; they must be from the other ship, the *Gale*. The *Sally* had sailed from Rotterdam two weeks ahead of the *Gale* but the two ships had arrived within minutes of each other. She hears one of the girls call out, "Catherine." The girl helping the woman looks up but does not smile.

That night, Elisabeth forgets to pray.

For the next five days, Elisabeth and her family huddle under a canvas shelter a few hundred feet from the beach. Nobody is warm but those in the middle are warmer than those at the edges. She sees no sign of any preparations for shelter, cooking or relieving themselves.

Twice a day, the English soldiers give them pease gruel and ship's bread to eat along with a mug of vinegar and water to wash it down. The men who are able to stand are divided into work gangs and sent to cut trees for poles and timber. They receive an extra meal of boiled salt meat and potatoes on the job. Stoffel is feeling better and this morning went into the woods with Christof and the other men.

She is dozing when she hears Stoffel's voice calling to her.

"Elisabeth, come, your house is ready. Come, you must move."

They are still weak and the walk over the hill seems endless. Finally, she sees a cluster of long sheds on a hillside some distance from the main harbour. They have canvas sidewalls and wood slab roofs. Inside, they have been divided into cubicles, one per family. Stoffel and Christof go back to working and leave Elisabeth to cope with the settling in. She looks about for someone familiar and finds Trudl Berghaus, a young farmer's wife who also had been aboard the *Sally;* she puts their bedrolls and trunks in the adjacent empty space. Trudl is sitting on her trunk rocking her young daughter. She looks up, half smiles.

"Hier sind wir," she says to Elisabeth.

Elisabeth tries to smile encouragingly. "Here we are indeed." she thinks as she and the children sit down on their trunks and look at each other. "And where would that be, I wonder?"

The older children, Maria and Peter, go out to explore their surroundings. Gertrud sits on a bedroll and begins telling Evie a story. Elisabeth looks around and takes stock. Their space is near the middle of two face-to-face rows stretching along a centre aisle. The floor is trampled earth littered with evergreen twigs and bits of woody branches; the inside walls are canvas and barely six feet high, the door a canvas flap. The outside walls reach to the roof making the space dark and foreboding. There is no sleeping bench nor table nor stool. The space is about eight feet by eight feet, small but twice the size of their shipboard quarters and with room to stand up. She looks up at the roof. Here and there the sky peeps through the roughly sawn timber. She looks up over their space. No sky. Good, no sky, no rain will pour in on them.

She can hear a woman weeping nearby and wonders if it is the weeping woman from the first day on the beach.

Trudl Berghaus scratches on the canvas and comes in. She looks around.

"You will have all your space to yourselves," she says. "We have to share ours; a young widow and her son are coming in with us."

"I'm sorry," replies Elisabeth, "however, it will be better than the ship, at least it doesn't move and we'll be able to walk in the fresh air. Now that the ground has stopped heaving under my feet, I welcome the open sky."

Trudl agrees.

They are interrupted by Maria who hurries in, breathless with news.

"A Captain Zouberbuhler is asking for all the women to come to the 'mess tent'. I think he means the cooking shelter. He says he has important information we must hear. He speaks German, so I could understand him."

She leads them to another canvas and wood structure. Inside are six fire pits with iron grates and eight tables. On one of the tables stands a small soldierly looking man in dark clothes and leather boots. His hands are clasped behind his back while he waits quietly for everyone's attention. Finally, he straightens and starts to speak.

"Guten Tag. Bonjour," he greets them. "Good afternoon. I am Captain Zouberbuhler."

Although most of the settlers are German speaking, a number are from Switzerland and speak French. Aboard the *Sally*, a quarter of the families had been French-speaking Swiss from Montbéliard. As a young girl, Elisabeth had learned French from an itinerant musician who stayed with her family over several winters. Her father had called him a rascal but her mother had loved his music. She had forgotten much during the intervening years; however, it is slowly coming back to her.

"I speak English, German and French. I, or another translator, will come here every day before the evening meal, to tell you what will happen the next day."

A babble of questions breaks out among the settler women, causing him to throw up his hands and command them to silence.

"Patience, be quiet, wait until I give you the information, it will answer most of your questions. Firstly," he holds up a finger, "cooking. This is where you will cook your meals and only here, in the mess tent. There will be no fires in the barracks, they are for sleeping. The soldiers will bring a portion of firewood in the morning and you may collect fallen wood from the forest."

A large woman in front shouts a question at him.

"Yes," he tells them, "you can eat in your own quarters but you must cook only in this place, and keep it clean."

Elisabeth agrees with him, keeping clean is important. As she looks around she can see that some of the women and children already look dirty and unkempt, potential sources of sickness and lice. One of the little girls catches her attention and Elisabeth's heart goes out to her; her face is marked with scabs, her cheeks streaked with tear tracks, her nose crusted and unwiped.

"Secondly, food," continues Captain Zouberbuhler. "You will be victualled every Wednesday in the morning. For today, the food will be cooked and brought here at three o'clock. Tomorrow, you will be checked against the ships' passenger lists and assigned your ration portions. The victuals are only to supplement your own food which you can buy in the market."

"What is he saying?" asks Trudl not understanding his translation. "What on Wednesday?"

"I think it is an English military word, I think he means food rations, provisions. He says we should buy our food in the market."

Trudl gasps, "We have no money for that!"

"Nor we," agrees Elisabeth.

They turn their attention back to Captain Zouberbuhler. "When you go to the marketplace, stay out of the way of the soldiers. And stay away from the fort, the men there are busy."

He marks off the points with his fingers.

"Thirdly, latrines. The latrines are in the woods." With his hand he points downhill at the end of the line of tents. "The latrines for the men are farthest from the tents. The closer ones are for the women and children." He steps briskly down from the table, ignoring the babble of voices and questions and walks from the tent to his waiting horse.

"Oh, Elisabeth, what will we do? We did not expect to have to buy our own food. We were promised rations until we have our own harvest. I am already hungry," says Trudl.

"I have some cold pease and bread left from last evening," replies Elisabeth. "Let's start a fire in one of these new hearths and feed the children, and ourselves. The men will have to persuade the English to abide by their promises, else we will starve before we harvest our crops."

Later in the afternoon, Stoffel and Christof return with armloads of evergreen boughs and straw to pile up for a bed. They have also found a few boards. Elisabeth lays them between the two trunks. They can eat at a table tonight.

The following day, Elisabeth is one of the first to arrive for the distribution of food rations. Several of the fires are already going, their small flames a welcome sight in the chill of the morning. A small voice behind her wishes her a good morning. She turns to greet the person and recognizes one of the four girls from the family who accompanied the weeping woman from the beach on the landing day.

"Good morning. How are you faring? Is your mother better? She was weeping when I saw her last."

"We are doing as well as others," the girl answers, "but she is not my mother; she is my mistress. My name is Catherine."

"I am glad to meet you, Catherine. I am Frau Baltzer, Elisabeth."

Catherine wears no shawl against the damp October cold. Elisabeth fingers the clasp on her own wool cape and is glad she insisted on her own girls wearing their wool capes onto the *Sally*. They had wanted to leave them behind, complaining of the burden and discomfort of wearing several layers of clothing at once. At various times they had slept in, on or under all of their clothes.

"I work for Herr Bernhard Herman, his wife is Margarete. She is not well. She was already frail and the voyage took the last of her strength. I hear you have some healing skills and I wonder if I could ask your advice for her."

7

"I have no special skills, only home remedies, but I will help you if I can," Elisabeth replies. "In these conditions it is not easy to either prevent or cure illness."

"The mistress is so weak she seldom rises from her bed, she coughs and struggles for breath. The master brought some syrup of horehound to ease her chest but it does not soothe her. She is weaker every day."

"The horehound should do her some good if she can rest and stay warm. If she has been sick a long time, it may not be enough. A physician might prescribe laudanum but I have none. Does she eat?"

"She lies on sheepskins, under several quilts, but still she shivers. I try to feed her pease gruel but she is not interested and turns away."

"After so many weeks, even the healthy are tired of pease gruel. If Herr Herman has some coins, perhaps he could buy marrowbones from the market. Now that we will have cooking fires, you could make some broth. It might strengthen her," suggests Elisabeth. "She may have lost heart after coming so far and being worse off than she was at home," she adds in a somber tone.

"Yes, you may be right, she still weeps. These conditions are not what we expected. Thank you for the suggestion about the broth. I will tell Herr Herman what you advise," answers the girl.

Elisabeth watches her walk away. She is a tall girl, a hand span more than five feet, thin and awkward with dark brown hair and dark eyes under straight brows. Her right leg appears to be shorter than the left and she wears a shoe with a thick sole on it. It looks heavy and painful.

"That cannot make her work any easier," Elisabeth thinks with a stab of pity.

Conversation among the women stops as two soldiers unload barrels of salt meat and canvas sacks of dried peas from hand-drawn carts while Captain Zouberbuhler sets out his ledgers and quills. Elisabeth can see no fresh vegetables, no cabbages nor onions to vary the routine of salt meat and ship's biscuit.

Elisabeth eyes the barrels of ship's biscuit. They are fist-sized lumps of flour and water dried hard that have to be soaked overnight and then boiled. When soft, they absorb the flavour of the salt meat or the molasses poured over it. She has even become accustomed to the sight of the weevils that infest it. It fills the belly. She sighs and straightens her shoulders; at least with a large family she will receive almost enough rations to keep them all fed.

She is entitled to full rations for three adults and four half rations in accordance with the ages of her children. At fifteen, her son Christof is expected to do the work of a man and receives rations as an adult. For a week this gives her 25 pounds of hard bread, 15 pounds of salt meat, 10 pounds of cured pork, 5 pints of dried pease, one and a quarter pints of vinegar, two and a half pints of molasses and the same of rum.

In response to her questions, Captain Zouberbuhler promises to acquire potatoes, cabbages and some turnip, if he can arrange it.

"Governor Hopson is hard pressed to feed his soldiers let alone 500 additional settlers. Remember, these rations must last the whole week," he admonishes them. "You must buy extras in the marketplace."

Elisabeth's lips tighten; she has no desire to spend her little hoard of coins on anything except the establishment of her new home. Neither will Stoffel. The promise had been to feed the settlers until they were able to feed themselves from their own animals and crops. The money Stoffel receives for his labours is all taken back to pay off his debt for their passage; there are no coins to spare.

Maria and Peter arrive to help her carry the rations. Peter has scrounged a used sailor's hammock with torn grommets and they use this to carry their rations. It is the same torn piece of canvas which covers the evergreen boughs beneath their bedrolls.

Elisabeth hangs the bags of dried bread and peas from the broken limbs on one of the rough poles which support the roof. The barrels and jugs go in a corner. Zouberbuhler had expected them to bring their own containers and she was fortunate to have been early enough in line that he still had a few jugs and barrels to give out. Their pound and a quarter of butter rests on a wood shingle. She sets it carefully on the lid of a trunk. Slowly, as though with a will of its own, it leans to one side and slips mindlessly onto the ground. She stares at her precious luxury now stuck with spruce needles, twigs and dots of earth. Against her will, her eyes lose focus and her throat closes against breath or speech. She has an overwhelming desire to be alone.

"Maria, Peter, take your sisters outside," she says in a low voice. "Dinner will be ready in two hours."

The children obey her order, something in her voice telling them that this is not a moment to protest her wishes.

She draws the canvas flap closed behind them, leaving herself alone for the first time in months. Her lungs feel starved for air; her breath comes in gasps, tears stream down her cheeks. Slumping to her knees, she rests her head on the trunk, her knees resting near the fallen butter. The sheer folly of their decision to leave all they know for the utterly unknown engulfs her. What will become of them?

"Lieber Gott, help me, help me, help me."

Unable even to pray, she pulls her shawl over her head and rocks herself as she would a child. She imagines her father arms comforting her as he did when she was a child, her mother's soft touch and reassuring hands smoothing away her girlish tears and her strong Stoffel holding her in his embrace. Gradually her breathing evens and her eyes clear. Stoffel is still her rock; each is firm in the knowledge that they can depend on the other. Elisabeth drives any lingering doubts from her mind. Together they can master this new world; together they will not only survive, but thrive. She rises, rubbing her knees where they have been pressing against the ground. Carefully, she slides the shingle under the butter and removes as many of the twigs as she can. This is not the moment to think of the future, first she must confront the present.

"Some things I can do; some I cannot. I will do what I can, and leave the rest to God."

It is already October, she must accept that they will be here until next spring at least; it is too late to settle on the land this year. She looks at the pile of brush on which they sleep and pushes aside memories of the thick eiderdown mattress and bedcovers they had sold for next to nothing. If they are to avoid illness she must find a way to keep them warmer, and to keep them fed and clothed for, she counts on her fingers, seven months at least, maybe eight. It is time to open the trunks.

Elisabeth slips her hand through a slit in the side of her outer skirt. Under her long skirt she wears two petticoats, one of quilted wool for warmth, the other of unbleached linen. Her long sleeved shirtwaist and bodice are also of unbleached linen. Under these, her pockets hang from a stout thong tied around her waist. The larger one contains a handkerchief, a vial of smelling salts, the keys to their trunks, a few brass pfennigs and her father's small folding pipe knife; the other is smaller and within its lining is sewn the few gold and silver coins she hoards against emergencies, against the time when Stoffel's coins have to go for other purchases, purchases for their farm.

She withdraws an iron key from the larger pocket and kneels in front of her trunk. From it, she removes her iron kettle oven and her covered skillet, a hefty chopping knife and a wooden stirring paddle. Time to stop making do with the tin pots they used on the voyage. Her hands linger on the small wooden box tucked into a corner. She strokes it gently. The tiny key for it stays in her pocket but for a moment she remembers the keepsakes it is guarding: a locket of hair, a brooch, a spray of dried edelweiss. This is not the time for dwelling on the past.

Elisabeth takes a careful portion of the rations to the cooking tent. There are women around most of the hearths but she sees a place near an older woman.

"Guten Tag," she greets her.

The woman smiles. "Bonjour Madame," she replies. "s'il vous plaît, il y a de l'éspace ici, près de moi," she says, gesturing to her side and moving her pot along the edge of the fire.

Elisabeth realizes she is one of the Montbéliard women from Switzerland. "Merci. I am Frau Baltzer, Elisabeth. Did I not see you on board the *Sally?*"

"Oui, I am Mme. Boutellier, Françoise, widow of Georges. I recognize you from the ship. How did you fare on the voyage?"

Elisabeth remembers Georges, an older man accompanied by grown sons. She is sorry he did not survive the journey.

"We all endured, thank God," she tells her.

"You are fortunate. I lost four children, two grandchildren, a daughter-in-law and my husband; only five of us are left. Perhaps it was ill fortune to start with thirteen souls; it is an unlucky number.

Elisabeth is unprepared to hear a tale of such calamity delivered in a flat and emotionless voice. There is no expression on the woman's face; it is as though she has been wrung out and left to dry, like a rag in the sun. She does not know what to reply to this story of misfortune so says simply, "I am sorry to hear such sad news."

The woman slowly picks up her pot.

"We had such hopes, such dreams." She looks at Elisabeth. "Now I feel nothing, not even sorrow."

Hearing of such loss makes Elisabeth ashamed of her own fears. Slowly, she cracks several handfuls of dried peas between two rocks and drops them into the water in her pot along with a few small pieces of cured pork and seven portions of ship's biscuit. Supper is started. At the end she will add a splash of vinegar for flavour and health. She sits on a piece of log, watching her iron kettle slowly come to a bubble, and counts her blessings.

"Elisabeth."

Trudl's voice claims her attention. She is coming into the cooking tent with an unfamiliar woman and a young man.

"Elisabeth," she says, "I would like you to meet Frau Appolonia Graff and her son, Christian. They will be sharing our quarters for the winter. They arrived on the *Gale*."

The women nod and smile at each other, the young man bows. He is a tall person, already showing that he will be a brawny man in contrast to his mother who is tiny in every way. She is short with small features and prim lips; he has a broad nose and a ready smile. The mother's eyes are pale blue, the son's are hazel; however, they share the same direct look from under straight brows. Elisabeth takes to the young man immediately. His open friendly face is in contrast to the somber dress and Calvinist demeanor of the woman. Elisabeth is minded to watch her frank and ready tongue.

"I am most pleased to meet you," she says to the woman. She smiles at Christian. "You are about the age of my son, Christof. You will meet him when the men return from work this afternoon."

"I would like to go and work with the men, too," he replies. "Perhaps I can go tomorrow morning," he says, looking at his mother.

His mother draws in a breath and compresses her lips.

"The debt for our passage was forgiven on the death of my late husband. There is no need for him to work," she explains to Elisabeth.

"He might enjoy being with the men and the other boys instead of the women and children," Elisabeth hears herself point out before she can seal her lips. So much for discretion.

Thankfully, Maria comes into the cook tent just then and she must leave to feed the other children.

"*Lord, forgive my hasty tongue and teach me patience*," Elisabeth asks God on the way back. "*Again*," she adds.

That evening Stoffel accompanies her when she goes out to the latrine. When Elisabeth lowers the canvas behind her, she feels familiar arms go around her shoulders and a rough beard brush her neck.

"Wife, it has been a long time, I miss our bed," her husband says in her ear. "Let us go into the woods a ways, I have need of you."

Controlling her breath, she replies demurely, "And I you, husband."

Privacy aboard ship had been impossible; there were no walls between the berths so that the air, such as it was, could circulate. Sharing the intimacies of marriage with family was one thing but with strangers another. Never shy in accepting her Stoffel's advances, she allows herself to curve into his arm and moves into the shadows with him.

November arrives with wind and snow. Elisabeth, Trudl Berghaus and Frau Graff sit around a table in the cooking tent, waiting for their turn at the fire. Christian Graff and Elisabeth's son, Christof, have become fast companions, going out to work with the men and talking endlessly around the cooking fires after supper. They are both cheerful young men, always willing to lend a helping hand to carry a heavy pot for someone and liked by many of the women, if not by the men, who have daughters. Marriageable young girls outnumber the available young men and the speculative eyes of mothers are quick to pick out likely candidates.

Appolonia Graff is worried. As a widow, she will not receive any land or support to set up a home. She admits to the other women, "My hope is that they will allot land to Christian even though he is only 15 years old."

"He is doing the work of a man, he should receive a land grant," responds Elisabeth. "Have you considered remarrying? A wise marriage can have advantages. There are many single men or widowers who are anxious to take a wife before we are settled into our homes."

"It will happen according to God's will," replies Appolonia primly.

"God's will sometimes needs our cooperation and help," replies Elisabeth frankly, hearing the unhappiness in her neighbour's voice. "I do not mean to offend you, and I am truly sorry for your trouble, but there is no room for sentiment in this wilderness. Besides, the choice will be better now than later."

Trudl gives a strangled chuckle.

"Elisabeth, you say the most outrageous things." With an eye on Appolonia's tightened lips, she changes the conversation. "I want to tell you about a disturbing meeting I had this morning."

"What happened?" asks Elisabeth.

"With whom?" Appolonia questions.

"A woman from the *Gale* came up to me while I was returning from the latrines. She asked me if I knew you, Elisabeth. When I said 'yes', she asked me if you had any herbs which would take away a pregnancy already begun."

"What?" exclaims Elisabeth. So many children had already died. Why would someone seek another loss?

Appolonia gasps in horror. "She would kill her child?" she asks.

"I told her I didn't know, but that I was sure you'd never give out such a medicine," Trudl says to Elisabeth.

"I should hope not," expostulates Appolonia.

"There are such herbs, but I don't deal with them, they're dangerous and often kill the mother as well. Do you think she's expecting a child?" Elisabeth asks Trudl, her healer's instincts on the alert.

"I think so. She looks as though she is quite advanced. She sounded desperate and very afraid. Anyway, her name is Thérèse and I advised her to talk with you. I don't think she will though."

Looking up, Trudl changes her mind. "Oh, there she is, the one with the black shawl. Appolonia, you and I should leave; perhaps she'll speak with Elisabeth."

As the two leave, the woman in the black shawl approaches Elisabeth apprehensively. Her shawl is wrapped over her head and hides her figure, the hand holding it closed is small and the fingernails are ringed with grime.

"Are you Frau Baltzer?" When Elisabeth nods, she says, "I'm Thérèse, Thérèse Kuche. I need your help. I'm at my wits end, or I would not ask such a thing."

As Elisabeth draws her away from the other women where they can speak more freely, she can see the swollen belly of advanced pregnancy.

"My friend tells me you're expecting a child, one that you do not welcome."

Thérèse nods her head and admits that it is so.

"When do you expect the birth?"

"Soon, I don't know the day, but soon."

In a sympathetic voice Elisabeth tells her, "My dear child, even if I had such a medicine or knowledge, I would not dispense it and, in any case, it's much too late now. This baby will come, you will have this baby. Soon, I think."

For all her care and concern, Elisabeth never coats the truth as she sees it, feeling that the sick do better when they face reality.

The young woman hides her face in her shawl and bows her head.

"Do you have other children? What does your husband say?" asks Elisabeth gently.

"He's dead, along with our baby daughter. Another man took me in but he doesn't want this child. He claims he can't be sure that it's his."

"Oh, what a tangle," thinks Elisabeth. There is no easy solution to this and it is well out of her power to help this woman. "I'm so sorry," she tells her. "I'm only a mid-wife; I have no means to change what has happened to you. I can help you deliver your child and tell you how to care for it, but I can't make you a maid again."

"Then I have no hope," she says and turns away.

"Talk with me a while, please," begs Elisabeth. "We must trust in God's grace, even under these circumstances. Many women here have children and no husband. They are making new families with other husbands, so can you. It is not like the homeland, we have to make our way here as best we can. Will the man not love this child when he sees it?"

The woman smiles faintly.

"I do not want another husband. There is no love for me in this life, not even God's. This baby should not be born."

"This baby will be born, soon by the look of you. It will need a mother and a father. You will have to do what you must to provide for it. An unwed mother, or a young widow, has little choice except for marriage, hopefully, to a good man."

"Thank you. At least you have been honest."

She turns away. Elisabeth watches her walk slowly out of the tent. Thérèse' bent shoulders and bowed head remain in her mind's eye. Although she appeared at first to be a mature woman, Elisabeth realizes she is very young. If the child is due very soon, it may be her dead husband's. If so, why would she not want it? She sighs deeply. She has no answer. There are those who find courage and those who lose it in the face of desperation. The look in the girl's eyes haunts Elisabeth the rest of the day. She hates the feeling of helplessness and failure, hates the apprehension that tinges her last memory of the woman.

That evening as usual Elisabeth and her family go to bed with the setting sun, all seven in a row on the canvas covered boughs, huddled together for warmth under their capes, bed covers and quilts. Stoffel guards one end and Christof the other. The boys sleep head to toe, their cold feet tucked into their brother's armpits. Next come Gertrud and Evie with their arms around each other. Maria lies head to toe with her mother who sleeps side by side with her husband.

Elisabeth closes her eyes, folds her hands under the covers and silently addresses God as she does every night.

"Holy Father, this is Anna Elisabeth. Thank You for taking care of us. We are truly blessed to have arrived alive and, with your help, suffered no more than we could bear. Others have endured so much more than we, I am grateful. Forgive me today's loss of faith; I know You will take care of us.

"Please, bless my sons, Christof and Peter, and my daughters, Maria, Gertrud and Eva. Forgive them if they stray and sometimes forget your commandments. They are good children. Bless and protect my husband for he is a good man and mindful of your ways. Take care of my angel babies, Katarina and Heinrich, who are in heaven with You. And, Lord, please, look after Thérèse this night," she adds. *"Amen."*

2

THE BITTER TIME

December, 1752–June 8, 1753

The hum of chatter is louder than usual in the cooking tent the next morning. Elisabeth asks one of the women what the excitement is about.

"Nein, not excitement, distress." the woman tells her. "We are talking about the young woman who hung herself in the night. From a tree, in the woods nearby."

"Oh, no," cries Elisabeth, the anguished image of Thérèse' face flooding her mind. She starts to rush toward the exit but is stopped by Trudl and Maria.

"No, don't go out there. There is nothing you can do; it is the woman from yesterday," Trudl tells her. "The one who spoke with you about her baby."

Stunned at the confirmation of her worst fears, Elisabeth sits on a bench and covers her face with her hands.

"It is not your fault, Mama," says Maria. "Trudl told me about her, you could not help her. Mama, there was nothing you could do. It is not your fault." She puts her arms around her mother while Trudl sits close in sympathy.

"I know. I just wish I could have done something, said the right thing to give her courage."

"It was too late for that; she made her own choices, Mama. You cannot save the world."

Elisabeth feels Trudl shift and allow another woman to sit down beside her.

"Frau Baltzer, ma chère Elisabeth," a soft voice addresses her gently. "Do not grieve. She had no more will to live, her heart was dead and she desired her body to follow it. But she allowed her son to live. See?"

Elisabeth looks up. It is Françoise Boutellier, the woman whose tale of loss had moved her the day before. In her arms she holds a tiny bundle.

"I want to show you a miracle," she tells Elisabeth, holding a blanket wrapped bundle so she can see it. "Out of the sorrow has come a new life, a symbol of hope and faith in the future. One life to replace those I lost." She looks up, "I call him Thérèse Alexandre. He will be welcome and nourished among those of my family who remain." She looks at Elisabeth with pleading eyes and smiles. In her arms lies a newborn baby boy. "There is no need to report him to the English, no need for him to go to the orphanage. Nous sommes d'accord, n'est-ce pas?"

Elisabeth opens her mouth to ask questions but the woman shakes her head.

"Non, non. Do not question the acts of God, He works in his own way. I was his instrument to save this life in the night, but I could not save two."

Elisabeth is washing the faces of her younger daughters against their wishes. The water is warm, but she is thorough and they start to squirm.

"Mama?" The pinched face of her youngest daughter, Evie, looks at her soberly. "Did God forget to have a birthday for Jesus this year?"

Gertrud hurriedly hushes her sister. Elisabeth looks at them in shock, the wash rag momentarily stilled. Had she forgotten Christmas?

"I'm sure it is not time yet. We can't have been here that long."

"It is in three more days," Gertrud tells her softly.

The days are passing in a blur of misery and struggle. The march of Sundays that separate the weeks have begun to run together. Taken aback at the passage of time, she reassures Evie that God has not forgotten. She smiles at her daughters.

"It may be a little Christmas this year, meine Lieblinge, but the birth of the Christ child will not be forgotten. We will spend a special day together."

After several hours of mental debate, she makes a decision. Today is as important as the future. Leaving the younger children in Maria's care, she sets out for the marketplace. Prudently, she notes the gnarled oak which marks the entrance to her path; she has never ventured this far into the town before. When she comes to a row of small shops and stalls, she slows and starts to look over the merchandise. In her pocket she has one of her hoarded silver coins, a small one, marked for emergencies. She reckons this an emergency. She will have to barter skillfully in order to buy even small gifts and food for her family's Christmas celebration.

In one shop she hears a man speaking German with his companion. Looking at him decorously from the edges of her eyes she sees a middle aged man, robust, clean, his clothes well tended. Not from the tent settlement then. The shopkeeper speaks to him in English. Unperturbed the man replies in English. Emboldened by the pressure of her errand, Elisabeth contrives to arrive at the door when he does, enabling a conversation.

After apologies and courtesies, she asks him, "I don't recognize you from among the settlers. Which ship did you sail on?"

He smiles and shakes his head. "I come from the American Colonies, not from Germany, although my parents did."

His eyes are friendly but she sees something in them that might be pity. Does she look that poor, that in need?

"Are you seeking something in particular? Can I direct you to a good shop perhaps?" he asks her politely.

She is suddenly conscious of how she must look to him: disheveled, hungry, even dirty. Embarrassment floods her face with red. She stiffens her back and raises her chin.

"I am in search of food and small gifts with which to celebrate Christmas. This has been a difficult year, my children and husband deserve a bit of festivity after the church service."

"You are very thoughtful. Let me help your plans by directing you to an honest shop."

He leads her along the street to a long narrow shop which appears to have collected all the bits and pieces no other merchant could sell. Bins and boxes clutter the aisle and counter, the wall is hung with tools and boots and pails, the shelves behind the counter overflow with dry goods and oddments. At the far end is hidden a small meat counter and barrels of vegetables. The man speaks to the owner and points at her. The shopkeeper nods his head.

"He will see you right, especially if you bargain well," he tells her. Raising his hat, he turns to leave. "I wish you and your family a pleasant Christmas and a happier new year."

"Thank you," Elisabeth replies, "you have been most kind. My wishes for a merry Christmas to you and your family, as well."

Gratitude and hurt pride struggle for supremacy in her heart. He has obviously brought her to a shop for cut rate goods, used items and odd lots, a place for bargains, but also a place for people who cannot afford first class goods. It is exactly what she needs and she is ashamed of her need.

"Needs must," she mutters to herself. "This is only temporary."

Returning home, she is pleased with her efforts, three lengths of ribbon for the girls' hair and three lengths of leather thong for the men to wrap their leggings. Four onions, a dozen potatoes and a cabbage. A pint of buckwheat flour and four eggs to make a sweet cake. And change in her pocket.

New Year is marked by the marriage of the widow Frau Appolonia Graff to Herr Philip Schmeltzer. Appolonia and Philip are so much alike they could be brother and sister. They are both terse in their manner of speech, but hard working and generous with their time to the church. It is a good match and Elisabeth wishes them well. Trudl will be glad to have privacy for her family once again; however, she wonders how Appolonia's son, Christian, will take to having a new father.

She soon finds out. When it comes time for bed on the day of the wedding, there is one extra head on the floor. It belongs to Christian Graff. He and her oldest son, Christof, have become inseparable over the past months. There is nothing to be done tonight. Morning will be time enough.

In the morning, Christian Graff admits that he is uncomfortable with his new stepfather. Elisabeth understands, but points out that Appolonia is his mother, and they are issued rations on the basis of his being part of the household. Those are the only food rations he will be granted and, if for no other reason, that makes it prudent to remain on good terms with his mother and stepfather.

"Go and tell them you thought to give them some privacy last evening but, now, would like to return home. You can stay out of their way most days. Soon you will be 16 years old, and can apply for a place of your own and rations in your own name. Try to be patient. In a few months we will be going to our new homes," Elisabeth advises him.

Christian's chin is squaring in stubbornness when Stoffel flings his arm around his shoulder.

"Come," says Stoffel, "I will go with you and reassure your mother that you were our guest last night and apologize for not telling her you were staying with us. She may have been worried."

His feet drag but it is impossible to resist the firm pressure of Stoffel's arm.

"Thank you, Frau Baltzer," he says to her. "See you at work, Christof."

"Mutter—" begins Christof.

"Nein," says Elisabeth firmly. "He has his own family and he must live in it until he makes his own way."

"As if I haven't enough family of my own," she mutters to herself.

"Oh, Mama," Maria says to her, "you feel everyone is part of our family when they are in trouble."

A bitter January wind ripples the canvas walls as Elisabeth sits stirring another pot of the endless dried peas and salt beef. Catherine joins her. Elisabeth greets her. Over the past months, she has often found herself next to Catherine around the cooking fire.

"I bear sad news," Catherine tells her. "Frau Herman died in the night. It is thanks to your advice and encouragement that she lived this long. I thought she would never see Christmas."

"I am sad to hear the news, expected as it is. You did all you could," Elisabeth consoles her. "How is the rest of the family?"

"Weary with the care of her, sorrowful at her death and relieved also."

"It is to be expected. How will you manage now?"

"The same as before, easier than before perhaps. Herr Herman will surely marry again with three daughters to rear. I only worry that I may no longer be needed."

"It is best not to fret before there is cause; I'm sure he will find you more necessary to him than ever before," Elisabeth comforts her. "Sufficient unto the day are the trials thereof," she quotes. "We've scarce enough to eat, the cold is bitter and we are never warm. Many are sick and dying. This is enough to worry about."

21

Catherine sighs but nods her head in agreement.

"You have been very kind to me. Thank you, Elisabeth."

Elisabeth is pleased to see her wearing a cloak; it is worn and too long but better than just her skirt and jacket. She wonders if it belongs to her master rather than her mistress.

"We must help each other if we are to survive to see our new homes and farms and begin the new lives for which we came so far."

Catherine murmurs, "You are right, we need each other," and returns to her duties.

The worry over food is constant and real. The English have continued with the victualling, but the settlers have been forced to spend some of their reserve coins. Except for Stoffel and Christof who are fed when they work, she ekes out only two meals a day for everyone else. Maria has fortunately found a job as maid to one of the Halifax families and earns two shilling a week, enough for a few wrinkled carrots, cabbage or a turnip and a few potatoes and the occasional piece of fresh meat. Last week Elisabeth had managed to persuade a butcher to sell her pigs' trotters at a reasonable price and she had made both stew and soup. There must be strengthening herbs in the woods, even at this time of year, but the plants are unfamiliar to her.

Captain Zouberbuhler had procured extra rum and molasses at Christmastime as well as extra bread and potatoes, but has been unable to persuade the governor to issue any remedies for the coughs and fluxes that plague the people. Elisabeth's only medicines are boiled water and vinegar, wool cloths heated at the hearth to ease a patient's chest and, occasionally, some goose grease to rub on their back.

Alone by the fire, her mind wanders back to her home, to the warm kitchen at the butchery, to her father's house and her mother's well stocked larder, to her own supply of herbal simples to mend the winters' ills. She wipes the tears that start at the memory. A longing for the familiar slips through her guard. She misses her friends, her family. She is homesick.

"*I will endure. With your help, God, with your help,*" she prays. "I will be strong," she repeats to herself.

Her thoughts turn to Stoffel. He has been increasingly silent and short tempered. She knows he is angry with the English government and claims they misled the settlers with their promises. Yesterday he became upset when he learned that the men who had arrived on earlier ships were earning 30 shillings a month toward their debt while those who arrived this year were earning 20 only.

"We should refuse to work until they pay us the same," he had declared last night before stomping off towards the latrines.

"Elisabeth. Elisabeth! Wife?"

She starts as her somber thoughts are interrupted by joyous shouts from her husband just as she has been thinking of him.

"Stoffel. What is it? Why are you shouting?"

He is standing at the opening to the cooking shelter with a happy smile on his face, gesturing her to come.

"Come and see. Come and see who is here."

She shifts the pudding to the side of the hearth and hurries toward the shelter tent. Stoffel is standing with his hand on the shoulder of a man a bit taller than he is and laughing as she hasn't heard for months. It is a joy to hear the boisterous chuckle and see his head thrown back and his arms waving in the old expansive gestures. She can't see the stranger in the dim light.

"Elisabeth. Here is Adam Schauffner; come from Germany last year with his wife. Adam from Pfalz who was in Rosenthal staying for the winter with Herr Goetz three years ago. You remember him," he explains excitedly, his words tumbling over one another.

Now she can make out his features and recognizes the broad shoulders and grey eyes in the smiling face.

"Herr Schauffner," she greets him enthusiastically, "you are indeed a welcome sight. And what a surprise to find you here in this wild place. Where are Margarete and die Kinder—?"

Stoffel cuts her off with a quick twist of his body and the offer of a hot toddy to celebrate their reunion. Hushed by his quick glance of warning, Elisabeth hides her surprised annoyance at her husband's rudeness and goes quickly to prepare their drinks.

"It is a great pleasure to see you again, Adam. It is warmer and there is more heat in the cooking tent. Go and find yourselves a place; I will bring your drinks," she tells them.

As she finds the mugs and pours a small measure of rum into them, she recollects the man who had spent a winter in Rosenthal. He and Stoffel had been inseparable, never seeming to tire of each other's company. Unable to find work he had returned to his farm in the spring. Yes, she remembers, he had been a farmer, but also a good carpenter. He had built some new shelves in their storeroom and repaired the kitchen table. She smiles. The old table had always wobbled on one uneven leg but Adam had made it firm again. She recalls him talking to the table as he struggled to make it steady, uttering a few choice words when he thought she was out of earshot. He looks older than she remembers and more reserved. She remembers a tall, strong man, blond hair, penetrating light grey eyes, a quick smile, always ready with a joke. She imagines they all look a little older now than they should. Margarete is the same age as she but a slight woman in contrast to Elisabeth's own robust frame. They had become all good friends that winter.

Elisabeth serves the men their drinks, rum watered down with a goodly portion of hot water and a dot of butter. She refuses their invitation to join them and returns to her cooking. She continues to watch them as they talk. What a relief to see Stoffel laugh and joke.

"Surely You do hear your servants, Lord. I am most grateful."

Eventually the two men wander outside to continue their reminiscing.

Stoffel is like his old self when he returns for supper. His happiness cheers everyone. Even the molasses pudding is devoured to the last morsel despite the fact that she had left it on the fire too long. The boys are on their best behaviour with no jostling or shoving and Evie forgets to cry when there is no more pudding. Maria, usually sharp of tongue when she is tired, is good humoured and pleasant. When everyone is settled, Stoffel and Elisabeth go out together. Elisabeth does not go outside their little encampment alone after dark, nor will she allow the girls to do so. There are tracks made by the constant passing of feet that lead from the cook tent, past the wood pile to the stream and around their canvas shelters to the latrines. A stroll in the woods is the only occasion that offers a moment of relative privacy.

"Now, Stoffel, you will tell me everything. How did you meet Adam? What has happened to Margarete that you did not want me to hear?" demands Elisabeth.

"I'm sorry, Elisabeth. I did not want Adam to have to explain it all again. Margarete is not well." He pauses, gently turning her to look at him.

"Their three children died of ship's fever within a week of each other and were buried in the ocean. She has not recovered from her sorrow."

24

"Lieber Gott," murmurs Elisabeth. "Oh, how could she bear such a thing? To lose all of them. This is an awful thing."

Stoffel puts his arm around her shoulders and rests his head briefly on top of hers. She feels his lips press into the shawl covering her head. He resumes his story.

"I did not go to work today. I was angry and needed to think. So I went for a long walk around the settlement, down to the beach where the ship put us ashore, along the edge of the woods from one harbour to the other. As I came to where the church is, I saw a man clearing brush at the edge of the garden lots. I gave him a wave and was about to walk on when he straightened up and waved back. Well, I thought, he seems friendly; perhaps I will stop for a while and speak with him. Just about then I heard him shout, 'Stoffel? Stoffel, is it you?' He came running and I recognized him. It was Adam."

"How happy you must have been."

"At first I didn't believe my eyes. It was a miracle. He came on the *Murdoch* last summer. They have a small one-room cabin, not much more than a Hutt, not far from the church, but they have not been attending services so we did not see them. Margarete will not go to church; she blames God for taking her babies. Adam says that she did not speak for months, not even when they landed here. Even now, she scarcely leaves the house and sometimes forgets to prepare the meals."

"I will go to her tomorrow. I will take some broth, and some molasses pudding."

Stoffel leans over and kisses to top of her head.

"My darling Elisabeth, your generosity matches your grace. She will surely recover with you to encourage her."

For a moment she allows her head to rest in the hollow of his shoulder.

It begins to snow the next day, big lazy flakes that drift down and cling to her eyelashes. As she returns to the tent village after visiting Margarete, her steps are slow, reflecting her concern at the changes in her friend. Margarete made an effort to be cheerful today but Elisabeth saw it was mostly false. None of the lanterns were lit, the shutters on the lone window were closed, mugs from breakfast still sat on the table. Her friend had not remonstrated with her when she lit a lamp and opened the shutters, cleared the table and heated the soup she had brought.

After eating both the soup and the molasses pudding, Margarete had seemed more cheerful, happy to reminisce about the earlier days. When Elisabeth tried to talk about their present situation, she refused to answer, turning the conversation immediately back to the past. Still, by the time Elisabeth had left, she was starting to prepare supper.

"She is hiding in the past," thinks Elisabeth worriedly, "hiding from what has happened. What can I do?"

As she returns to their crude shelter, she wonders how she would cope if such a tragedy happened to her. In the cooking pot cradled in her arms she carries a cabbage, seven potatoes and seven carrots, produce from Adam's garden. A small treasure of ordinary things.

Easter Sunday, April 22nd, 1753, dawns with a milky sun and a translucent sky. Ground fog and hoar frost cover everything. Despite her efforts and those of the mother, another child had died during the night. Elisabeth can still hear the mother's sobs. So many have died in the winter, the old, the children, even some of the strong men had fallen ill and not recovered.

Every morning she runs her eyes over her family, checking for signs of illness. They have been fortunate, no one has been seriously ill and they are better off than many folk. Her prayers of thanks include Adam who continues to share his supply of vegetables with them instead of taking them to market. She believes the admonition of her mother, and her mother's mother, to heed what nature provides by way of food and medicine. If we ignore what God provides for us, we sicken, physically and spiritually. Good food, fresh air and cleanliness were precepts they had drilled into her.

Ignoring her family's reluctance, she is inflexible about her housekeeping routine. Their bed covers are aired whenever the sun shines and the floor is sprinkled with vinegar every week. She has Stoffel and Christof bring fresh boughs and more marsh grass for them to sleep on. She makes them wash themselves all over once a month and rinse their mouths every day with the salt water from the bay. They have come this far; they are not going to fail now. If only the weather would warm up. They need sunshine to dry out their clothes and bedcovers.

And their shoes. Elisabeth looks at her feet. All their shoes are in the same condition, the top leather worn nearly through and the soles patched. Last week she had approached one of the officers in charge of rations with a request for shoes. She still seethes at his answer.

"If you Germans would stop hoarding your coins and expecting Governor Hopson to provide everything, you would go and buy yourself new shoes and all the other things you constantly complain about," he had railed at her.

She gives her bonnet a final brisk tug and steps out of the tent. The sun breaks through the overcast sky and highlights her family, standing carefully in the dry patches on the track and waiting for her. Love and pride fill her heart.

"Dear God," she realizes with despair. "How thin they are. How shabby they look."

Their clothes do not fit. The boys' pant legs as well as the girls' skirts are too short, their stockings have as many holes as mends, their capes are shabby. And their hats! She hides a smile, Stoffel's is drooping on his head like a wet hen.

"You look wonderful," she tells them. "How proud you make me."

Despite their smiles, their faces are pinched and red with the constant cold and wind. They look like—like the refugees that came through the villages back home during the wars. She stares for a moment at her precious family. Stoffel and Christof, the father and son are very alike in looks and manner. Burly men of medium height, with strong arms and wide shoulders, their large hands hanging uncomfortably out of their Sunday jackets. The sun glints off their blond hair and makes their blue eyes squint. Peter, only nine years old, dark and slight and very different from either parent, resembles Stoffel's grandmother. He is her dreamer. Maria, her oldest daughter, also resembles that side of the family with her brown hair and dark eyes. She is no dreamer though but a person of action. Impatient and quick minded, she is always speaking and acting before she has time to think. She is often sharp tongued and always regrets it too late. Then there is Gertrud and Eva, little Evie. Evie had been born too soon, tiny and whimpering. Elisabeth had expected her to die in infancy. She is slow to develop; at five she is still happy with her rag dolly and her own thoughts. Elisabeth often thinks of them in the same thought as they are always together, Gertrud, Evie's protector and Evie, her adoring companion.

"I smell," complains Gertrud.

"We all smell," answers Elisabeth. "God does not mind."

"Maybe God has no nose," suggests Peter. "If God has no nose, maybe he has no ears and if he has no ears how does he hear our prayers?"

"God can hear what is in your heart," replies Elisabeth in a no question tone, "and He does not have endless patience. Come, we will be late."

The text that Sunday is on the merit of accepting God's will, of not questioning his designs even when we do not understand the reason for it. Elisabeth likes neither the pastor's tone nor his choice of words; it sounds as though he is saying that people like themselves are not intelligent enough to understand God's will. As she does not consider herself a person any less intelligent than the pastor, she stops listening and thinks about the direction God's will might have for them.

She does not believe that God expects them to be like sheep, blindly following and accepting whatever happens. She believes that the Lord helps those who help themselves, that people have an obligation to make the most of the opportunities God provides. Sometimes an opportunity comes disguised as a misfortune and one has to be alert to find the path God lays out before one. And sometimes, she believes, things just happen of their own will and are not an act of God, that God only takes a hand when it is needed. She knows that they will need God's grace mightily before this ordeal is over. With that thought she bows her head and prays, in gratitude for their continued survival, in apprehension for the months ahead and for blessings on the new life she carries in her belly.

After service, they walk to Adam's house for Easter dinner.

Margarete is having a good day and the meal passes in happy chatter and shared tales. When all is cleared away, they rest, cozily warm with the nine of them squished into the little house built for two. Outside it has started to rain again.

Suddenly, Christof asks Adam, "Tell me about the Indians and these Frenchmen the soldiers are so afraid of. We learned nothing about them before leaving home and we have seen nothing of them here."

"They are very real," Adam assures him. "The English have other forts. They have been attacked and soldiers killed, mostly by the Indians. How much do you know of Nova Scotia history?"

"Very little," admits Stoffel.

"Can you tell us some of it?" Christof asks him with a nod of permission from his father.

Adam begins. "A hundred and fifty years ago, the French came to find new opportunities for commerce; some of them stayed behind and settled here. They call themselves les Acadiens, the Acadians. They survived by becoming friends with the local Indians, called Mi'kmaq. Over the years, France and England have fought over Nova Scotia and it changed hands several times. Now it is governed by England but the French do not accept that."

"I thought the French lived in a colony called Quebec," interrupted Stoffel.

"Yes, they live there as well and that is still governed by France," explains Adam.

"Sorry for the interruption, please, continue," apologizes Stoffel to his friend.

"The English have been attacked during the last few years by both the Acadians and their Indian allies. So they want to establish loyal Protestant farmers around the colony to offset the French threat."

"Will we be in danger of attack if we accept the English farm land?" asks Elisabeth.

"Maybe," Adam answers. "I expect they will build another fort to protect us."

"How did you learn this?"

"I sell vegetables to one of the doctors at the fort."

"How soon will we be allowed to go to our farms?" asks Stoffel.

"I asked but he didn't know," Adam replies.

In the fickle manner of Nova Scotia weather, the sun shines hot and yellow in a blue sky on Easter Monday. The snow melts from the sides of the hills, the ice leaves the edges of the streams and the paths become muddy. The children greet the day with shouts and laughter. The men leave their winter cloaks at home and the women cover every shrub and tree with bedding and washing. There is little cooking that day. All the pots are needed for washing.

On a Wednesday in early May, Captain Zouberbuhler is accompanied by Herr Hoffman as he supervises the distribution of food rations. It is unusual for both of them to supervise the victualling but they are reviewing the lists, crossing out those who have died and adjusting the ration accordingly. As Elisabeth steps forward to collect her share, she overhears Hoffman say to the Captain that this may be the last time he has to spend a morning in this foul place. The Captain quickly interrupts him with a sharp look at Elisabeth and continues the conversation in English, knowing that she cannot understand that tongue. Whatever they are saying obviously concerns the settlers.

"When are we going to be given the land we were promised?" she asks Captain Zouberbuhler directly. "The weather is warming and the seeds need to be planted if we are to have any harvest this year."

"I would tell you if I could but it is still not decided," he finally answers. "Not too long now, this spring," he adds with a kindly smile.

She watches Hoffman. He lowers his eyes and fusses with his ledger.

"Ja, ja, you will be told," he mutters.

"They know. It is decided," she realizes, "but for some reason they will not tell us yet."

After the food is stored and she is once again alone in their space, she removes a pair of scissors from the trunk and carefully snips open the stitching holding her small pocket closed. From inside, she extracts a small cloth bag which she slips into her everyday pocket. Several times as she prepares their food and airs the bed covers, she puts her hand into her pocket and checks for its presence. There are seven of these little bags, each with a gold coin secreted inside, kept separately so they will not make a noise and betray their presence. Money hoarded from the sale of her dowry gifts and jewelry, her pewter dishes and the carved wedding cupboard built by her father.

As they talk during the supper meal, Stoffel remarks that the soldiers are piling stacks of lumber near the docks and are busy building what looks like rafts of timber. Christof reveals that a soldier told him they were for blockhouses, pre-built walls so that the soldiers can quickly erect them when they are needed.

"There are more ships in the harbour, too," adds Maria. As her mother opens her mouth to ask her daughter what she was doing down at the harbour, Maria quickly forestalls her by explaining, "I was looking for Peter."

Peter, eager for excitement, asks, "Are the Indians going to attack Halifax?"

"I've heard no rumours of Indian attack among the men and they would be discussing it if there were," answers Stoffel. "How about you, Christof?"

"No, nothing. Maybe they are going to push inland or along the coast and put up another fort."

"I heard Frau Riegel and Herr Kohl talking together last week about what they might need to start a homestead and yesterday they got married without having a celebration," Maria says suddenly. Frau Riegel is the widow with five children whom she had been helping for the past few months. "He was saying that one of the soldiers heard that we were to be moved to our settlements soon and they should be married before that happened so there would be no trouble over getting a house. And yesterday they did."

"Why didn't you tell us before?" asks her father.

"I thought it was just talk. Everyone talks about building their new home."

"I think we should prepare ourselves and be ready to move," says Elisabeth. "Captain Zouberbuhler said today that we would move this spring."

"But when this spring," wonders Stoffel.

The next day, Elisabeth is at the market as soon as the stalls open. By mid-day she has traded her coin for three short handled garden hoes, a large iron cooking pot with three legs, two wooden washtubs, a straight sided crock with a wooden lid, a sheepskin, and an old but serviceable hearth grate and standing spit.

"This handle is broken," points out Stoffel as he dubiously turns one of the hoes in his hands.

She also unwraps from a piece of cloth, a fine curved adze.

"For making bowls and troughs from our own trees," she says. "And the handle is strong. Anyhow, you can easily put a new handle in the hoe head. The tubs are used but fine, they do not leak even though they are old. I made the shopkeeper put water into them and let them stand while I looked for other things."

"The tyrant of the marketplace," he teases her. "And a sheepskin," exclaims Stoffel. "What can we do with a single sheepskin? We have no baby to keep warm under a sheepskin. Or were you thinking to pad my chair which I haven't made yet?"

"No, not your chair and I think there will be little time to sit. And you are right, Stoffel, we presently have no one small enough to need a single sheepskin—but we will, shortly," she answers. She smiles at her husband, wondering if this will be welcome news.

She places a hand gently on her stomach. The layers of clothing have disguised her increasing girth and hidden her pregnancy from her family. Stoffel holds still for a moment and then lifts his head and looks at her. His eyebrows are raised. At her nod, he embraces her and beams with pride. He is a generous man and a patient father, never happier than when his table is crowded with his children and his lap warm with a newly swaddled baby.

"When?" he asks.

"If it pleases God, not before we arrive at our destination."

He kisses the top of her head and proclaims, "We make good babies."

Elisabeth smiles on the outside and prays on the inside, "*It is easy to make them. Please, God, help me to keep them alive.*"

When the women gather on Wednesday, May 16th, they are told that Governor Hopson has ordered that their men cease working and prepare themselves to be moved to their farms. They rush to their quarters. Elisabeth smiles to herself. She was right to have begun collecting what she will need so that, instead of the panic displayed by the other women, she can calmly complete her careful preparations.

The women's voices rise in apprehension and excitement.

Captain Zouberbuhler calls out, "Wait, don't you want to know where you are going?"

The women look at him in sudden silence. Desire and anxiety show on their faces.

"You will all be settled together around a bay 50 miles southwest of Halifax. It is an old Acadian village, now uninhabited, with 300 acres of cleared land. A place we call Lunenburg."

"When are we leaving?" shouts one woman, chorused by others; their departure day is the only thing that interests them.

"You will have ten days to prepare, maybe a few more, but you should be ready in ten days. In a few days, a gathering of everyone will be held to tell you more."

True to his word, on the 28th of May, the military commander calls the heads of the settler households together to draw lots for home sites in the new community. The town is laid out like a military encampment, streets and lots marked out without thought to terrain, each house site identified by name and number. Stoffel draws Rudolf Division, Section G, Lot 9. Their new home has a place.

The military officer in charge of their transportation and the building of the town of Lunenburg is Captain Charles Lawrence. He tells them that the first group of ships will leave the next day; any of the settlers who are ready should give their name to his aide and as many as can be accommodated will leave with the first flotilla of ships. Elisabeth smiles to herself. She is ready and urges Stoffel to hurry and sign up.

She dreads putting foot aboard a sailing vessel once again even though Adam Schauffner assures her that it is a voyage of little more than a day. Adam is not on this voyage; he and Margarete will come in the second flotilla. When rain and fog, then lack of wind, and then confusion among the fleet of small ships delays the voyage and keeps the passengers aboard for ten days, she is hard pressed to keep from demanding to be rowed ashore. Only the knowledge that this is the last sea voyage she will make, keeps her on board. She leaves most of the chores to Maria and curls up on her quilt, alternately raging or praying to a God who seems to have stopped listening. Doesn't He understand that she will **not** have a baby aboard ship?

On June 7th, the winds shift from southeast to southwest and the flotilla of vessels carrying 600 of the settlers and most of the materials for building the new town of Lunenburg leave Halifax harbour.

"Thank You, God," Elisabeth prays. *"I know that You have not brought me this far only to let me die before my time. Soon we will have a new home, a new baby, a new life. Give me strength for the toil ahead. Amen.*

3

LUNENBURG LANDFALL

June 9, 1753–June 19, 1753

Elisabeth prods Stoffel with her knuckle.

"They've dropped the anchor. We're here," she whispers. "Let's go on deck."

Silently they ease out of their bedroll and creep up the ladder leading to the deck. Elisabeth's hugely pregnant belly barely squeezes through the hatch opening.

"It's about three o'clock," he murmurs over his shoulder. "The stars are still out."

"Hush, they'll send us back down if they hear us."

The deck is busy with sailors lowering and tying down the sails. The British soldiers are lined up on the foredeck listening to instructions from Colonel Lawrence. Other settlers slowly drift up from below decks and soon the rail is lined with people eager for their first glimpse of their new home. As the starlight fades and the pre-dawn glimmer strengthens, the dim light reveals a broad protected harbour surrounded by low but steep hills much of it covered in large trees. The land is cloaked in long shadows.

"How mysterious it looks," she reflects to Stoffel.

He puts an arm around her shoulders and pulls her closer.

"It's just the lingering night, the sun will show us more welcome," he assures her. "Look along the eastern horizon, a new day is beginning. Smell the air; it is filled with the scent of pines and fir. This is what we have come so far to find."

Briskly, Colonel Lawrence organizes the settler men into working parties. They begin to ferry building materials and supplies ashore, leaving the women and children aboard the ships. There are only four oared boats per vessel to transport the smaller goods ashore and it is slow work. The kegs of nails are heavy. Elisabeth sees one fall into the water and sink. As a lad jumps in and tries to retrieve it, she watches carefully until he is hauled back on board. The timber is tied into rafts and rowed ashore; some of the men and boys jump into the water and hitch a ride with the timber. When they reach the shore, many of them run away up the hill and into the woods, leaving the work of bringing order to the landed cargo to the soldiers.

Elisabeth loses sight of Stoffel and her sons who have joined the working parties. The ship is hauled as close to shore as possible, staying just off the bottom as the tide falls. Some of the women have managed to reach the shore as well. Elisabeth finds herself a place at the base of a mast where the forward sail has been tied around its boom, sits down and prepares to wait. Her two younger daughters collect around her. Maria returns to the hold to make sure their bedrolls and trunks are still safe.

Elisabeth gently places her hand on her swollen belly and feels the baby stretching and turning. It is restless and ready to leave her womb.

"Another day, two if you can manage, little one," she tells her unborn child, "just another day or two."

A few minutes later, Maria approaches her and asks if a young woman travelling alone can stay with them. A short woman with green eyes and red curls escaping her bonnet is standing demurely behind her; her shawls hide her figure, the hand clasping them is clean. She looks about 25 years old.

"Good morning, Mistress," she greets Elisabeth in English.

"English? What is an English woman doing aboard a ship of German and Swiss settlers?" wonders Elisabeth.

"Wer ist sie? Who is she?" Elisabeth asks Maria. "Ist sie ein englisches Fräulein?"

"I'm not sure but I think so. She seems to know the soldiers." Maria bends toward her mother's ear, "I think she is someone's mistress," she whispers. "She has no one to stay with; she is alone. I found her hiding in a corner behind the trunks."

Elisabeth shrugs in acquiescence; befriending a soldier's girlfriend will only cause trouble, but minor compared to the other obstacles that lie ahead.

"Frau Baltzer, Elisabeth," she says as she points to herself. "What is your name?" she questions with her hands.

"Miss Victoria Downing, Victoria."

"Guten Tag, Fräulein Donig." She has energy for no more and gestures for her to sit.

All day the cluster of women and girls cling to their little space around the mast. Several times the soldiers gesture for them to get below deck but Elisabeth refuses to move, setting her chin and speaking to them in German. The men ignore them after a few times. They are too busy to fuss with the little group. Elisabeth studies the land, rests and gathers strength for her impending ordeal.

The ship dips and rises in the slight swell. The sun is shining. In the warmth of its glow, their new home seems more welcoming. Curving rocky headlands protect the harbour and frame the view of the country that undulates beyond the shore. At the western head of the bay is a sweep of beach fronting low forested hills. As the tide recedes, it reveals a stretch of mud flats on which birds squabble and fight for food.

The men land timber and goods in the broad curve of the bay where the beach is narrower and the water deeper. Here the hill rises more steeply and an old cleared area is surrounded with tall evergreen trees. The shore continues its curve around to a rocky point to the east where another low section of narrow beach is backed by an area of marsh and wild grass. Here and there are open patches of cleared land covered with low growing scrub and a tangle of wild plants backed by steep hills and tall trees. Perhaps the land beyond is flatter and better suited to farming, but for now she straightens her back, giving the restless baby more room.

A sizeable log and timber building, partly hidden by trees at the base of the westward slope of the hill, catches her attention.

"Look," she tells the others, "there are people living here."

She had believed this place abandoned, but at least one family including men, women and children are living here. A man comes out of the house and stands on the beach as though waiting to be greeted. The others remain close to the building or at the edge of the woods. She identifies two men and several older boys, two women and six or seven children. They must live here, alone in this isolated place; there are no other dwellings. Eventually, three of the Englishmen walk over to the man and there is shaking of hands and introductions. It appears that they are not surprised to find him here. They talk for some time, with much waving of hands and pointing here and there. Apparently satisfied, they part.

Filled with curiosity, Elisabeth continues to watch. A woman collects water from a stream; the other spreads a few clothes on the bushes to dry. The children chase each other and throw sticks for a dog. Elisabeth wonders who these people might be. An English family living alone in the wilderness? She squints to see them better. They don't somehow look English. A curious thought springs to mind. Could they be Acadian? Do they pose a threat?

"Who can those people be?" she wonders aloud.

No one answers.

At nightfall the soldiers round up all of the settlers who fled to shore and force them back onto the ships where they are given their first and only meal for the day. Victoria stays with them, helping Maria with the younger children and with securing space for the family. Stoffel raises his eyebrows but Elisabeth merely shakes her head at him, saying only, "Fräulein Donig." As usual he does not question her judgment when it comes to such matters; over the years he has learned to acquiesce to Elisabeth's wisdom in the matters of women and children.

The next morning, everyone is roused at three o'clock to resume unloading the ships. This time Elisabeth holds Stoffel's arm in a tight grip and insists that he get her ashore.

"They're not taking the women yet," he protests, trying to shake loose of her hand. "The soldiers spent all day yesterday rounding up people hiding in the woods. Until the blockhouses are up and the palisade built we have no protection from Indian attack. Stay here, you and the girls will be safer on the ship. The boys can come with me."

"I am going ashore. Our baby is starting its journey into this world and I will not have it happen on this filthy ship."

"It is not time. You are just impatient and restless. In a few days we will all be ashore. There is time, my dearest."

"And you, of course, are experienced in such matters and can tell impatience from the pangs of birth at a glance. I need your help to get off this verfluchte Schiff or you will be delivering this child yourself on this very deck."

The glint in her eye and set of her chin signal her determination to have her way. Elisabeth is usually the soul of calmness; however, Stoffel knows from experience that she can become vocally forceful and fiercely obstinate when delivering her babies. His face mirrors his consternation and uncertainty.

Victoria is watching the intense conversation. She puts her hand on Elisabeth's belly and raises her eyebrows. When Elisabeth nods her head, she waves Stoffel and the boys ashore and signals Elisabeth and the girls to wait here. The men leave with guilty relief. Victoria quickly returns with a red-faced young soldier in tow. He takes them to the offshore side of the ship where a raft of timber is being assembled. The men in charge of the raft protest, but the soldier overrides them, and the women are handed down onto the raft. The men are French-speaking settlers from Montbéliard who, once they accept their additional cargo, guide their clumsy craft to the beach farthest from the soldiers. One of them helps Elisabeth to shore and raises his hand in benediction.

"Que Dieu vous bénisse, maîtresse."

"Et de même pour l'enfant aussi," another one calls to her.

"Merci Messieurs, merci pour vôtre aide," she calls back.

The little party ignores the shouts of the soldiers farther up the beach and disappears into the woods. Victoria helps Elisabeth across the rocks and up a short steep embankment. Not far from the shore is a patch of brier roses and wild alder bushes behind which the forest opens up into a small protected glade of grasses, violas and ferns shaded by an old elm tree. The hill slopes more gently here and the curve of the land will conceal them from the soldiers and working men. Victoria and Maria help Elisabeth settle onto the ground.

"Je suis désolée, Madame," apologizes Victoria to Elisabeth. "Je ne m'était pas rendu compte que vous parliez français. Moi aussi, je parle français."

Elisabeth pats Victoria's hand.

"No, no, you forgive me," she replies, "it did not occur to me either that you might speak French."

Victoria and the girls quickly collect a pile of fresh grass and settle Elisabeth onto it with her back resting against a rolled quilt. Inside the quilt are several clean cloths, Elisabeth's small, sharp birthing knife and some clean twine. These she hands to Maria.

"Keep them clean. They will be needed."

"Yes, Mama. I have watched you."

Victoria lays a comforting hand on Maria's arm, "I have delivered one or two. We will do fine." Her tone and smile give Maria confidence.

Victoria gestures to the younger girls. "Collect some more grass, a big pile," Maria shows then how, partly to keep them busy, partly because she isn't sure how much they will need.

They sit on either side of Elisabeth and prepare to wait. In a while they help Elisabeth to remove her outer skirt and jacket. They leave on her long petticoat and sleeved chemise and wrap their shawls around her shoulders.

They chat desultorily and take turns playing with the younger girls. During the day, Victoria reveals that she is the mistress of Captain Sutherland, second in command of the transfer party. No wonder the young soldier on the ship had been so helpful and so embarrassed; it is risky to disobey one's Captain, but also risky to anger his mistress.

Gradually, Elisabeth learns her story.

"I was born in the American Colony of Georgia." she tells them. "My father was a school teacher; he is the one who taught me to speak French. He didn't remarry after my mother's death. Because he was a keen horseman and kept a fine stable, the English officers often left their best horses with him, and were often invited to our house. That's how I met Patrick. I was young, only fourteen, and he was very handsome in his uniform. He was always kind, including me in their conversations. I was in love from the first time I saw him."

"But how did you come to Halifax?"

"He was with the Gibraltar Troops who replaced the New England soldiers at Fort Louisburg in 1745. They transferred to Halifax when it was returned to the French four years later. I followed him. Wherever he goes, I will go."

"Will you marry?" asks Elisabeth, thinking how she would feel if one of her precious daughters went traipsing off after some soldier. "Does your father approve?"

"No. I heard that he died of a fall from a horse soon after I left. As to our marrying, I no longer believe that will happen but, perhaps, if he stays here—".

Another pain interrupts their conversation. Elisabeth has no herbs to ease her delivery, only her courage and experience to rely upon.

She looks up through the branches of the graceful tree and silently tells her baby, *"No roof but God's for us. Thank goodness it has stopped raining. You will be born onto a pile of fresh grass and wrapped in an old petticoat. Others have done it, my little one, so can you."*

Tonight she will make a tea of the raspberry leaves she collected in Halifax to ease the flow of blood. All will be well.

As the sun begins its westward descent, the pains tumble one after another with scarcely time to breathe between them; Elisabeth clutches her daughter's hands and beseeches God to see her safely through her travail. Finally, a gush of blood and water stain the earth, followed by a tiny head. Four weeks before her time, Lunenburg's first citizen arrives with clenched fists and a squall of indignation.

Victoria firmly ties the cord with the twine. She holds it for Maria to cut.

"This is the first time I have done this," she tells Victoria, her eyes beseeching assurance.

"You are doing well. Make a clean cut now; it is tougher than it looks."

The young woman and the girl rub the infant clean with a cloth wet in sea water and wrap the tiny infant closely in a worn, but clean, petticoat and shawl.

"Well?" demands Elisabeth. "Have I another son or another daughter?"

"A girl, a beautiful little girl." laughs Maria. "We have a sister," she calls to the others. "What is her name?" she asks her mother.

"Sophie Elisabeth," she answers and holds out her arms.

As the others gather the bloody grass and push it under nearby brambles, Elisabeth rests and nestles her daughter to her breast.

"Thank You, God," she whispers.

Eventually, she rises and walks into the cold water of the harbour to wash herself before placing a cloth between her legs. She loops the ends over the thong which secures her pockets and puts on her old skirt and jacket. Like other women of her time, she wears no pantaloons under her skirt unless the weather is very cold but, because she cannot spend her confinement in her bed, she staunches the heavy bleeding with a cloth.

As darkness falls they quietly join the last of the settlers being rounded up to spend another night aboard ship. No one except Stoffel notices the extra little bundle in Elisabeth's arms.

"She is safely here," she tells him, "She was too eager to arrive so she is small, but she has fine lungs, our little Sophie Elisabeth."

Stoffel strokes her soft baby hair and murmurs, "Willkommen, Sophie Elisabeth; meine kleine Bettina, may God bless and watch over thee always."

The moon is still bright in the sky when they are awakened by the calls of the soldiers. It is Captain Zouberbuhler who climbs down the ladder into the hold and tells them to collect their belongings and gather on deck. They are going ashore today.

"Keep your belongings together," he advises them, "and hold on to your children. You will be taken ashore aboard the timber rafts and I don't want any of you to fall into the water. Don't crowd about. Wait your turn. Everyone will be taken ashore today," he reassures them.

As people begin to push and shout at each other at the foot of the ladder, he blocks the way up the steps, "You will go in an orderly fashion," he commands them. "Everyone will be taken today; there is no need to push. When you reach the shore wait on the beach. Wait on the beach," he repeats in a firm voice.

Despite his words, Elisabeth is jostled as the people surge toward the ladder. They are desperate to leave shipboard life behind. Eventually, she makes her way up the ladder, cradling tiny Bettina in her arms and bracing her elbows protectively. The deck is crowded with people and bundles and trunks and children. Many are jumping into the water and making their own way to shore. Women are herding children and making piles of their goods, the only things they own in the world. Elisabeth can see some of the people already on shore carrying off their trunks and pots into the woods; others are sitting on them and shooing away anyone who comes too close. Colonel Lawrence has erected two large wooden roofed shelters, similar to the ones in which they spent the winter in Halifax, and the soldiers are urging the women and children to come into the shelters. They are not being very successful.

One woman shouts at a soldier, "Nein, they are dirty," referring to the single men and a few of the less industrious families who have gathered in the tents. "We don't want to live with them. They are full of lice."

Elisabeth looks over the people who have taken shelter in the tents. Indeed, it appears that it is the more shiftless of the families that are happily setting up under the wooden roofs. Some of the people she knows, the Berghaus', the Kohls, are heading for the woods.

"Where are you going?" she calls out. She is exhausted and wonders if she can walk the distance.

"To the woods. I have an axe and we will build our own shelter. No more tents," one answers.

"We want a place of our own," another woman calls.

Stoffel is climbing the hill towards the woods when he hears his name called. It is Bernhard Herman.

"It is no good to go to the woods, they will bring us all back anyway and by then there will be little space in the tents. There is neither blockhouse nor palisade to protect us, thus, they will only force us to come back here where they can guard us. We should find a clean place and take it for ourselves; there are enough of us together to keep out the dirty ones."

"Ja, it is a good idea," says Elisabeth to her husband. "Let us stay together here in the shelter."

She isn't going to say so, but she is bone tired after the struggles of yesterday, and climbing the steep hill lumbered with bed rolls and a new baby is more than she wants to attempt. The Herman's little maid, Catherine, also looks tired and the three girls are slumped on the ground. The daughters had cared constantly for their mother, but make little effort to help Catherine to run the household.

"Here is a corner not taken," she says pointing out a section of the second tent facing the setting sun. "You are five and we are nine with Victoria, and here comes Pieter Bubechoffer with his wife. Let us stay here," Elisabeth proposes to Stoffel.

Pieter had made the voyage on the *Sally* with them and Elisabeth had mourned with the young farmer when his wife and child died before arriving in Halifax. It had happened to so many of them, but there was no returning. Those who had lost husbands and wives were remarrying among themselves and forming new families. His second wife is the widow Sabina Catherine Himmelman, a good woman, practical and steady.

43

"We will not be here very long," Elisabeth assures herself. "Soon we will build our own little house and plant our garden."

The tents are hastily erected shelters with a wooden roof and canvas sides. There are no separate quarters, just large open spaces. As usual those who had arrived together choose to gather together and, by nightfall, the Berghaus' and Kohls have returned to join them. Christian Graff and his parents arrive with Christof and so they become a large group all together.

True to his word, Colonel Lawrence only allows food to be issued to people in the tents; the ones who have to be forced back from the woods by the soldiers receive nothing which leads to much grumbling and complaining.

Victoria, who now seems a permanent addition to the Baltzer household, reports that the soldiers are not happy with the settlers either because they are shooting off their rifles at every shadow. Stoffel, who had been issued a rifle when he boarded the ship for Lunenburg, has already taken an unsuccessful walk through the woods looking for fresh meat for the pot.

"They are afraid one of the settlers will shoot them by mistake," she tells Elisabeth.

Aware that Elisabeth can speak French, their friends think nothing of her and Victoria using this language and accept her as another friend of Elisabeth's, maybe from Switzerland, another unfortunate widow.

As they sit quietly, gossiping or dozing or speculating over their futures, they hear footsteps approaching. Elisabeth is resting against her bedroll and feeding Bettina. She looks up at the interruption. It is Captain Zouberbuhler, whom they all recognize, and with him is Captain Patrick Sutherland, the aide to Colonel Lawrence.

"Victoria," she whispers sharply, "c'est ton ami, le Capitaine."

Victoria utters a startled, "No!"

Elisabeth smiles, she suspects that the Captain presumes his lady love is safely stowed away back in Halifax and that this meeting will be a complete, and maybe not a welcome, surprise. She watches as Victoria tries to make herself inconspicuous.

"She is going to have to do more than pull up her shawls to keep that mane of red hair unnoticed," she speculates to herself.

It is obvious that Lawrence's aide is inspecting the camp and has brought along Captain Zouberbuhler to translate for him. Many of the men and older boys rise to their feet while the women remain watchfully where they are. In fact, he does have a message to convey, work on the defences will resume tomorrow at four in the morning and no one is to venture into the woods on pain of withholding of rations. As the Captain is about to pass by, Peter Baltzer inadvertently knocks his foot against a tin washtub causing Captain Sutherland to look more closely at the silent group. Victoria's red hair glows in the light of the setting sun.

"Vict…, Miss Downing," he bursts out, "you are here."

"Good evening, Captain. I am here, as you see," she responds in English, "and in good company."

Elisabeth watches as his face registers total surprise, delight and consternation. As he is restoring order to his expression, Victoria rises gracefully to her feet. None of the others had even suspected she might have a connection to the English officers and to find her addressing this one familiarly, and in English, is a discomforting revelation. Who has Elisabeth brought among them?

Victoria formally introduces the people around her.

"May I present Mrs. Elisabeth Baltzer, her husband, Stoffel Baltzer and their children; Mr. Herman and his daughters; Mr. and Mrs. Bubechoffer; Mr. and Mrs. Adam Kohl; Mr. and Mrs. Nicholas Berghaus; Mr. and Mrs. Philip Schmeltzer," she says in English, gesturing to each of the families in turn.

She then turns to the group of settlers and says, "I would like to present Captain Patrick Sutherland, aide to Colonel Charles Lawrence and second-in-command of the building of Lunenburg."

No one speaks except for Sebastian Zouberbuhler who is busily translating. The Captain bows as do the men, the women bob and nod in varying degrees of welcome. It is the first time they have met Captain Sutherland although they know he is one of the key men in deciding their immediate fate. The faces of the settlers show a range of emotions from near hostility to curiosity to pleasure. Sutherland makes formal responses of greeting and thanks them for their work on the defenses. Stoffel boldly asks him, "When will we be allowed to start work on our own land?"

"The surveyors are still working; some of the house lots are not suitable and have to be reassigned. They are too wet, too rocky, or too steep. We plan to have everything ready by the time the flotilla with the second group of settlers arrives from Halifax", Captain Sutherland answers him.

The men shuffle and murmur in response. It is not the answer they want, but at least it is an answer, the first they have received.

Victoria stands silent, her chin and lips sending messages of stubborn determination. Not knowing what to say, Captain Sutherland tips his hat in farewell and walks away into the night without speaking directly to her. Curious looks arise among the settlers at the presence of the English stranger in their midst. Is it good or bad to come to the attention of the English Captain? And who is this woman Elisabeth has befriended? Trust Elisabeth to ignore the proper way to do things.

"I didn't tell him I was coming on the first boat," Victoria admits to Elisabeth. "I was afraid he would insist that I stay in Halifax until he is established here. He will never be established, he will always be sent somewhere else. He says it is no life for a woman to be a soldier's wife, au contraire, I think it is no life to be a soldier's mistress. I want him to stay here, even if he goes away and then comes back—as long as he comes back. He will not stay angry. He was pleased to see me. Did you see his face?" Nervousness makes her sentences run together.

Elisabeth had. So had the others. They will soon decipher the relationship between the woman with the red hair and the English Captain. Their acceptance of a "fallen woman", an English fallen woman, in their midst might be grudging. It all happened very quickly and she hopes that most of the girls have indeed been asleep and not eavesdropping. She knows Maria will be all agog for she never misses anything; in any case, she already likes Victoria and is a loyal friend. Stoffel is another matter, he can be prickly in matters of proper behavior and she has not told him that Victoria is a soldier's mistress. He knows she is English, but assumes she is a widow or a wife separated from her husband by duty. Elisabeth has not corrected his conclusion. Because of her recent childbirth, Stoffel is sleeping with the boys and they can't speak together privately without going outside. To forestall a discussion until everyone becomes accustomed to Victoria's presence, Elisabeth returns to her sleeping place with the girls and pretends to sleep.

By morning, Victoria has acquired two allies at least. Elisabeth hears Sabrina Bubechoffer telling Appolonia Graff, quoting from the Bible, "Judge not, lest ye, too, be judged," and backs it up by being openly friendly with the young English woman.

Then, over breakfast Christof tells Stoffel, "I see it this way, Papa, this is a new land and everyone who is able and willing to work will be needed. This place has made many people do things they would never have done before. And—and it can't be a bad thing to be a friend of the friend of an important officer."

As a result, no one openly disapproves, at least not in front of Elisabeth, and Stoffel holds his peace.

Watching Victoria help Maria tidy up their space, Elisabeth tells them, "I am glad you are here, you two are making it easy for me to have this baby. You are pampering me."

"Without you I would be alone," Victoria tells her. "And Maria is a great companion," she adds, smiling at her. Maria smiles back. Lack of a common language seems to be no obstacle.

"Rest, Mama, there is little enough to do until we can build our house. Victoria and I enjoy having something to do."

"The rain seems to have stopped for a time, I feel like taking a walk. I'll take Bettina. Is it alright if I leave you in charge of the others for a while?" she asks them.

"Yes, of course."

"Be careful."

While still in Halifax, Elisabeth had looked carefully at the surveyor's map which had been put on display during the distribution of the house lots. The town site is on a slender peninsula lying between the main bay to the south and a smaller bay on the north. Along its length is an irregular rocky spine marked with gullies and streams. The broad protected Lunenburg Harbour has a narrow rocky beach; the other, called Back Harbour, has a shore of grasses and rocky ledges. The blockhouses will be located at either end of the rocky spine and the palisade will stretch between the heads of the two bays. Beyond that, as far as she can see, is marsh land with reeds, grasses and bushes backed by tiers of treed hills.

Here and there, perhaps where the Acadians had their houses and gardens, small fruit trees are in bloom.

"I would like one of those on my land," she thinks.

Her immediate interest, though, is the hill in front of her leading upward from the main landing area before sloping steeply down to Back

47

Harbour. This is where most of the cleared land is and where the house lots are being surveyed.

She wraps Bettina in a shawl and sets out to climb the hill. Following the gentlest slope as much as she can, she finds an old trail that wends eastward and then northward to the top of the ridge. Here the hill flattens slightly and the water of Back Harbour is just visible through the trees. A breeze caresses her face and she holds it up to the sun as she sits on a felled log at the edge of the woods to rest. It is not raining as it has most of the time since their arrival.

This would be a nice place for a house she thinks, high enough for the sun and the breezes and for the rainwater to run off quickly. Resuming her ramble, she walks westward along the top of the ridge. She notices painted stakes with letters and numbers at regular intervals. "These must be the lot markers," she thinks to herself. Three men are using instruments to measure out more land and one is pounding in more stakes. They speak to her in English and wave her away. Ignoring them, she takes the paper with the letters and numbers of her house lot written on it out of her pocket and shows it to them. The man who seems to be in charge shakes his head and motions her along, but one of the younger men who is carrying the stakes points back the way she had come and smiles. Elisabeth thanks him. Even if he is wrong, she will hold that thought in her heart, a little house at the top of the hill, all their own.

Lost in her day dreaming, she finds herself moving down the western end of the ridge towards the fresh water brook. To her right, the men are building the palisade. She continues to where several small rivulets converge and lead to the harbour. She has never been this far from the landing site, nor had she intended to wander so far, but she does not want to become lost and by following the stream to the beach, she will arrive back at the tent site.

Ahead she hears voices, the sound of laughter and the chatter of children. Some of the others must be also enjoying the day. She pushes her way past some small saplings and bushes and steps into sight with a greeting on her lips.

"Guten Tag," she calls out with a friendly wave of her hand.

The small group of women and children fall silent at the sight of her; Elisabeth stares in consternation. These people are strangers. The older woman wears a white mop cap and has her skirts tucked up into the top of her apron; she is barefoot. Two small children are playing naked in the stream. The younger woman reaches to pull them close to her. The women have been washing roots and leaves that they must have gathered in the woods.

An older woman stops what she is doing and looks up. After a minute she replies, "Bonjour Madame. N'ayez pas peur, do not be afraid. We are happy to meet you."

Elisabeth resettles the baby closer to her. As her surprise recedes, she realizes they are speaking French although the words have an unfamiliar pattern.

"Bonjour Mesdames," she returns their greeting.

They must be the people from the house at the end of the bay, the people who live here already. Earlier she had decided that they must be English people, a small group who had moved out from Halifax and chosen to live on their own in this isolated bay. Why are they speaking to her in French? Elisabeth does not know what to do. She is some distance from the camp and too far away from the men working on the palisade for them to hear her shout. Are they friend or foe? The older woman walks toward her with her hands held out and a smile on her face.

"Do not be afraid," she repeats. "We will not hurt you. We are happy to meet you. You have your new baby with you. Is all well?"

Elisabeth is confused by her pattern of speech. Perhaps she is misunderstanding the French and is worried about giving offence.

"Your baby, la petite, she is doing well?" the woman asks again.

"My daughter is well, she is sturdy," seems the best answer. "Her name is Sophie Elisabeth," she adds. She reveals the baby's face and says, "We call her Bettina."

The woman smiles, makes the sign of the cross and repeats, "Bettina.

"French," realizes Elisabeth, "and Papist." The truth dawns on her that they are, indeed, Acadian, not English.

"You live in the house at the edge of the woods?" she asks the woman, pointing in the direction of the old dwelling.

"Yes," the stranger answers, "with my husband, Paul Guidry. This is my daughter, Jeanne, and her children. A nephew of my husband, Jean Deschamps, lives with us, too. I am named Anne Muis d'Entremont."

"I am Frau Baltzer. We came on the boats, from Germany."

She chides herself for stating the obvious. Naturally, the women know already that they came on the boats, but Elisabeth is rattled; these are the enemy of the British who brought them here and she worries that she has put herself and the baby in danger. They are only women and children, she reminds herself. The other settlers are only yards away. The woman speaking to her has made no threatening moves and simply remains still and smiling. Her eyes are dark and search Elisabeth's face calmly. They seem to express nothing except curiosity and patience.

"Frau Baltzer," Elisabeth repeats, pointing to herself. "Elisabeth."

"Bienvenue, Elizabette. Anne," the woman replies, tapping herself on the breast. "Je m'appelle Anne Muis d'Entremont. There are many of you," Anne continues. "Are all of you going to live here in Merlegueche?"

Elisabeth ponders the worried look on the woman's face as she answers, "Yes. The English have brought us here to build houses and farms and make a settlement. They are giving us land to build our houses and make our gardens. Why do you call this place Merlegueche?" she asks. "We are told it is named 'Lunenburg'."

"No. Here, this place," answers Anne, "is Merlegueche." She half sighs and explains, "This is our village that was named Merlegueche by the Mi'kmaq. We were eleven families. The others moved away after the English came to Halifax."

Elisabeth begins to understand. This is their village, their home, and it is about to be invaded by 2,000 strangers who will claim it as their own. No wonder her questions express concern.

"She is right to be worried; life will change for her, too, as it has for me," she thinks, then asks aloud, "Who lived here? Who were the other families who used to live here?"

"Mi'kmaq and Acadian people. This has been an Indian village for many generations."

To hear such names dropped casually into ordinary conversation shakes Elisabeth's composure and she has no response; she has many questions and does not know how to ask them without giving offence.

"Mi'kmaq?" she questions the unfamiliar word.

"The Mi'kmaq are the native people who live in this area, the local Indian people."

"This is an Indian village?" she ventures, bemused with the idea that they are moving into an Indian village to live. If she understands the woman rightly, her Lunenburg is actually an Indian village called Merlegueche.

"Indian and Acadian. Together we lived here for many years," Anne replies.

Elisabeth looks around; there is no sign of habitation.

"But nobody lives here," she replies.

"Mais oui! We live here. People visit, family and friends. We are the only ones now who stay for the winter. Now that you have come, they will not return."

The women drift into a slow walk along the streamside back to the beach. At one point Anne stops to take a closer look at baby Bettina, smiling and stroking her cheek with her finger. The baby regards her calmly while Elisabeth takes a cautious chance to study the woman's face. Her hair is black with grey streaks and is pulled back into a tight bun at the back of her head. She has wrinkles at the corners of her brown eyes and at the ends of her smile. Her skin is dark as though she has been out in the sun a great deal, her hands are dark, too, and rough from hard work, the nails are pared short. She wears no jewelry.

"I saw you, in the little glade over there, when you were having the baby," confesses Anne, looking at Elisabeth woman to woman. "I wanted to help you but I thought you would be afraid of me. I know some of the plants to ease the pain; my mother taught me. She learned from an Indian medicine man."

Elisabeth has no response to this statement. Indeed, she would have been afraid, and the other women would have put the stranger to flight. The Acadian women stop to put on their shoes which they had left under a bush. Elisabeth admires the footwear.

"These are beautiful," she tells the woman with genuine admiration. "And so soft," she compliments her, stroking them with a finger.

They are of leather, rather like a low boot but without a heel, and are resplendent with colourful bead decoration.

Anne holds them out, explaining, "Shoes, called moccasins with Mi'kmaq decoration from porcupine quills and glass beads. These are from deer hide."

Elisabeth is interested in how they are made. Their own shoes are worn through and many people are forced to go barefoot. Before she can ask more questions, however, three men wave to them from the door of the house.

"My husband, Paul," explains Anne, waving back, "and his nephew, Jean Deschamps. The English people call my husband Old Labrador, and his nephew, Cloverwater. Cloverwater works for the English Colonel Lawrence. The other is an Englishman. Will you meet them?"

Suddenly, tired from her walk and the burden of new information, Elisabeth regretfully refuses the invitation to be introduced to the men watching her so carefully from the doorway.

"No, I must prepare hot food for my family," she apologizes as she walks away to the safety of the tents and people she knows. She turns. "Good-bye," she says. "I would like to meet you again," surprised to realize that it is true.

Bursting with desire to discuss her day, she is disappointed to find that Captain Sutherland has removed Victoria to elsewhere.

"Victoria said not to worry," Maria tells her. "She will visit tomorrow."

Elisabeth wants to share her afternoon's adventure. Had she actually been talking with an Acadian who is, possibly, married to an Indian? She does not understand at all what she has learned. Today has turned her thinking upside down. She does not feel at ease discussing these things with her Stoffel or the other women. Also, she doesn't want her wanderings curtailed.

Victoria comes by the tent a couple of days later.

"Where have you been?" Elisabeth asks her abruptly.

"Patrick has found me a position with the van der Hydes who have been allotted a private section of one of the wooden tents," her face revealing her surprise at Elisabeth's tone.

"Why? Why a separate space rather than all together like the rest of us, and why does he not let you stay here with us?"

"Because they will live there until their house is built so they need a more permanent space."

Elisabeth raises an eyebrow.

"Because they are close friends of Governor Hopson and because he is an official translator and because he is wealthy," she patiently explains further.

"So is Captain Zouberbuhler," points out Elisabeth, "and he sleeps with the soldiers in the barracks tent. His family is waiting in Halifax."

"He is not married to Mrs. van der Hyde and, despite his languages, he is considered a common man while the van der Hydes are a better class."

"That does not explain why Captain Sutherland did not leave you here with us."

"He doesn't think it is a good idea to be too friendly with a particular family of settlers. He must be seen to be even handed and not favour some over others." Victoria looks upset at the sharpness of Elisabeth's voice.

"He thinks we are not good enough," Elisabeth concludes. "That we are dirty trouble-making Germans like that Colonel Lawrence thinks. Can he not see that we are not all the same? That we did not come as slaves and only wish to be treated fairly and in accordance with what we were promised." Strain and fatigue have shortened Elisabeth's temper.

"Dearest, Elisabeth," protests Victoria vehemently, stung by her new friend's outburst, "he does not think that at all, nor do I. You know that. He wants to stay here, maybe to be in charge when Lawrence leaves. He must be seen to be fair and he must obey the instructions from the Governor as Lawrence orders him. A soldier cannot always do what he personally wishes."

"I'm sorry," apologizes Elisabeth, even more so when she takes time to register the look of distress on Victoria's face. "Forgive me. I spoke out of impatience, a serious fault of mine. It is only my worry speaking and the fact that I was missing your presence. Of course, you must do as he wishes and I understand his thinking. He does not know us as you do. And, I admit, some of the young men are troublemakers. One de Brisé has been bringing a boat from Halifax with rum on board as well as his cargo of boards and selling it to the men. There's been some drunkenness in the tents and fighting at night. Some of the single men hide in the woods and carouse there, too. They complain about the work and make the rest unhappy."

Victoria puts her hand on Elisabeth's shoulder, "You are forgiven. I am sorry things are so difficult for you; you must be desperate to be out of here and building our own house. I'm sure it won't be much longer. Here, let me hold the baby. " She is relieved that Elisabeth has calmed. She stores away the name de Brisé to tell Patrick, he doesn't need any more trouble than he already has.

Elisabeth surrenders the baby to Victoria and settles to cut up some cured pork to add to the soaked bread for their supper. It is not as salty as the beef and does not need to be soaked for hours ahead time. At least Colonel Lawrence has issued a few rations to supplement the daily distribution of pease gruel.

"What do you know of the people who live in the old house by the stream?" she asks Victoria.

"Only that Colonel Lawrence finds one of the men very useful in gaining information about the movements of the Indians. I think he calls him Cloverwater, a strange name. Patrick tells me he is an Acadian coastal pilot who spends most of his life aboard his ship sailing along the coast from bay to bay trading goods and carrying news. He has a wife and family inland somewhere."

"So he is trusted to warn of a pending Indian attack, although he is one of the Acadian people?"

"Yes. He knows the Acadian villages and Indian trails and has friends among them who pass along information. Not all the Acadians hate the English. They, too, only want to farm their land in peace."

"We saw no Acadian villages along the coast during the voyage from Halifax."

"They are farther west and north; however, we could pass the Indian villages without seeing them. They hide from the English and do not live out on the coast except to fish in summertime."

"They used to live here, I think," says Elisabeth. "This place is called Merlegueche by them and by the Acadians who used to live here. They left when the English came to Halifax. This was a mixed Indian and Acadian village. I met them," she admits, looking up at Victoria, "the people from the old house. I think they are Halbblut, half-bloods, part Acadian and part Indian. Yet Colonel Lawrence appears to trust them with the safety of the town site."

"You met them? How? What were they like?" Victoria asks eagerly.

Elisabeth surprises herself by realizing, "They were very friendly, and nice. I liked them. I hope I meet them again."

She does not tell Victoria everything, not the part about Anne seeing her while she was delivering Sophie Elisabeth. That is too private a moment, yet, it has built a bond between her and the Acadian woman, Anne.

Rainy day follows rainy day. Even Stoffel is becoming short tempered. One evening, as they huddle under the leaky roof, Herr Herman brings welcome news.

"We are to have Sunday as a day to worship," he tells them. "Apparently, some of the men demanded it and Colonel Lawrence granted their request. Already they have started to clear a place. It is on that saddle of land in the middle of the town site."

At this Stoffel is more cheerful.

"A day to worship and tend to our own affairs. You have brought welcome news, my friend."

On Sunday, they gather for worship in the open air. They stand under grey, but for once not raining, skies. This is the first time Elisabeth has encountered the minister sent to head the new community's religious life. He is the Reverend Jean Moreau, a former Catholic priest now converted to the Church of England and who, thankfully, speaks English, French and German.

"His task will not be easy," ponders Elisabeth. "We all have our different ways. In fact, we are not at all alike even though we may seem so to the English. Mostly we are Lutheran, but also there are followers of Calvin, Zwingli. And then, there are the English with their ways. And the Swiss."

As they are ending their service a cry comes up from the shore.

"The others are coming. The ships are arriving."

It is June 17th and the second flotilla of ships is coming into the bay with the other settler families. People are eager to see friends and greet the rest of the arrivals. As soon as the benediction is ended, they head for the edge of the beach.

"Adam should be on board. I will be happy to see him again," exclaims Stoffel. "Now they will have to give us our land, there is no more room. Three times as many people are arriving than are here now."

Stoffel, Christof and Peter go hastily down to the shore. Stoffel is eager to greet his friend. Over the winter, their friendship had not only been renewed but cemented in shared hardship. Elisabeth, after sending Maria and the girls to keep a little space in their tent for him and Margarete, follows more slowly.

Following the random drawing of lots in Halifax, there has been much exchanging of house lots so that people from the same region, or friends made on the voyage across the Atlantic, can build their homes close to each other. Stoffel and Adam have arranged for people they know to build in the same section of land and he wants to be sure their plans are still intact.

Peter is the first to recognize Adam standing at the ship's rail and they wave happily to each other. Elisabeth is happy to see Margarete able to climb down the rope ladder herself and make her way to shore.

"Her health must have improved, even in ten days. Perhaps the anticipation of her new home is buoying her up," she thinks happily to herself.

With the arrival of the other ships, the relief of no rain and a day off work to tend to their own needs, the mood of the settlers improves even though the next day, it rains again. Rivulets of water trickle among the trees and rocks, gathering volume as they flow to the shore and the ocean. They even flow through the wooden tents in which the people are sheltering. It is impossible to stay dry.

Elisabeth and Margarete celebrate their reunion as best as they can and crowd in together. Everyone else has friends moving in, too, and the space becomes impossibly crowded. The desperation to move into their own places increases to the boiling point. Fortunately, the surveyors finish their work on Monday, June 18th and Colonel Lawrence announces that the settlers may move onto their land the next day.

Colonel Lawrence wakes the settlers in the pre-dawn darkness of Tuesday, June 19th, and orders the heads of households to assemble in front of the barracks to have their lots recorded and receive their garden lot assignments. With all the trading of lot assignments among the settlers, few of the receipts presented match the records made in Halifax. Colonel Lawrence, frustrated with the problems of language and time, capitulates in exasperation and simply records the number presented on the settler's receipt. Those without a receipt receive the lot recorded in Halifax. Elisabeth has safely kept their receipt in her pocket where she similarly stores away the new receipt for their garden lot. Adam has secured the lot next to theirs.

"Elisabeth, Maria, you and Peter go and find the lot. Then send Peter back to me where they are giving out the boards and nails," Stoffel happily orders his family. "You can carry our things and secure them under a tree. By night we will have our own little house."

For the first time since her meeting with Anne, Elisabeth climbs the hill. Peter runs ahead, searching for the stake with their lot number painted on it. When he reaches the top of the hill he shouts back to his mother, "Here it is, here it is." When she reaches him, she is delighted to see that it is not far from the place where she had stopped on her walk. It is near the northern edge of the town, yet not too far from the protection of the blockhouse. They are in a little cluster of house lots with other families that they know.

"This will be a fine place for our house," she exults. "Peter, go and help your father; we will be safe here."

Rain falls without ceasing. A steady drizzle of heavy drops that penetrates every layer of clothing, trickles down their necks and under their collars, soaks their skirts and trousers, turns lips and fingers blue with cold, and renders bedding musty and smelly. Elisabeth wraps the baby in her sheepskin, thinking that the tiny bundle is the only dry and warm body in Lunenburg this day.

The women sit in the shelter of a large fir tree, keeping their trunks and bedrolls dry as best they can while the others clear trees and shove aside rocks, trying to find a spot sufficiently level to function as a floor. Stoffel and Adam decide to work on both lots in tandem, clearing a space for the supports for the walls of one and then the other. Their section of lots is shared by the people with whom they have been sheltering. The families are sharing the labour and come running to help when a shout goes up for more hands. A few trees come down, a lot of rocks are moved, brush cut. Thankfully, the English have issued them more tools and all of them can help, even the girls and Elisabeth. Margarete is not strong enough, but seems content to look after the baby.

The men help each other carry the boards up from the waterfront, 50 boards and 250 nails per household, some bricks and shingles. Maria and the girls insist on doing their share, but stop after carrying two boards up from the waterfront. Green lumber in 10-foot lengths more than a foot wide is heavy and the hill is steep.

"Is there limestone for mortar?" Elisabeth calls to Stoffel.

"No, it did not arrive."

"No hearth?"

"It will have to be outside for now. We will have one soon, do not fret. We will have a roof."

By nightfall, they have a one-room house, 10 feet to a side and six feet high at the eave, with a low sloping roof and a door secured with leather hinges. There is no window opening, but it does not matter as they have none to put in. Stoffel has built a wide low shelf along one side of the single room. No more sleeping on the ground. It has been an advantage to have many hands to hold, fetch and carry, even Gertrud and Evie have done their share, carrying drinks to the others and holding the ends of boards.

They gather inside. For once, no one has anything to say. They stare at the primitive walls.

"Tomorrow, we will push moss and mud into the chinks. It will do until we have mortar," Elisabeth comments.

"First, we must thank God," Stoffel tells them.

They hold hands in a circle while Stoffel prays aloud.

"Dear Lord, Father and Protector of us all. We thank You for your mercy and guidance to us, your children. We thank You for allowing us to live in your grace and love, for your forgiveness of our sins, and most especially this night, we thank You for bringing us all alive and safe to this place. We ask You for your continued protection. We ask You to bless this house and all who live in it. Thank You, Lord, for all your mercies. Amen."

Elisabeth lovingly spreads her quilts over the boughs on the sleeping shelf. It will be the first time in thirteen months that they have slept under their own roof, the first time they have been more than two feet from other people. They are alone. This is theirs. It is so quiet, no talking, snoring or rustling of another family beyond the canvas. It is wonderful. Exhausted, everyone falls asleep before the stars break out from behind the obscuring clouds.

4

FIRST PLANTING

August, 1753

Victoria finds Elisabeth cradling Bettina in the shade of the elm tree near her garden lot. The August sky is greyly translucent but, thankfully, it has stopped raining for the first time since Sunday service, five days of endless drizzle, foggy mornings and damp evenings. Elisabeth looks up at the sound of her approach.

"Welcome," she greets her. "Do you have the afternoon free, or are you coming to tend the van der Hyde garden?"

The settlers had been quick to prepare their assigned garden lots and plant their first vegetables. The English had distributed seeds and many of them had brought seeds from home, vegetables and flowers to remind them of the old country. The summer is passing rapidly and anything they can grow will be urgently needed during the months ahead. Elisabeth is no different. Christof and Peter had been sent to clear away the growth of plants and bushes from their garden lot on the day after their house was built.

"No, not today. I have been taking advantage of the dry day, going for a walk while Mrs. van der Hyde prepares for dinner with Colonel Lawrence this evening," she explains. "I've laid out her clothes and cleaned the house. She's hired one of the Swiss women to do the cooking tonight. I went by your house and the girls told me you were here. Your garden looks well despite the lack of sunshine," she adds.

"At least I don't have to water it," Elisabeth comments, "but see how the marsh is encroaching into the garden."

Sure enough, with all the rain in the eight weeks since they landed, the marsh is as high as it had been two months ago. The garden plot is

40 by 30 feet and located at the lowest point of the communal gardens, just at the edge of the reedy marsh which separates it from the salt water of the harbour. It is a sunny protected spot, but with so much rain the water is not receding, and the reeds and sedges grow right to the edge of Elisabeth's labouriously created vegetable garden. The government supplied them with seed potatoes, cabbage, turnip, oats and barley seed. Elisabeth has planted oats, barley and vegetables for the winter. There is enough grain to make seed for next year, but not enough to grind flour for home use; the lot is too small for more.

"It is a good thing I planted the potatoes on the higher ground, they would be rotting. We should have come here a month earlier; we would have a larger harvest this fall. We will not be able to feed ourselves through this winter from such a small garden. The English will have to continue giving us rations," she goes on, revealing the worry on her mind. "Have you heard anything about continued victualling?"

"I know the food will be short," Victoria agrees, "but Governor Hopson did not wait for final approval from England to move us here. When he realized we could not be settled into Acadian communities, he settled us all here as quickly as he could arrange the ships. Don't worry, I believe he will decide again in our favour and continue rations."

"The Acadian threat, the Indian threat. They live peaceably enough together, why can't we all?"

"Because, England and France are quarrelling over whose territory this is. The fight carries on, even here," explains Victoria.

Elisabeth's understanding of political and military affairs is limited to what Victoria tells her. Without the information that she relays from Captain Sutherland, Elisabeth feels she would be completely ignorant.

"We are far from the Acadian lands," Victoria continues, "and, so far, the Indians have not tried to attack us here. We seem safe here, but still we need the soldiers to protect us."

Elisabeth apologizes. She hates to put Victoria between the settlers' and the English view of their situation. For the English, it is a matter of solving the Acadian situation, for the settlers it is a matter of receiving their land grants and building their homesteads. Their interest is in the development of their farms, not in saving English pennies.

"Patrick is worried about completing the blockhouses and the palisade, and having the storehouses finished before winter. The last boats that arrived from Boston brought more brick instead of the finished timber and rations that were expected. This has slowed the construction and left the food stores nearly empty. And, I'm sorry to say, some of the soldiers have been getting their hands on rum which has not helped."

"Everyone is hungry, even the soldiers," agrees Elisabeth. "Perhaps one of the ships will bring us some shoes," she muses, looking at her earth covered feet. "Even if we have a little money, there are no merchants to sell us either food, or shoes. And we are tired. It is too much to work all day on the defences and then all evening on our own land."

To take the sting out of her next words, she put her hand on Victoria's arm, "I don't want to hurt you, but living with the van der Hyde's, you don't see how we are suffering."

"Perhaps if I talk to Patrick," begins Victoria hesitantly.

"No, no, I am not telling you this to have you talk to Captain Sutherland," protests Elisabeth. "We have sent people to talk to Colonel Lawrence. He can see by just looking that we have no shoes, our clothes are in rags and people who are sick are not getting well as they should. Surely he will do something."

"What can he do? He has his orders."

"He ignored his orders when he allowed us to have some of the bricks to make a hearth and some of the shingles for our roofs; he didn't make a fuss when we took some of the limestone for mortar. He only gets angry when he thinks we are being lazy. Some of the young men are bored with working and sleeping and working with no let up and, of course, some are just scallywags. They get drunk and make trouble and disobey the soldiers' orders and run off into the woods. When he is angry he thinks we are all like that."

"The soldiers are still afraid of being attacked by Indians. I heard Patrick telling one of the guards that they are planning to send Cloverwater on a reconnaissance across the province to Piziquid," says Victoria.

"Cloverwater. Thoughts of him have gone to the back of my mind, and of Anne Muis d'Entremont; there have been many things to do in the last weeks. She will think I am avoiding her," remarks Elisabeth shaking her head at her neglect. "I wanted to learn more about them."

"She might welcome your company. Nobody talks to them," says Victoria. "The officers sometimes talk with the older man, Old Labrador they call him, asking about harbours, trails, and directions from which

Indians might attack." She pauses. "They don't talk to me either," she adds quietly with her face turned away.

"What do you mean?"

"The other women, even the women who speak French, the ones from Montbéliard."

Elisabeth pats her hand in commiseration. What was there to say? She knows her fellow women and their prejudices against unmarried relationships.

"Give them time. We are all wrapped up in our own affairs. They will get to know you and accept you, I am sure."

The friends sit in silence, watching the butterflies and bees flitter about the cabbages and potato blossoms, listening to the gulls screech overhead and the sea wind sough through the marsh grass. Elisabeth tells Victoria that she is pleased with her experiment of drying cut marsh grass in the sun and using it for mattress bedding.

"You're so clever at doing things, I never seem to see the obvious. I see flowers for their beauty, not for their useful nature," Victoria tells Elisabeth.

"You make me sound a boring sort of person," replies Elisabeth. "I see their beauty, too, but when they are beautiful and useful, how much more their splendour."

Victoria hugs her friend. "Never boring, mon amie, never boring."

A man who has been weeding several gardens away shoulders his hoe, gives his vegetables a last look, and slowly walks toward them. As he nears, he lifts his hat and gives them a nod. With the shadow of his wide-brimmed hat hiding his features they had not recognized him, but as the light reveals his face Elisabeth remembers him. He is the lay pastor who led the Lutheran meeting this past Sunday afternoon. The German-speaking Lutherans have taken to holding their own service after the morning Anglican service; in fact, some families have stopped going to the morning service and attend only in the afternoon. She forgets his name. The women stand as he comes closer. He will pass very close to where they are sitting and they do not want to be caught in so casual a position.

"Guten Tag, meine Damen," he greets them. "I see you are enjoying this fine weather."

"Good day to you, it is indeed fine to feel the sun after so much rain," responds Elisabeth. She waits for him to introduce himself.

"Permit me to introduce myself. I am Melchior Seiler. I met your husband at service last Sunday, Frau Baltzer, while you were talking with some of the other ladies," he says to Elisabeth. He smiles in the direction of the baby, "Surely the youngest of the Lunenburgers," he comments.

"Indeed," she affirms. "Bettina is perhaps the first born of the new community. She was born the day after we made landfall."

Turning to Victoria she translates into French. "This is Monsieur Seiler who takes service at the Lutheran meeting." Switching back to German, she introduces Victoria.

Victoria replies in English, "I am pleased to meet you."

"Ah, you are English. I am most pleased to meet you, Miss Downing," he answers in perfect English.

They are surprised when the man answers in English and they smile at the mixture of languages they have used to speak to each other.

"I have seen you with Colonel Lawrence," says Victoria, "talking with some of the ships' captains, I thought you were one of them."

"I have sailed on many ships but I have never been Captain," he replies, laughing. "I am an old friend of Sebastian Zouberbuhler, from Carolina in the American colonies. It is his garden I am hoeing," smiling as he repeats his information in German for Elisabeth.

Both women nod. Captain Zouberbuhler has become more than the mere translator he was in Halifax, and is regarded as a valuable ally to both the military and the settler communities, an important man for a friend. And friends enough with this man for him to be sharing the garden work.

"I was born in Georgia, but I have been to Carolina," says Victoria, "with my parents when I was a child. It was lovely. My father taught school and hoped to find a position there, unfortunately, it did not come to be," she concludes.

"Yes, it is beautiful there. My children are there with their families. Well, I must be getting back," he continues. "Good afternoon, Miss Downing; Guten Tag, Frau Baltzer." He lifts his hat again and makes his departure.

Victoria prepares to return to her work and the evening's chores at the van der Hyde house but Elisabeth remains staring after the man they have just met. There is a speculative look on her face.

"I have seen him before, that is why he was so familiar at service last Sunday. Now I remember; he is the man I saw coming out of the house of Old Labrador, the day I met Anne Muis d'Entremont," she tells Victoria.

"Are you sure?"

"I am sure. He knows them. They must be friends for him to be in their house," continues Elisabeth. "How could a person from the American colonies know these people? According to Anne, they had nothing to do with the English until the surveyors from Halifax arrived this spring. They do not even speak English, and he no French, apparently."

"It is true they do not speak English," concurs Victoria. "Patrick spoke of using a translator with the one they call Cloverwater."

"A riddle to be solved," comments Elisabeth.

The women part where one path leads up the hill and the other down toward the larger houses nearer the water. There are no houses on the waterfront itself as that is reserved for ships' docks, warehouses, landing jetties and soldiers' barracks. It has become a busy place over the few weeks they have been here. Ships arrive from New England, especially from Boston, with building supplies, salt meat and potatoes, and from Halifax with messages from the Governor and more supplies and soldiers. A few of the soldiers have families and they are beginning to arrive. There is much building going on, more houses, some shops, storehouses for the supplies and a larger dock. Already trees are being felled to supply masts for the navy ships. Stoffel has felled two of the tall white pine on their lot and sold them for cash to the timber merchant. With the money he was able to acquire a felling axe and enough extra bricks and mortar to build an indoor hearth.

As Elisabeth reaches the top of the hill she slows down to look at their home. It is still only one room, but it has a door and a shuttered window, and the land about the house has been cleared of brush and tall plants. In a sunny south-facing corner near the back door she has dug up a bed for some of her kitchen herbs, sage, dill, caraway. She brought the seeds wrapped in muslin and sewn into oiled silk bags to protect them from moisture on the voyage. She has also planted feverfew for headaches, some elecampane and horehound to help with the winter illnesses that will surely strike them down. To one side, the boys have constructed a lean-to of boughs to keep the rain off the wood they gather for fires. Elisabeth smiles at the slightly unsteady washstand beside the door her younger son proudly made. Peter is learning to be quite a good carpenter. He will be 10 years old soon, and already provides another pair of hands to do the work.

Inside there is still no floor but the dirt has been packed smooth and swept clean. One wall has the hearth and sleeping bench. There is a table and seven maple blocks for seats and extra shelves for storing food and their few dishes. The chinks in the walls have been stuffed with grass, moss and mud. A window opening has been cut into the wall opposite the door, and the pieces made into a shutter, so she can more easily clear out the smoke and freshen the house.

"A small Hutt, but it is our own," she thinks. Pride of ownership makes her smile quietly to herself. It is a start, a beginning.

Inside, Maria is waiting for her. Gertrud and Evie are visiting with Trudl Berghaus whose house is on the southern side of the same block. "Peter has gone with Christof and Christian to help carry stones for the walls of the English storehouse," she tells her mother. "Have you heard? Colonel Lawrence has agreed to pay everyone who works on the defences one shilling per day. He also is increasing the rations by two pounds of bread and extra molasses every week. He took away the rum ration to pay for it."

"We will miss the rum; however, the bread is welcome. Do you think Peter will be paid? He is too young," Elisabeth asks her daughter.

"He can try. He likes to be with the men."

This is true Elisabeth knows. When he comes home, he is full of stories about what he saw and heard. Sometimes she doesn't know if his tales are true or make believe; they always sound plausible.

"May I go out for a while?" Maria asks her mother.

"Where are you going? Who is going with you?" she asks her daughter, still apprehensive of the dangers that could befall. "I don't want you going alone into the woods or near the soldiers' camp."

"Anna Herman, Philip Herman's sister. We are just going for a walk in the open woods around the gardens and along the ridge to the blockhouse. I will return in time to help with supper," she promises.

"Philip Herman? A relation to the Bernhard Herman for whom Catherine works?"

"I don't think so. If they are, it is distant; however, they are still Hermans."

"Speaking of the Hermans, if you are going toward the gardens, take some of the fermented buckwheat batter to Catherine. I have plenty and she can use it to start more. She was asking about it yesterday and I promised her some."

"Mother," protests Maria in exasperation, "you don't even like her. She is always asking you for things, implying she is better because Herr Herman is richer. Did you know he hired a washerwoman? I saw her on Monday stomping the sheets in a huge tub."

"Maria, for shame, I don't dislike anybody. I don't dislike her. I feel sorry for her with all that work to do and three growing girls to look after. And Herr Herman is such a quiet man, still living as though he had a house full of housemen and maids to wait on him."

Elisabeth sighs in frustration as she puts a generous portion of pan bread batter into an enamel bowl, covers it with a clean cloth, and hands it to Maria. Catherine has been a perplexing question for Elisabeth. Her initial instinct had been to reach out in sympathy to the overworked girl only to be rebuffed and then, a few days later, Catherine would come asking for advice and support. Elisabeth does not know what to make of her.

"Here, take the bowl to her. When it has grown she will give me back some to keep it going. I have only enough flour for one more meal anyway. Who knows when we will receive more?"

One of the Boston ships had brought some ground buckwheat and barley flour which the women were overjoyed to receive. Unfortunately, there is no constant supply. They receive little grain and, anyway, there is no grinding mill as yet. Ship's bread pounded into small pieces, soaked and beaten with eggs, can be cooked in the skillet as a relief from pease pudding. She doesn't have her own chickens yet but Trudl has promised her a few fertilized eggs when the time comes. Food is becoming a serious problem; the increased rations will be welcome.

Anna is three years older than Maria and is allowed more freedom. With her infectious laugh and impetuous nature, she appeals to Maria's sense of adventure. Maria enjoys being the younger of the two instead of the older; not always having to be watchful and responsible as she is for her younger sisters.

Today they plan to go beyond the garden lots and explore the far side of the low headland that protects the eastern side of the harbour.

Afterwards, they will return along the top of the ridge, passing close to the eastern blockhouse. Neither one is unaware that the young soldiers on duty might be out practicing their drills or working on the foundations of the blockhouse. Of course, they will ignore them as young ladies should.

Maria and Anna obediently take the dough to Catherine. The Herman's house has four rooms downstairs and two more under the eaves reached by stairs instead of a ladder; it has both front and rear doors and there is even a glass window in the parlour. Catherine opens the door.

"Oh, it's you two. What do you want?"

"I've brought some of the fermented dough that you asked my mother for," answers Maria. "She made enough so that she could share it with other people," hinting to the girl that she would be willing to take an exchange.

It irritates Maria that her mother often gives away things they could have used themselves.

"Oh, yes, I did."

She reaches out and takes the bowl.

"Thank you, your mother is generous. Tell her I will have the bowl ready for her to collect when she passes on her way to the garden. I want to show her the new wool cloth that Herr Herman has had sent from Halifax to make cloaks for the girls. Now that we have a laundry woman, I have time to sew for the girls. They were so cold last winter."

"How generous of him. I, too, remember the cold of last winter," answers Maria. She also remembers her envy of the fur lining of Frau Herman's winter cloak. Guiltily, she says a mental, *"Forgive me, God,"* having momentarily forgotten that the poor woman died of the cold.

"We are going to the garden lots and must hurry if we are to finish with our work," Maria tells Catherine, eager to get away for her walk with Anna.

"Your mother just came from the garden lots. She was with the English mistress of Captain Sutherland."

Maria hears criticism in her tone.

"Her name is Miss Victoria Downing. She is a schoolmaster's daughter and well educated. She speaks French," Maria defends her friend, ruffling at the implied disrespect to both her mother and her friend. It angers her when people speak against her and, after all, Catherine is only a maid.

Victoria always treats Maria as though she were an equal and Maria considers her a friend. Maria can read and write German, but not French, so the two women converse in a made-up mixture of languages which seems to bother neither of them.

Maria grabs Anna's hand and says to Catherine, "We must be going. I'll tell mother that you want to show her the cloth. Good bye."

Anna will not let her friend sulk and soon has her laughing at her outrageous mimicking of the characters of Lunenburg, pretending to admonish her with the exaggerated piousness of old lady Grittel and singing off key like Herr Buche. They come out of the woods midway along the garden lots. The shore they want to explore lies on the other side. It takes them fifteen minutes to reach the top of the ridge so that they can see the other side. A swath of lowland covered in trees, scrub and rocky shoreline stretches ahead of them.

"Oh, bother," complains Anna, "I thought there might be a pebble shore so we could explore and look for flowers and relics of sunken ships and things."

"You mean treasure chests with gold coins and jewelled rings," scoffs Maria.

"Why not?" pouts Anna. "I've heard stories about such things."

"So have I, in fairy tales. Sometimes you don't act 17, Anna."

"Sometimes I'm not 17, Maria. Anyway, I plan to be a young girl until I am an old woman. I'm just going to skip all those boring years."

They are climbing cautiously along the ridge when Anna, who has scrambled atop a rocky hillock, calls excitedly to Maria, "Look, over there, I see a column of smoke. I wonder what it's from?"

"It's probably fog," dismisses Maria, "no one lives over here."

"It's not fog; it's smoke. Come and see for yourself."

Maria climbs up beside her friend and looks where she is pointing. It does look like a thin column of smoke, rising up several hundred feet and dispersing in the wind.

"Let's find out what it is," urges Anna.

"There's no pathway to follow," protests Maria, a little quiver of anxiety tickling her neck.

"We'll go down toward the shore, there, where the land narrows. If people are going back and forth there will be a path. We can follow that. If we come across anyone we can just say we were following the path."

"I have to be home in time to help mother get supper ready," protests Maria, worried about what might be causing the smoke, and who.

"Don't worry. We won't be long," Anna assures her.

They find a rough path along the base of the ridge. After a time, Maria suggests that they turn back. She is afraid they will be late returning and her parents disapproval will fall on her head. She doesn't mind a severe reprimand from her mother, but when her father becomes angry with her, his disapproval can be painful. In that regard, he does not discriminate between his sons and his daughters. Stray out of line enough to upset their mother into telling him and they would feel the leather belt. And her failure to return on time would upset her mother.

"Five more minutes, just past that tree with the grey bark," Anna cajoles.

As they reach the tree, they hear voices, men speaking German.

"How long does it take?" asks one.

"I'm not sure. Melchior said up to one day for large ones, a few hours for smaller ones," answers another. "These are sort of middling, maybe six hours."

"Someone has to tend the fire and keep it smoking," says the first voice.

"We can share that. I'll stay today, you can stay next time," answers the second. "You go on home now so no one comes looking for us."

The girls hear footsteps start along the path. Discovery is certain; they turn and try to scramble behind some trees and bushes. Maria is quick and crouches down behind a little shrubby of young spruce, unfortunately, Anna catches her foot on a root and tumbles to the ground.

"Well, well, what have I found here?" says a man's voice. "Spying on us are you?"

Anna tries the innocent approach and answers, "I was just following the path and it led here. I think I am lost. Can you tell me how to get home?" She opens her eyes wide at him, in what she hopes is an innocent gaze.

"You didn't find this path by accident," he answers, unmoved by the naive glance. "Even I can hardly find it and I know it's here. Does your mother know where you are, wandering in the woods alone?"

"Oh, yes, I told her where I was going, and I—"

The man interrupts her with a scoffing laugh.

"You don't have a mother. You are Philip Herman's sister. I doubt he knows you are here, and his wife would never give permission for you to be so far from home alone."

Maria can't leave her friend to face trouble alone and steps out into the pathway.

"She is not alone, and we are not lost. I know exactly how to get back to the town," she tells him firmly. She turns to her friend and says calmly, "We should go. My father and brothers will be waiting for us."

Suddenly, the man stares at Maria in consternation.

"Maria Baltzer," he exclaims in an irritated tone.

"Tobias Wirth," she says at the same moment. Tobias is a neighbour and knows that she is not allowed to wander this far.

By this time the other man has heard the voices and is arriving on the scene. Maria recognizes him from Lutheran service, a young man about 24 years old, but does not know his name. She recalls that he is one of the singers, his voice strong and melodious which, if she listens hard, she can pick out among the others. She likes to listen to it.

"I know you are not allowed to be here young lady," states Tobias, "but, seeing as you are, who is your friend, Maria?"

Anna has regained her tongue. She could not be considered a beauty, being tall and less than slender with a tendency to giggle; however, she is lively and has infectious smile. Her pale eyes are ringed with long dark lashes; her brown hair has hints of gold and is long and lustrous when not confined to its cap. She is an impetuous woman and intriguingly blunt.

"I am Anna Herman," she states without waiting for an introduction. "My brother *is* Philip and will probably be most annoyed that I am late in helping his wife prepare the meal. Do not detain us any longer."

"Miss Herman, I apologize that I did not recognize you immediately. May I introduce my companion, Johannes Bauer," he replies with a gesture toward the young man who has joined them. "At the risk of delaying you further, I would just mention that we will not reveal our meeting in this isolated fashion and trust you will both be as cautious. To ensure that you do not become further lost, I suggest we return at least part of the way together."

With as much dignity as she can muster, Anna nods her head and indicates to Maria that they should start back along the pathway. Tobias takes the lead and they are left to match as best they can his long stride and rapid passage over the stones and roots that strew the trail. He has nothing more to say and merely indicates with a wave of his arm the route back to the garden lots while he turns toward Back Harbour.

Maria and Anna look at the westering sun and hurry faster.

"Say we were delayed with picking flowers," admonishes Anna.

"We have no flowers," points out Maria.

"Well then, say we were investigating a likely spot for some of those herbs your mother is always looking for."

"She will ask to be taken there."

"Well, we will find a place before she does," replies Anna in exasperation. "Don't say anything." After a pause, she asks, "Is he married?"

"Johannes?"

"No, not that boy. The one with the dark hair, Tobias, Herr Wirth."

"His wife and daughter died on the voyage; he has two young sons," Maria answers shortly.

It is the other man who is on her mind. It is as though blinders have been ripped from her eyes. She remembers vividly the fair hair that curls around his ears and falls over his brow, his deep blue eyes edged with dark lashes. His mouth seems to—*his mouth. Lieber Gott, what is she doing thinking about a man's mouth?* She has never looked at a man's mouth before except her father's and then only to determine whether it is going to smile or frown. They part with a wave and walk on with thoughtful looks on their faces.

Maria arrives just minutes before her father and brothers, but it is long enough for her mother to confine her to their property until Sunday service and promise a longer discussion about her tardiness in the near future.

Sunday arrives and Elisabeth has had no time to talk to Maria. On the way to meeting she notices that Maria has put on her shawl despite the day's sultry heat. When questioned, Maria answers impatiently that her best jacket is too small.

"It fit last week," retorts her mother.

"It is too small this week. It does not fit properly."

Elisabeth looks at her daughter in bemusement; Maria has never cared how her clothes fit. What has wrought this sudden concern?

The church now has several rows of squared log benches for the women and children. The men stand to the sides. The wealthier families gather together towards the front. She sees the van der Hydes in the front row, but there is no sign of Victoria. Elisabeth finds a seat on the last row for herself and the girls. Melchior Seiler is leading the service again which reminds her of the questions she has about his connection with the half-blood family.

Since meeting Anne Muis d'Entremont, she has learned from Victoria, who questioned her Captain about them, that they are indeed an Acadian family. No mention of the Indian connection which Elisabeth suspects. If she had known, she would have been too terrified to talk with the woman; however, she remembers her pleasant face and welcoming manner. Her curiosity is aroused and she is determined to learn more. Was it Pastor Seiler that Elisabeth had seen coming out of the old house and, if so, what is the connection between them? Elisabeth decides to ask him outright at the next opportunity.

Beside her on the bench, Maria is intent on the service, especially on the singers. Elisabeth hears her sigh and looks over at her. Her daughter is staring at the little group of singers who have gathered together at the front of the church. She is staring at one singer in particular and there is a blush of red staining her cheek. A disturbing insight occurs to Elisabeth and she stifles a groan of concern and exasperation. With all the work and worries of building a home and developing a farm, a daughter in the throes of hero worship will require even more patience. Her oldest daughter is quixotic at the best of times and her transition into womanhood is likely to be tempestuous.

Maria and Peter are her only two children with dark hair and brown eyes, a legacy of Stoffel's grandmother. They are slighter and finer boned than the rest of them, more restless and quicker tongued; they are independent minded and more adventurous. Maria is only 14 years old, a natural age to be interested in young men but too young to be married, another two years at least. Her father will put a stop to any undue attention paid to his Maria. Who is she looking at so intensely? One of the younger men looks up, directly at Maria who drops her gaze and blushes. Johannes Bauer. So that is the young man who has caught her fancy. Now, how did that happen? Her talk with Maria is obviously long past due.

Melchior Seiler steps forward from among the singers and clears his throat to begin the sermon for the day. He has chosen Matthew 18: 20, "Lo, I am with you always, even unto the very end of the age." He elaborates on the idea that Jesus Christ is always present and the gathering together in worship confirms his presence, here, as it did in Europe. He reassures the people that Jesus protects and guides them in their struggle to build a home in the Lunenburg wilderness just as he did before; that he knows their pain and losses, takes it into himself and, if they have faith, he will strengthen them to endure it. Elisabeth has heard this particular sermon before and listens with only half an ear while using the time to think about the pastor himself.

He is a good height with a solid build, grey hair clubbed back with a leather thong and grey-blue eyes, clean shaven with long side burns. Out of doors he habitually wears a leather jerkin with wool britches, leather shoes, shirt and hose, a hip-length wool jacket or, in the rain, a long great coat and always a plain leather hat with a broad brim. He looks like what he purports to be, a respectable Lutheran of maturing years come up from the American colonies to find a new start. He is friendly with the settlers, moves easily among the English officers and men, visits and dines with the wealthiest of the German colonists, talks easily with ordinary settlers and leads Lutheran service. He is obviously educated, knowledgeable and travelled. Why has he come to this out of the way frontier? Where does the half-blood family come into the picture? Well, there is one certain respectable way to meet a man who has no wife and, if he is both the Christian and the friend of Sebastien Zouberbuhler he proclaims himself, it will not hurt to have him see the conditions under which ordinary settlers are living.

As the last "Amen" is chorused, and Herr Seiler raises his arms in benediction to intone the final "Go in Peace," Elisabeth moves swiftly to where he will stand to shake hands with the departing congregants. She is among the first to greet him as he takes up the accustomed position, Stoffel is just behind her with Christof and Peter.

"A most appropriate thought for this morning's sermon Pastor Seiler," she says. "And most timely for our circumstances." Without waiting for him to thank her and side-track the purpose of the conversation, she continues, "I want to thank you for leading our services, your words are most comforting and thought-provoking. To show our gratitude we would welcome you to share our dinner today, after you have finished here. Our home is humble but our hospitality will be from our hearts."

Behind her, she hears Stoffel inhale sharply, but it is masked by Seiler's answer.

"You are most kind, Frau Baltzer, Herr Baltzer. You are very generous. I would be delighted to accept your invitation and will come in about an hour, after I have spoken with the other worshippers. Thank you very much."

"What are you thinking?" demands Stoffel as they start their walk up hill to their house. "He is an important man, what are you doing inviting him to our little cabin?"

"It is all right, Stoffel, even the best houses are still humble, only bigger. I meet him sometimes in the garden lots and we smile. It is time we met properly. Besides, he has no wife to cook his Sunday meal."

"We have no good ale to set before him and only salt meat."

"We have good rum and cold water, and I have made a good boiled dinner. It will be fine, Stoffel. And there are some wild berries."

"I shall have to stay and talk instead of going to look at the land at the head of Back Harbour with Adam," he grumbles. "We found an old trail there and planned to follow it for a distance this afternoon, before it becomes too dark."

"Ask him to join you and Adam," replies Elisabeth.

He makes a sound under his breath. Trust Elisabeth to rush ahead without thinking a matter through carefully. He doesn't like to have his plans changed suddenly, nevertheless, he can see the advantage of knowing this man better.

Herr Seiler is a pleasant guest, talking and joking with the men, smiling and courteous with the girls, even holding Bettina on his lap and letting her play with his watch chain. He brings with him a bowl containing eight eggs explaining that one of the ship's captain's had carried them from Halifax, a gift from people he knew there. There are more than he requires for his simple needs and would be honoured if

Elisabeth would accept them. She protests, though not too strenuously. Eggs are more precious than gold, the hens of Lunenburg being sparse on the ground and prone to hiding their eggs in the woods.

Later, after the three men take their walk, Stoffel returns in a good mood, happily describing the deer tracks they had seen and speculating on the chance of killing one for the pot.

"Melchior seems uncommonly knowledgeable about the woods and various ways of hunting and trapping. He has a solid grasp of the scriptures, too," comments Stoffel as he washes his hands and arms before coming to the table for supper.

Elisabeth smiles. He has become "Melchior" instead of Herr Seiler. Now when she meets him at the gardens, it will be reasonable for her to talk with one of her husband's friends.

After Gertrud and Evie are in bed that evening, Elisabeth takes Maria with her to help scrub out the cook pots with sand and grass.

"Now," she says to her oldest daughter, "tell me about your day with Anna Herman and your little walk in the woods."

"It is very simple. We walked beyond the gardens and came to a path," she explains, "—an idea Pastor Seiler had, an experiment to build a smoke house to preserve meat and fish. They kept it secret so others would not come with their ideas and suggestions; they want to it to be their own success. Then Herr Wirth walked us safely back to the gardens. No harm was intended nor done."

She admits only the name of Tobias Wirth, their neighbour, but Elisabeth already guesses the other person's identity, Johannes Bauer. What interests her most is the mention of Melchior Seiler. His presence is becoming more frequent in their lives, always turning up in the garden lots when she is there, taking church services, talking with the settlers and being mentioned by Victoria as a confidante of Colonel Lawrence. And a visitor to the Acadian house.

It rains for the next three days. The fourth day is warmer but without much sunshine. Everyone is damp and bad tempered with the inactivity and discomfort. Elisabeth tries to cheer everyone up by making a pudding with some of the eggs, soaked bread, fat rendered from the salt pork, molasses and a rum sauce. The fire needed to bake the pudding in the iron skillet overheats the house, on the other hand it does dry out the bedding as well as some of their clothes.

The fifth day dawns sunny and the morning fog burns away quickly. Peter has gone with Christof and Christian to bring back more wood for the fires they will need this coming autumn and winter. Stoffel has gone with Adam to work on the western blockhouse. His wife, Margarete, is minding Bettina; the other girls are cleaning the house and then will pick some more of the red raspberries and the dark blue berries that grow at the western end of the town site. Elisabeth sets herself to restore the garden lot after the rains have washed away the earth covering the potato plants. Too much light will sunburn the developing tubers and they will develop a greenish tinge. Her mind on the morning ahead, she does not see the figure waving to her from the Herman house.

"Yoo hoo. Please wait," calls a voice.

Elisabeth stops and turns. It is Catherine, waving to her from the pathway of the Herman house, a bowl in her hand. Elisabeth walks back to the waiting girl.

"I wanted to return your bowl. Thank you for the starter, it worked very well. Mr. Herman enjoyed the griddle cakes very much," she says. "Do you have a minute? I wanted to ask your advice about some of the girls' dresses."

Elisabeth opens her mouth to say that she is too hurried this morning, but before she can say anything, Catherine has turned away and is leading the way up the path to the back door. Elisabeth sighs and follows. On the large table in the kitchen are three piles of material, a heavy worsted for jackets, linen for petticoats and English linsey-woolsey for dresses in sombre blue, green and burgundy. Elisabeth guesses the cloth has been selected by Mr. Herman to make winter garments for his three daughters; girls would not likely choose such dreary colours.

"What seems to be the problem?' she asks Catherine, struggling to subdue a surge of envy. "It is fine material."

Catherine runs her hand over the pile of folded cloth.

"Yes, very fine," she answers. She looks at Elisabeth with her head half turned and says, "Did I tell you that he gave me his wife's winter cloak? Apparently she asked him to do that. Isn't that a grand gift?"

"Indeed, it is a grand gift," agrees Elisabeth.

Catherine smiles to herself as though she can already feel the soft fur on her shoulders.

"It's not the new cloth that I wanted to discuss with you, Elisabeth. It is about the girl's old dresses that I called you in," she explains." They have outgrown some of their dresses; however, the material is still good, too fine to make into aprons or covers or cloths. I thought of your three girls who are nearly the same ages and sizes. They must be growing out of their clothes as well and wouldn't mind wearing the dresses of friends. You could alter them so no one would see they are hand-me-downs. Wait here, I'll fetch them," she tells the older woman.

Catherine climbs labouriously up the stairs to her sleeping room and returns with an armload of dresses, at least four or five. Elisabeth strokes the soft material and admires the colours, brighter and finer than she can afford for her daughters. The dresses are of soft, durable fabric, and not worn through with holes and repairs. Anger flares through her body. Hand-me-downs for her daughters when she is the one who always takes clothes to the needy? She does not need handouts. Tears threaten to show themselves. *"Be not prideful,"* she reminds herself. Swallowing hurt pride and anger in the face of her daughters' desperate need for new clothes, she holds out her arms to accept them.

"Thank you, Catherine. You are right, and very generous, my girls are in need of new dresses and will welcome Herr Herman's gifts."

"It's not charity, Elisabeth, I want to give them to you. They are a gift; it is my pleasure to give them to you instead of to strangers," says Catherine.

"Thank you, Catherine," she repeats, trying to mean it. "It really is very kind and thoughtful of you. The girls will be most happy. It is a most thoughtful gift."

Laden with the bowl and the dresses, she goes home to store them before she can return to the garden. Her neighbours will think she is taking in laundry. *"Be not prideful,"* she reminds herself again as she puts the dresses safely away. She is upset and surprised at her strong reaction to the gift. She has never coveted anything in her life; however, she coveted some of that fine cloth for her family and is troubled by her turbulent feelings.

Arriving in the garden at last, she sets to work with her hoe, hilling up the potatoes, restoring the earth that has washed down in the rain, and picking up some sticks and limbs that clutter the ground. Anger mixed with guilt still war in her mind; guilt that she is not truly grateful for the thoughtful gift, anger and hurt pride that she needs the gift. And to Catherine of all people; Catherine who surely understands the gall of charity. Had it been deliberate? No. There is no need for Catherine to give them to her. There are many other families in need of clothes for their daughters. She should be grateful. The gift was meant in kindness; the dilemma is hers.

Exasperated with her own conflicting thoughts, she turns her face to the sun and says aloud, "*I am sorry. I asked for your help and You gave it to me.*" She returns to hoeing, "*In your own way as usual,*" she mutters, hoeing the cabbages vigourously. "*I'm sure You know best. I will endeavour to learn the lesson You are teaching me,*" she apologizes out loud.

"He usually does, know best I mean," remarks a voice behind her.

Startled, Elisabeth gasps and turns around, the hoe gripped in both fists.

"Whoa, I mean no harm," Melchior utters quickly as he steps back.

"Herr Seiler," she exclaims. "Nor I," she reassures him, lowering the hoe. "It is unsettling times and I am unsettled with it," she apologizes, not entirely meekly. He had not only startled her, but caught her at a private moment.

"Let's begin again," he says. "I wish you good morning. I also want to thank you for the kind invitation and the most excellent dinner on Sunday. I enjoyed meeting your family. Your husband is a most practical man, an excellent merchant I suspect."

"Yes, he was a successful butcher with many customers in the old country. Much respected."

"And you with him, gnädige Frau."

Elisabeth bows her head in modest acknowledgement.

"It is a beautiful morning to be out in God's world is it not? I was pleased to hear you addressing Him. It is something I do quite frequently myself when happy or troubled or just because the sun is shining."

Elisabeth looks at him intently. Is he mocking her? His face is solemn.

"You are a lay pastor, I am a woman. I know it is improper of me to question his will; however, I confess, it is my habit to speak with Him when I am confused in my thoughts."

"On the contrary, it is in no way improper. It is an excellent idea and one more of us should follow. There is a difference between questioning his will and seeking clarity and understanding; however, I am willing to listen also, if you would talk with me."

He not only gives her his attention, but sets to with a will and begins hilling the potatoes and weeding the cabbages. He even checks them for cabbageworm, squashing any invading worm relentlessly between his strong fingers. In the half hour it takes to tidy the garden, Elisabeth reveals her dilemma over the dresses and her worries over Maria.

"I wonder if we are talking about false pride," he asks her. "For some, it can be easier to give than to receive. Learning to accept a gift with gratitude means acknowledging one's need of the gift, acknowledging that one is not sufficient unto oneself. I suspect that you, Elisabeth, are always a giver and have little experience of being the recipient. Perhaps you are not comfortable with it."

Elisabeth doesn't know how to answer these arguments. The truth in them stings her.

"Perhaps I am guilty of pride; too much self pride, too little humility," she admits reluctantly. "I accept that Catherine meant to be a friend and acted out of friendship. I feel bound to tell you, however, that I do not like false humility in people, Pastor Seiler. I prefer the honest smell of the cow byre to the sweet stench of sanctity," Elisabeth tells him with a tinge of asperity in her voice.

Melchior laughs out loud. "I have never been called 'Pastor Seiler' in quite that tone of voice before. You are angry with me, Elisabeth. I am sorry; I stand rebuked. I was not claiming to be void of false pride, indeed, quite the opposite. I was thinking only that we all will find ourselves in need of help from time to time as we build our lives here and must learn to accept it with grace, as it is meant."

After a minute, Elisabeth tells him, "Yes, you are right. We need to help each other; that lesson has been born out many times already. There is no shame in that. Thank you."

"I hear that you know of our efforts to build a smoke house," he tells her. "I also hear that it was Maria and her friend, Anna, who stumbled upon it."

"This man knows altogether too much," thinks Elisabeth to herself. Aloud she says, "Yes. I was not happy to hear of this adventure. The girls were much too far from the settlement. If you please, tell me your version of the event and how you learned of it."

"Johannes told me of their meeting," he explains, and goes on to tell much the same story which Maria had told her.

"What really is going on in that shed?" she asks outright.

"As they told her, we are learning to smoke fish, in the way of the Indians and Acadians."

For once Elisabeth has nothing to say. He is smiling quietly to himself. Elisabeth knows that he guesses what she has been thinking, that they were running a still, making alcohol to drink. She decides to take back the conversational initiative.

"How do you know so much about the Indians and the Acadians?"

"I don't know very much, only what I hear from others."

"I know that you know Cloverwater and his uncle, Old Labrador. I saw you there, coming out of their house," she states, no longer beating about the bush, but confronting him directly with her suspicions. "How do you come to know them?" she challenges him.

"I might ask how you came to see me?" he counters.

"I know Anne Muis d'Entremont, Old Labrador's wife," she exaggerates boldly.

"Ahh, yes. I should have known two healers would meet sooner than later. How do you speak?" Then he answers his own question. "You speak French, of course. I heard you with Miss Downing."

"I might ask you the same question, but I doubt the answer is the same."

"You are right, I do not speak French but I do speak Maliseet, another of the Algonquin languages very similar to Mi'kmaq which is the local native tongue. It is similar enough that we understand one another. The Guidry-Labradors and the Mi'kmaq have intermarried for several generations, and so they all speak both French and Mi'kmaq. Don't look so surprised, the Acadians and the Indians have been friends for 150 years."

Elisabeth returns to an earlier statement he made. "Anne is a healer?"

"Yes."

"I should have guessed. Why do you think I am?"

"Because of the way you stroke the leaves of the wild plants and smell your fingers. Because of the fact that you could successfully deliver your child alone in the forest and have no one guess your secret. Because of the blue berries you served on Sunday. Because you did not immediately deny it."

"You are observant," she answers.

"As are you."

They fall silent. This unusual man both intrigues and unsettles her. Few people are so frank in their words, or encourage her to reveal her thoughts so unguardedly. Elisabeth has so many questions, but this is not the occasion; she has been here longer than needed to tend the garden.

"I must leave, there is food to prepare," she says, tapping the dirt from her hoe on a nearby rock. "Good bye. Go in Peace."

"And you also," he replies.

The girls are delighted with the dresses and spend all their spare moments carefully picking apart seams and sewing new ones. Elisabeth and Maria do most of the sewing while Gertrud picks apart the seams, saving as much of the thread as possible. Evie carefully collects all the leftover pieces. In the end, they each have a new Sunday dress. Two of the dresses have been reworked into long shirts for Stoffel and Christof, while Peter has to make do with a shirt cobbled from the remains of shirts belonging to his father and older brother. Elisabeth saves all of the scraps and pieces of their worn out garments to sew into quilted petticoats and vests, the new material sewn onto the thin places in the older garment to make it warmer.

Maria has had very little spare time to go on walks with Anna. In fact, it seems that Anna is content to spend her afternoons helping with the redesign of the dresses. This puzzles Maria until she realizes that Anna frequently visits the back of the lot where it abuts that of Tobias Wirth, and it is not to use the privy. "So that is the way the wind is blowing," she muses, "at least for Anna." She has seen no sign of Tobias being interested in remarriage but decides not to interfere; Anna is of age and the availability of young men is limited.

After one such foray, she overhears her brother Christof remark to his friend Christian, "I doubt she'll have much luck there. Yon Tobias is a crafty one and I've heard him say he'll not take another wife."

"He has two young sons to rear," replies Christian.

"And relatives to do the rearing," answers Christof.

"Ja, that's true."

When Maria carefully rephrases the information and mentions it casually to Anna, her friend admits that she knows this but considers him a handsome devil with a ready smile.

Maria sighs and pricks herself. Her mother guesses, wrongly, that handsome Johannes Bauer has come to her daughter's mind and astutely holds her tongue, nonetheless she mentally determines that her Maria will need to be kept busy for the next year. Fourteen is too young to be thinking about marriage and children. Young love should be confined to long looks in church where it can lead to nothing more than languishing sighs.

One afternoon, as Elisabeth is piecing bits of cloth into a vest for Maria, Victoria arrives in great excitement.

"I have wonderful news. Patrick is to be placed in charge of the town site when Colonel Lawrence leaves at the end of the month. Governor Hopson is returning to England and Lawrence is to become Governor in his stead. Imagine, Patrick will be in charge. I am so pleased for him, now he will surely stay here," she exclaims. "Now things will get better, you will see."

"I'm really pleased for you," Elisabeth responds to her friend's news. "It's what you wanted."

"I have more news, too. Colonel Lawrence has requested that a general store be built at the bottom of Duke Street at Montague Street. So that we can purchase a few things like pots, and cloth, and tools. He is ordering the ships' captains to stop dealing directly with the settlers and plans to set up a proper broker for selling produce and buying supplies. And, the shipment of boots has arrived from Boston."

"That is indeed fine news," says Elisabeth. "Worth another of my dwindling hoard of coins," she thinks to herself.

Commerce she understands, being from a family of merchants. Her own father had been a broker in the wool trade. It is good news that the town's commercial life is improving.

"He has established a fixed price for some of the items," Victoria goes on, "to prevent the settlers being cheated because they can't speak English. I'm going to have my own room, too, and not have to work as a maid. Patrick said I could send for my things from Halifax as soon as he is confirmed in position."

She looks as happy as a little girl with her first hair bow. Elisabeth smiles at her and is happy, too.

Recently, Elisabeth thinks more highly of Colonel Lawrence than she had at first. True to the rumour, he increased the food ration. The extra rations are bread and molasses, not much, but it allows them to have a meal before starting their day as well as one about midday and another after the heavy work is done for the day. The rum ration is eliminated for a time to allow for this, but the trade-off is acceptable; it will be restored. Now that the work on the defences is nearing completion, Lawrence is better disposed toward the Germans and is doing his best to see that they are ready to face the coming winter. He has convinced Governor Hopson to continue to send the increased rations plus some shoes, blankets, potatoes, flour, shingles, and bolts of warm material. Those who have earned some money can purchase at least a few supplies.

"Oh, Elisabeth, we will be able to buy necessities and maybe something pretty. I'll keep watch and when it is open we can go, together. It will be such fun. I will buy something special for my new place."

Elisabeth drops her eyes for a moment to hide her sadness; she would like to buy something special, something not essential, for her new place, too. Then she pats Victoria's hand and says, "Yes, we will go shopping when the store is open."

They sit in silence for a time; Victoria is putting a deep hem in one of Evie's dresses. She is a fine seamstress, her stitches small and neat.

"Maybe they will sell thread," comments Elisabeth, "embroidery thread. I used to do good work," she adds, pointing to a finely embroidered edging along a scrap of kerchief she is sewing into a pieced undervest.

"You still do fine work," counters Victoria with a thoughtful look on her face. "I was considered quite a fine seamstress; I designed a wedding gown once, for the daughter of a big plantation owner. Do you think people might buy our work?"

Elisabeth's curiosity about Anne Muis d'Entremont does not abate but there is precious little time to visit her. She wants to know more about the smoked fish project, about Seiler's background and the half-bloods, about Anne and her healing methods. Also, she wonders about the absence of Melchior Seiler these last three weeks.

The answer to the smoked fish comes sooner than she expects.

As she is setting out the plates for their meal her son, Christof, comes in with a leaf-wrapped bundle which he places on the table. It smells of fire smoke and old boots.

"Here, we should try some of these for dinner tomorrow," he tells his mother.

Not a person fond of smelly surprises, she tells him sharply, "Take them out of here until we have eaten. They smell like old boots. What have you brought into the house?"

Christof knows his mother and merely answers, "Smoked fish. The Indians taught the Acadians how to catch them and preserve them by smoking them. Melchior taught us."

"I'm certain they shouldn't smell like that. Take them back until you and Tobias and the other boys learn to do it properly," she orders.

Christof stares at his mother in surprise, not at the brusqueness of her words which mean nothing except that he has caught her off guard, but at her casual acceptance of the smoke house with which he had hoped to surprise her.

"You know about the smoke house? I'm supposed to be the one with the surprise. How do you know about the smoke house?"

Maria has been watching from the doorway.

"We all know about the smoke house," she informs her older brother haughtily. "Johannes told me."

"Johannes? What is he doing, telling you such things? We are perfecting our method. These are herring, fresh caught and smoked immediately. They are quite good, we tried them," he explains. "And only a few of us know about the smoke house," he adds. "Until we can smoke them reliably, we don't want many people knowing."

"Where did you get the herring?" asks his mother, shooing him out the door with his bundle.

"Peter caught them, with Tobias. Then the five of us smoked them. Melchior helped us build the smoke house."

"Peter! You have to go out in a boat to catch fish. What was Peter doing out in a boat?"

"Catching fish for us to smoke," answers his brother laconically. "Melchior told us about how the Acadians catch and smoke fish to keep it from spoiling. So Christian and I, Peter and Johannes decided to try it. Tobias heard us talking about it and joined in. Tobias knows about fishing and had already brought some nets and floats from Halifax. One of the captains let him use a shallop to set a net in return for a week's ration of rum from all of us."

Not certain how to respond, Elisabeth finishes readying for their meal in silence; finally, she tells him, "If it works, we should have one of our own."

Christof smiles to himself; his mother has an uncanny instinct for when an argument can't be won and always supports an idea she thinks might be useful. "It will have to be next year," he replies, "the herring run is finished for this year."

The herrings glow golden bronze in the mid-morning sunlight when Elisabeth gingerly picks away the leaf covering the next day. They smell smoky, not fishy. She has eaten herring pickled in vinegar and salt with some onion and peppercorns which traders sometimes brought in from the Low Countries. She wonders if these have been salted in which case they would need soaking first. She pokes one with her finger. It is firm to the touch but not hard. She licks her finger with her tongue, just smoky and, well, a bit fishy, but not fishy. Quite good actually.

"I see our little experiment has been revealed," says a voice behind her.

The herring jumps from her hand, but she catches it deftly. "You are making a habit of doing that," she replies recognizing the deep timbre of Melchior's voice. Rising, she turns and continues, "Welcome back, Herr Seiler. Perhaps next time you will approach from the front."

"I apologize if I startled you, Frau Baltzer. I just spoke with your husband who is helping with the foundations of the armory. He said that you were at home today." His amused smile belies his apology.

"Yes, alone for a few moments, until the girls return from helping Frau Schauffner with some housekeeping tasks."

"She is poorly?" inquires Melchior.

"No more than usual. She does not have reserves of strength and needs more rest than some."

Melchior tells her, "Adam has spoken with me; he is concerned about her continuing delicacy. He wonders if she might be expecting another child."

Elisabeth lowers her head and feels the heat on her cheeks. She is not accustomed to a man who speaks so frankly, even though he is a pastor and twenty years her senior.

Melchior continues, "I speak to you openly because she is your friend and you will be helping her through her labours. And, I suppose, I am your minister and so privileged to speak honestly."

"She has not said, but I think you are correct. If she is, I will help her."

"That is good." Switching topics he says, "I have a present for you, from Anne." He holds out a container made of white papery bark, "Dried blueberries."

She takes them in her hands and raises her eyebrows in question. "They look like the ones I picked earlier in the summer, on the edge of the barrens."

"Yes, they are. These are dried in the sun. They will remain edible for many months if they are kept dry. They are considered very beneficial for good health."

"I thank her very much. I have nothing to give in return," she replies.

"You can give her your friendship. There are not many women in her household, none when the others return to their villages for the winter. You can learn much from each other, you can share your healer's knowledge."

"I would be very happy to do so," Elisabeth answers. Then she is honest enough to speak what is on her mind, "I think they are not liked by many of the settlers who regard them with suspicion. I will do nothing to make people scorn Stoffel or my children."

"I understand. However, people are very busy with their own affairs and will not notice very much. You can tell them the truth, that you are learning the local plants to use in healing their ills. They will accept that."

"Will you tell me how you know them?"

"Yes, but first I will tell you how to cook smoked fish. You can fry them in fat or boil them gently in water. You can add some to cooked pease or potatoes. They are very tasty. I hope you enjoy them," he concludes and with a tip of his hat departs.

Elisabeth sighs in exasperation; once again he has avoided her question.

5

THE HOFFMAN INSURRECTION

September, 1753–February, 1754

Food is on Elisabeth's mind. Not because she is presently hungry, but because she fears that they will be very hungry before spring comes again. She reviews their situation.

The constant rains finally halted during the third week of September. Peter and the girls helped Elisabeth harvest their first crop, most of which would be eaten before the new year. Still, she had made one crock of sauerkraut, shredding the cabbage and putting it down with generous sprinklings of salt between the layers.

The smoke house venture is successful, but there is too much to do and the building of a permanent one is postponed until next year. Christof and Christian shoot a deer. The boys stretch the hide and dry it but they don't know how to tan it, so the hide lies stiff and smelling where they nailed it to the side of the house. They will have to depend heavily once again on English rations.

Today, Elisabeth is carrying the tough discarded leaves from the cabbage back to the garden where she returns them to the earth to enrich next summer's crop. As she looks back at the harbour, she thinks about other changes occurring in the town. Colonel Charles Lawrence has returned to Halifax where he is Governor of Nova Scotia. Captain Patrick Sutherland is now in charge of the new settlement. Work on the defences has halted for the winter which means that the men are able to work their own land, but have lost their source of ready money; consequently, people will be unable to purchase much food and will suffer dearly before the long winter runs its course. Many have inadequate housing and scant harvest to supplement their rations;

everyone's clothes are worn out and their health is already compromised by the last years' of hardship. Discontent is growing in the community and the settlers are blaming the English for their grim situation. And the cold weather approaches rapidly. This morning Stoffel announced that the water in the wash bucket had frozen solid overnight.

The rest of the morning, however, brings good news. Both Margarete Schauffner and Sabina Bubechoffer come to Elisabeth and ask her to deliver the babies they are expecting in the new year. However, the women's reactions to their state are very different. Sabina is beaming with pride and happiness while Margarete clings to Elisabeth's hand and weeps.

"I don't want this child. What if it dies? I can't watch another child die," she whispers. "I thought I would die myself when they tossed the bodies of my children overboard." She raises her eyes to Elisabeth's and confesses, "I tried to throw myself into the ocean after them but Adam wouldn't let me go. I was so angry with him."

Elisabeth holds her in a gentle embrace. "It was a terrible time," she murmurs.

"I think of them every day, I imagine I can hear their laughter. It is not right; God should not have allowed it to happen." Anger still tinges her voice as she remembers. "I don't want another child; I don't want to replace my lost babies with another."

"It was a dreadful thing, a tragedy; there are too many little bones in the ocean."

Elisabeth is distressed at her friend's losses but nothing can change what happened, nothing can make it less painful. She can feel Margarete spiralling into a black sadness again, not wanting to live, but a new life is on the way; to carelessly lose it would also be a tragedy. She has no herbal remedy for this; she has only friendship and her own love for life to share.

"Margarete. Margarete, dear friend. You are sick with grief and mourning; it is making you see the world darkly, but the darkness is in the past. A child is a gift from God, a blessing even though it may be difficult to see it that way at first. Adam is a good husband who loves you; he'll cherish this new child and you for bearing it. Fretting will do you both harm. You'll never forget your other children, but it is time to think about the one that's coming. I'll help you when your time comes," Elisabeth reassures her.

"Oh, Elisabeth, you have so much courage and I have none. I am ashamed of my weakness, but when I reach for courage it slips out of my grasp. Poor Adam."

"My dear friend, stop worrying. It will only make you worse. You have plenty of courage or you would not be here. Adam is an intelligent man; he does not blame you for what happened. No one is to blame for what happened; sometimes tragedy just happens, even to good people."

Elisabeth rises to bring two tin cups to the table. "Here, I've brewed us some raspberry tea, just like at home. Drink some. It will help you feel calmer."

"You brought raspberry tea from home?" inquires Margarete in surprise.

"Nein, it grows here, too. I picked the leaves and berries myself and dried them. See? This land has things to offer us, we will be well."

Elisabeth frowns in worry as her friend leaves. Women need a streak of toughness to survive at the best of times and this is not the best of times.

A goodly number of the women are expecting babies and many will turn to her for help; her reputation as a healer and midwife grew during the terrible winter in Halifax, and had continued. Aside from raspberry or buckwheat tea, she will have little except her skill and comfort to offer. She takes the soft leather bag in which she keeps her simple tools and empties it on the table. She inspects them carefully: a small sharp blade to cut the cord; linen thread, boiled and waxed, to tie the cord; her stitching needle and flax thread should the mother tear too much; a small tin funnel to help her hear the baby's heartbeat and two clean lengths of linen to wipe the baby—what swaddling comes after will be as the family sees fit; a flint to light the lantern; a vial of rum to restore strength and a large clean apron to protect her skirts. She has only a sliver of soap to wash herself and the woman, but she and Trudl Berghaus plan to make a supply for the winter as soon as her husband borrows a large kettle. She will keep some of her share aside for this purpose; she believes that her habit of cleanliness contributes to her healer reputation.

By November the weather turns consistently cold and morning snow covers the ground. Soon it will not melt in the warmth of the day.

On November 11ᵗʰ, the men return from church repeating rumours about the London Board of Trade and Plantations, the company of Englishmen who recruited them as settlers. Apparently, a group of the Swiss settlers have written to the Board complaining about the lack of food and poor conditions under which they are expected to live. Jean Petrequin, one of the Swiss Protestants, claims to have received a letter from a relative in London informing him that promised supplies have arrived in Nova Scotia, but Governor Lawrence is refusing to disburse them.

"Are you sure?" Elisabeth asks Stoffel. "Have you seen the letter?"

"I saw the paper; John Hoffman was waving it around and he said he had read it. Petrequin cannot read so Hoffman read it to him."

"Petrequin. I don't know him. Where does he live?"

"I don't know."

"What else did you hear in church this morning?"

Maria spoke up. "Johannes said he heard the same thing."

"Johannes? Johannes Bauer? Why would he be talking about such things to a little girl like you?" asks her father brusquely.

"I'm not a little girl," she protests indignantly. "Next year I will be old enough to marry. And he speaks to me every Sunday after church." She raises her chin stubbornly but will not meet her father's gaze.

"Marry!" her father is sputtering. "No daughter of mine will marry when she is still a baby. I will talk to this Johannes."

"No," protests Maria. "Mama—".

"One thing at a time," interrupts Elisabeth, seeing the frown developing on Stoffel's face. "Is this the same John Hoffman who used to dole out the rations in Halifax? He's not honest; he tried to short ration us. You should find out more before you set your mind."

"Johannes says the men are meeting and will force the British to give us what they promised," Maria informs them, pleased for once to know more than her parents and proud that Johannes confided such information to her. "Ask Christof, I see him and Christian talking with Johannes sometimes. He knows about it," she adds, looking pointedly at her brother.

"Ja, they talk big, but what are they going to do?" he asks.

"What do you know and do not tell me?" demands Stoffel of his son. "What is going on and I do not know about it?"

"There is nothing to know," Christof defends himself. "They only talk."

Elisabeth fears that talk may lead to action. She does not want her men involved; neither does she want to miss out if any advantage can be gained. Is it young men's talk or not?

"Stoffel, invite them here, Johannes and two or three of the others. So you can hear what they are saying; they will talk freely around the table," entreats Elisabeth.

It is the only way in which a properly modest woman can hear what the men are saying and know what to advise. "It is so complicated being a woman," Elisabeth muses to herself. It would be much simpler if she could ask Johannes directly what they intended. She is certain they are up to something. On two occasions during the past week she has seen Johannes and some of the other younger men, mostly unmarried men, entering Tobias Wirth's house and not reappearing for several hours. This might explain what was going on. She had thought they were drinking and bragging to each other in the way men do. Melchior who often slipped enough information into his conversation to satisfy her curiosity had disappeared again, off on his mysterious trips.

Three days later a small group of men including Johannes Bauer, Tobias Wirth, Stoffel, Christof, and two others meet at the Baltzers. Tobias' face is flushed as he speaks angrily against the English treatment of the settlers, claiming that the Governor has deliberately withheld part of their settlement supplies and is keeping it for himself. Johannes repeatedly urges them to "take action." An older man rails against the Swiss, claiming they have taken land that rightly belongs to the Germans. The fourth man claims to be a friend of John Hoffman and to have seen the letter written to Jean Petrequin.

Elisabeth is refilling the jug of hot water and rum that sits by Stoffel's elbow and at this statement nudges him to follow up this opening.

"What exactly did it say?" he asks, having been primed by Elisabeth for this opportunity.

"Exactly that," the man replies, "Hoffman read it to me himself."

"Hoffman again," mutters Elisabeth under her breath as she turns away.

"How come it's the Frenchies that are talking to the English to get better treatment? There's more of us Germans," complains another man.

"Ja. It's them that'll be hivin' off the best land if we don't stick up for ourselves," agreed another.

"We need to show the English they can't push us Germans around."

The tempers of the men rise as they review all the slights and grievances they hold against the English. Their suspicion of the French-speaking settlers, especially Petrequin, grows as they realize they really do not know what is going on and what has or has not been said by the Board of Trade.

"Some of the Swiss have already left to join the French up at Louisbourg, what if Petrequin leaves with the letter?" asks Johannes. "We'll have no proof that we're being cheated if he disappears."

This thought puts a match to the fuse and they start calling for action, but they cannot agree on what to do. Elisabeth anxiously realizes that her efforts to gain information may have worsened the situation. Her first reaction is to get the men out of the house so she can persuade her family not to do anything rash. When she indicates that the rum is finished they settle into glum silence and finally the others depart for Tobias' house. Stoffel goes out to fetch more firewood and Christof settles onto a stool next to the hearth with some hot berry tea. These are the same dark blue berries she found on the headland and that Anne had sent to her. With their deep purple colour and tart taste she regards them as a blood strengthener and makes each of them drink a cup once a week as a defence against the rhumes and fluxes of cold weather.

"They are pretty riled," he comments.

"Ja," Elisabeth agrees.

"They might be foolish," her son adds.

His mother stops tidying away the jug and cups and turns to look at him, "What do you know, Christof?" she asks.

Christof is 16 years old and has entered the men's world and assumed a man's portion of responsibility for the family welfare. He and his mother share the same point of view on the family; it comes first, before any individual in it. In the last year, he and his mother have come to understand that they share this feeling of family priority and their willingness to sacrifice themselves for it. It is an unspoken understanding but one they can rely on. Elisabeth is proud of her son and grateful for his strength and young wisdom. She often wonders how he can be so like his father and yet so like her when she and Stoffel are so different, he silent and pragmatic, his day bound by the hard work it requires, she bursting with ideas and questions, her day often interrupted by musing and wondering.

"It was a mistake to have them here, I should have considered the consequences more carefully," she says.

"No. It'll be fine. We'll stay busy with our work until they calm down. What can they actually do?"

Elisabeth does not answer. She has seen people do ill-considered things before, during the European wars. "Should I talk with Victoria?" she wonders to herself. Maybe Patrick can do something to reassure the men.

The meeting has clarified for Elisabeth that no one except Hoffman has any knowledge of the contents of this letter to the illiterate Petrequin; however, it has done nothing to dampen the anger among the men. Their anger is directed mainly at Petrequin because they feel the letter proves that the French-speaking Swiss have acted unilaterally behind the German-speaking settlers' backs by writing directly to the Board of Trade. Consequently, at this point the Germans are suspicious of both the English Governor and the French-speaking settlers. One thing the men do agree on, the letter to Petrequin is proof of their being cheated, therefore, Petrequin and the letter must not disappear until the German settlers can talk to the English authorities.

In the end, Elisabeth does not have a chance to talk with Victoria. On the morning of December 11th, the community wakes up to discover that a group of the men, including Johannes Bauer, have kidnapped Petrequin and locked him in the blockhouse where they intend to keep him until the English authorities give them the goods and lands they were promised when they were recruited. Shots are exchanged but no one is killed. Captain Sutherland tries to talk to the settlers and bring some understanding to their complaints, but it is to no avail; they will not listen to him, suspecting him of being part of the plot. On December 22nd, Governor Lawrence sends Captain Monkton in command of 200 armed soldiers to Lunenburg to restore peace. Monkton quickly subdues the rebels and calls for a complete return of the arms that the settlers had been issued in Halifax.

Stoffel is angry at the loss of his rifle which he carried not only for protection against Indian attack but for hunting animals. He is complaining about it when there is a knock at their door. It is Johannes Bauer.

"Ah, here he is, one of the hotheads that caused us all the trouble and lost us our rifles," he says. "What are you doing, knocking at my door?" he asks in irritation.

"I have come to apologize to you and Frau Baltzer for my hasty actions following the afternoon we all met here. I fear I have caused you some embarrassment and, maybe, some trouble. Captain Monkton's soldiers asked me about you, about our meeting here."

"How do they know about that?" Stoffel asks him roughly.

"I don't know. Gossip. I assured him, repeatedly, that you had nothing to do with the rebellion." He looked away from Stoffel and added, "Actually, I told him it was a prayer meeting, that we were meeting to discuss religious matters."

"You young whelp, what have you done to my reputation?"

"Nothing, Herr Baltzer, nothing. They know you had nothing to do with it. I know it was a foolish thing to do, to act before we knew what the truth was. Now we know the story and we were all duped."

"What are you telling me? How were we duped?"

"Apparently, the story of the letter is a fraud. There is no letter. That man, John Hoffman himself was the instigator of the wild accusations. For some reason, known only to himself, he stirred up the French and the Germans against each other and against the English. He has been arrested and sent to gaol in Halifax. Monkton has gone back to Halifax."

"He made fools of you, is what he did. And I nearly believed it," growls Stoffel to his family. "And, now I don't have a rifle."

The morning of January 6th, Three Kings Day, Elisabeth rises early, earlier than her usual pre-dawn hour. It is still dark when she stirs up the bed of embers and feeds it dry birch bark and bits of spruce bough to spark it into life, ready to catch at the larger logs of birch and maple. It has been a cold winter with snow falling nearly every night since Christmas Day. It is beautiful when the sun shines on the fresh snow, but the hills are treacherous and falls are common. Only yesterday Peter came home with a badly bruised arm which, fortunately, wasn't broken. She had wound a strip of wet canvas around it. It seemed better by bedtime. Mornings are cold in the small cabin. The floor is frozen earth which turns to mud if she keeps the fire too lively; it is a constant balance between being cold and having a dry floor, or being warm and walking about in mud. Elisabeth had tried laying the deerskin on the floor but it just became dirty and the house was no warmer so she hung it over the door opening.

"That blessed piece of leather" Stoffel calls it, but it keeps out some of the cold fingers of wind that blow in when the door is opened.

Keeping warm is always a challenge. Stoffel and the two boys each have a long quilted vest to wear under their shirts and she and the girls have a quilted petticoat and bodice over their long chemise. Their jackets and cloaks are threadbare and she has no wool to knit them stockings so they line their boots with moss or bits of canvas or rags. The men tie rabbit skins over their boots when the snow is dry; when it is wet the skins are of little help. Some days they wear both their Sunday clothes and their workaday clothes to keep out the cold. Thankfully, the English had sent them a load of boots and shoes at the end of last year. Nights they crowd together on the sleeping bench for warmth.

Food is a problem. They have enough for two meals a day. If they are careful they will survive until the next rations arrive. Christof and Peter learned from one of the older men how to set snares for rabbit, otter, muskrat and beaver, and are becoming more consistent at bringing home two or three a week. Melchior told her that the quill covered porcupine was also edible, but she has not had the confidence to try it yet. With over two hundred families hunting in the near woods, it is becoming more difficult to trap food animals.

On this morning, as every morning, she is searching her mind for a way to keep her family warm and fed. And healthy. Disease has been the enemy every day since their departure from Germany. Hungry, cold people succumb to illness and the weak do not recover. In this, the remaining few coins in her pocket are of little use. There is nothing to buy and neither simple herbalist nor expensive doctor to call upon who can protect her family, the bone cutter who tends the soldiers is ignorant of all but gross injuries. Her simple skills are their only resource. And good food and a warm bed are her first priorities. Few of the families are any better off; those who have more wealth have brought in supplies from Halifax or Boston, but they account for a tiny percent of the population of Lunenburg. Even the English soldiers are suffering in their barracks.

She moves the big three-legged iron spyder to the side of the hearth where the fire is blazing merrily away and adds a larger split of maple which will burn more slowly and create a steady heat for cooking. She adds some pork fat to the spyder, fills it with potatoes, turnip and salt pork and moves it nearer the fire. It is her one new purchase since coming to Lunenburg even though it had meant another raid on her special pocket. By putting a lid on the spyder she can bake a flat loaf of bannock bread, when she has flour, or a pudding of bread and molasses or fry up a hash of leftovers.

This morning's breakfast will be the leftovers from last evening's supper. The routine of the day rarely changes; up between five and six, warm up their insides with a drink of hot water, molasses and a float of pork fat; home chores for three hours; breakfast of leftovers and a hot drink of water and rum; work for six hours followed by supper, a discussion of work to be done the next day, family prayers; then to bed to keep warm and rest for the trials of the coming day.

As she reaches for the flat ended stick which Stoffel has shaped into a stirring spoon, a sudden pounding at the door startles everyone awake. Alerted by the urgency of the knocking, she opens the door immediately to find Melchior preparing to rap his fist on the door again.

"We are up, we are up," grumbles Stoffel, feeling with his stockinged feet for the wooden shoes he has carved for them to wear in the house.

"What's the matter?" asks Elisabeth, looking at the pinched lips and narrowed eyes under the flaps of the wool cap.

Melchior removes his fur mittens, but makes no move to take off his boots.

He looks at Stoffel while directing his request to Elisabeth.

"I come to ask for your help. A friend of mine has come with his granddaughter to visit with Old Labrador and Anne. His granddaughter is expecting her first child and he wanted Anne to help her, but her time came early and she has been in distress these past two days. Anne is exhausted and I beg to persuade Elisabeth to come with me. I am afraid for both the child and the mother, things are not progressing well."

Stoffel nods his head, "She will go whether or no I say so. Of course, my friend, she may come with you. She will come to no harm with the old Acadian as long as you are with her."

It takes them many minutes to reach the house through the snow. Elisabeth looks closely at the house, curious about how it differs from hers. From the outside it looks much the same except that it has more windows, an overhanging roof and is much wider. It also has a stoop with three steps leading to the front door.

Melchior gives the door a peremptory knock and ushers Elisabeth in. There are several people in the warm kitchen but he deftly removes her cloak and moves her toward another room. Inside the room, Anne is sitting on a stool wiping a cloth over the forehead of a figure whose eyes are closed in a face grey with fatigue and pain. Anne looks up and wanly smiles her greeting to Elisabeth. She is too tired and worried to beat about the bush.

"The baby is bottom down, but one foot has entered the canal. She is too weak to push and has given up. I'm afraid she is dying."

Melchior adds to the explanation, "The English surgeon from the barracks will not come, he says he does not birth half-blood brats."

Elisabeth is not surprised that the man holds that opinion; such prejudice is common. She looks around the room. It is clean and the folded cloths are plentiful and clean; the bedclothes are rumpled and stained with smears of blood but have been changed since the waters broke.

"Is the baby alive?" asks Elisabeth, setting out her small array of equipment and tying on her big apron. "May I examine her?"

Anne nods permission.

Elisabeth puts the small tin funnel wide end down on the mother's swollen belly and the small end to her ear. She holds up her hand for silence, a redundant gesture as everyone is holding their breaths. Even the mother is silent, barely groaning when the contractions strike. Elisabeth can hear the baby's heart beating rapidly, but strongly. At least the infant is still alive.

"I have given her tea of squaw root twice and dare give her no more, but she can't push hard enough to expel the baby," says Anne. "He was nearly here when she fainted and he sucked back into the womb."

The girl on the bed gasps raggedly and groans. A powerful contraction causes her to arch in pain and then collapse back into a limp heap. Melchior appears with a basin of hot water and soap for Elisabeth to scrub her hands, and then returns to the other room.

"Do you always wash your hands?" Anne asks Elisabeth.

"Yes, so my mother taught me." While washing her hands, Elisabeth tells Anne, "We must get the baby out. I don't think she knows what's going on any more and can't help herself. Tie her arms to the bed posts, she will pull and make herself push when the pains come."

The women hurry about their tasks. Anne ties the girl's limp arms to the bedposts with pieces of torn cloth; Elisabeth raises her legs with rolled blankets and crouches at the foot of the cot. She sees a tiny foot. Placing Anne's hands above where the baby's head must be, she asks her to push down steadily when the contraction begins. She herself carefully inserts a hand into the canal and feels for the other leg; she wants to grasp it at the hip by hooking one finger between the leg and the baby's tummy. There is only a moment before the next contraction begins. As Anne pushes down Elisabeth can feel the pelvic bones grind into her fingers, but she touches the baby's bottom and finds the bent leg.

Another contraction follows swiftly and Elisabeth slaps the woman's leg, speaking loud orders to push, trying to rouse her out of her lethargy. As the girl struggles at the cloths confining her hands, she automatically bears down.

As a third wrenching contraction begins, Elisabeth calls to Anne to push the baby down while she urgently pulls with her fingers. This is one of the last chances, for if the baby is trapped in the canal it may suffocate and die. The contraction ends and the baby starts to draw up, Elisabeth has only one finger around the baby's bent leg and feels it slipping.

"Nein, nein," she commands the universe, "one more time, bitte mein Gott, one more time."

Anne pushes as hard as she dares on the baby's head position. At the next contraction Elisabeth cries, "Maintenant! Jetzt!". With a grunt she falls to her knees with a bloody but kicking infant boy clasped in her apron. Anne quickly ties off the cord and cuts the baby free of his mother. Leaving the baby to Elisabeth, she turns her attention to the mother who is lying unmoving on the cot. She scoops the afterbirth into a basin and packs dried moss between the mother's legs before covering her warmly with blankets and wiping her hands and face of sweat.

"Let her rest, I will watch over her," Anne tells Elisabeth. "You tend to the child."

The baby stops mewling and closes his eyes as Elisabeth fixes a band around his middle, wipes him with a wet piece of flannel and wraps him tightly in a swaddling blanket. She lays him next to his mother but she weakly pushes him away. Her eyes never open to look at the new life she has paid so highly to deliver. Anne takes the baby from Elisabeth and gestures for her to follow.

She rinses her bloody hands and removes her stained apron. In the urgency of the birth she has noticed very little, but now the sombre atmosphere seeps into her consciousness; the cries of the baby have brought no one into the room nor smiles of happiness to Anne's face. She looks at the young mother more closely; she can't be more than a girl of 14 with straight black hair and high wide cheekbones. The pallor of her skin is the colour of tanned hide. Elisabeth realizes that this is an Indian girl and her infant likewise. But the birth of a boy out of the near death of both should be a joyous occasion in any family. "What is going on? What has Melchior dropped her into?" she asks herself.

They move into the other room again where Anne hands the baby to a man she has not seen before. He and the other men stand in a circle and unwrap the blankets from around the child.

"A boy," says the first man, "and alive. It might have been better had he died."

"To let him die by doing nothing would have been a sin of omission, murder in God's eyes," states Melchior unequivocally.

"It is Half Ear's child. See? He has the cropped earlobes of his father. The girl tells the truth; her brother is the father," says the stranger in a sad voice.

Elisabeth stands helpless and confused by the door to the bedroom. The men are speaking Acadian-French and some other language in low tones and she cannot decipher the conversation. "Why is there no joy in the room?" she questions. The unknown man has rewrapped the child and handed him to a woman standing quietly to one side. She is neither young nor old and has the same straight black hair as the new mother, but her eyes are light brown and her skin is almost fair. She takes the child and turns away to put him to her breast. "A wet nurse. There was a wet nurse already waiting; they had never intended for the mother to have the child," she realizes with astonishment. She takes a breath to speak but closes her mouth when she sees Melchior give his head a single sharp negative shake.

"Care for my granddaughter," commands the stranger. "I will return for her," he tells the others. He gestures to the woman who is cradling the baby and turns to depart. She lifts a large pack to her back, settles the infant into a carrying sling over which she drapes a fur cape and follows the man out into the night.

Anne turns to Elisabeth.

"Thank you," she says. "I was at my wits end and torn with the dilemma of saving the mother or the child. And you did both, I am grateful."

"The child was ready to appear. I did nothing you would not have done."

"No. I was exhausted. It was your energy and sureness that turned the tide."

They return to the bedroom and inspect the mother. She is resting and the bleeding is normal. Anne replaces the bloody moss with clean. Elisabeth is curious about its deep yellow colour; Anne explains that she has soaked it in tansy tea to prevent infection. Tansy is a powerful herb, one that can abort a baby or kill the mother; this way it is not ingested and is safe. Sensing Anne is impatient to have her depart, Elisabeth packs up her things and reaches for her apron.

Anne takes it away from her, "I will boil it, and the bed clothes; no blood trail must lead any evil here. We will burn the birth sac. The boy will have to make his way without his ancestors."

Elisabeth looks at her without understanding.

Anne takes her hands in hers and holds them, "At least the boy will have a chance to live; a sister cannot have her brother's child. The infant will be abandoned in another village where someone may take him as their own. The girl will be married into another tribe where she is not known. Perhaps they both will live. Come, Melchior will take you home."

At the door, Anne hands her a bundle of tanned hide. When Elisabeth starts to protest at the large size, Anne shakes her head and firmly pushes the bundle into her arms. Elisabeth is perplexed at her treatment and a little annoyed. She has come through the snow without breakfast, succeeded at a difficult delivery and is being rushed out of the door. Anne is looking at her with begging eyes and a plea on her face, so she merely smiles an understanding which she does not have and leaves with Melchior who sets a stiff pace. She suspects he is trying to prevent her from asking questions. The wind has dropped and the sun is shining; the return trek takes only a few minutes.

When they reach her door she says firmly, "Come in for a hot drink; it seems you have landed me in a heap of mystery and I want to know what."

Melchior acquiesces with a nod of his head.

"Yes, you deserve to be told about the sad affair in which I involved you. Stoffel should know as well, but it is not for children's ears."

Elisabeth puts the heavy bundle on the bed and disperses her children about the neighbours on various errands and then, with a cup of hot water and molasses in front of them, she, Stoffel and Melchior sit at the rude table. Melchior begins.

"This is a matter that could fetch us all a bit of trouble with the English if it becomes known. They tolerate Old Labrador and his family because they are useful, but they never forget that they are Acadian; they only suspect that they are also part Mi'kmaq, but it is true. Anne may be pure Acadian, but Paul and his nephew are at least half Indian, probably more. They see the advantage in having peaceful relations with the English and hope that the English, the Acadian and the Indian can live together peaceably. So they cooperate with the soldiers. But the English never really trust them. They use me as a go-between because I can speak to them in Maliseet, a language close to Mi'kmaq."

"Where did you learn to speak an Indian language?" asks Elisabeth.

"In Maine, where I lived for a time and where I met Noel Rousse, the other man who was there tonight. He is an Acadian and the young girl's grandfather."

Elisabeth remains silent and he continues.

"Indians and Acadians lived together in Merlegueche for several generations. When it became too dangerous for them to be so close to the English, they left, all except Old Labrador. The names Guidry and Labrador have become interchangeable, Jean Deschamps is John Labrador, or Paul might be Guidry or Labrador. These people have lived independent of any government or laws except their own for a hundred years. They live by their own rules and are fiercely independent.

"Noel Rousse, the man you saw last night, is an old friend of mine and of Paul's. He is Acadian, but lives in Maine, near Quebec. He and one of his sons, Gilbert, married Mi'kmaq women from Nova Scotia.

Those women are the same family as Keskoua, a Mi'kmaq woman who was Old Labrador's first wife. That is how they know each other. Azelie, the young girl whose baby you delivered, is Gilbert's daughter and Noel's granddaughter."

"Now Anne is married to Old Labrador. What happened to Kesk-oo-aa?" asks Elisabeth.

"She died."

"Oh. I am sorry, continue."

"Noel's grandson, the brother of Azelie, is called Half Ear because he has no ear lobes. He has always been in trouble. He's a man now, probably about 17 years old. When Azelie finally had to admit she was pregnant, she accused her brother of raping her, not once, but many times. Her father refused to believe her, refused to believe that his son could be so evil, so she ran away to her Grandfather Noel. He brought her here, to Anne, to help her with the birth because she is young, only thirteen."

"Thirteen?" gasps Elisabeth. "She is a child herself."

"Yes, she is a child herself," agrees Melchior. "Incest is not accepted among the Mi'kmaq. The girl and the child are dead to their families; no one, not even a distant relative will offer them care."

"What happens to the boy, the father?" Elisabeth asks.

"I don't know, that depends upon the family or the village. His crime will be handled as they decide."

Elisabeth purses her lips, angry that the girl should be so harshly treated and suffer so much only to be rejected while the boy might not pay any price.

"Now that the baby is here, it is obvious that it belongs to Noel's family. His grandson has these ears with no lobes, none of the girls have these ears, which proves Azelie's story."

"Anne said that they will be sent away, the child taken from the mother," says Elisabeth.

"Yes, but they will have a chance. The child will never be told where he comes from and if the girl says nothing, no one will know. Noel and the elders of the family will hold a meeting and talk about what to do with the offender. We may never know what they decide. To have let the child or the mother die, by not doing all we could do to save them, would have been a sin against God. That's why I came for you."

"You must know them well for them to trust you so intimately," comments Elisabeth. "How long have you known Old Labrador?"

"Only since we came here, but I knew he would be here. I came to Halifax because of Noel Rousse. I've known him for many years and he knows Old Labrador. With these connections, I sort of loaned myself to Colonel Lawrence as an advisor on French and Indian affairs.

"The Indian and the Acadian people have a mutually beneficial relationship. Noel and I, we wondered if we could influence events between the Indians and French and the English to maintain this working relationship. Noel collects information by travelling through Maine, western New Brunswick and Quebec, while I travel through Nova Scotia and eastern New Brunswick. We meet to exchange information and make plans on what to advise the English."

"You are spies then," accuses Elisabeth, "but for whom?"

"No. We are spies for no one. I give the English honest information. All I do is try to influence Lawrence to take actions that allow for peace instead of war. There are those who want to control North America: the French, the Catholic Church, the English, some of the Indian tribes. England and France, especially, are at each other's throats over the boundaries of their territories in North America."

"So you have told me," murmurs Elisabeth.

"We came here to get away from war," exclaims Stoffel.

"What does that have to do with us here in Lunenburg?" Elisabeth asks. "We're only farmers and families who want to build our homes and work fields and live peacefully with each other."

"The next war between England and France will be fought in North America. Both countries see these colonies, including Nova Scotia, as a source of wealth, of fur, of timber, of fish. Already some of the timber we cut here is being used to make masts for English naval ships. And beaver pelts are shipped to Europe for the making of hats and fur coats and, of course, the fish for food. So England and France want to finally settle the boundary dispute and establish control over as much territory in North America as possible. And the church has involved itself, Catholic and Protestant wanting to dominate each other. English Halifax and French Quebec City each want to be the centre of power. Lunenburg was founded by the English to be a Protestant centre, whatever troubles come will affect us."

"We left our home to live a peaceful life, I don't want to fight a war," protests Stoffel, "I want to build a farm and live my old days with my sons around me."

"None of us want war, but already some of the Swiss settlers have fled to French territory fearing that the English may win the war."

"I did not realize I was so ignorant. I feel I know nothing," murmurs Elisabeth more to herself than to the others. She looks up and says, "And what if there is war and the French win? What will happen to us then? Will we have to worship in the Catholic faith again?"

Memories of the hardships caused by the years of war in Europe are sharp in her mind. Stoffel lays a hand on her shoulder, "If it happens, we will survive, this is our land now. Besides," he jested, "who, but us tough Deutsche would want to farm among the rocks and salt water?"

Elisabeth smiles wanly and, excusing herself, says, "I must be about my housework if we are to eat today."

Melchior rises to leave. As he takes his farewell of Stoffel, he says, "Your wife was very brave today, but it might be best not to speak of these events to people whom you do not trust absolutely. The English soldiers are more and more distrustful of the Acadians every day. And of the Indians. Settlers who are thought to be too sympathetic towards them may find themselves in trouble. It would be best if no one knew that Indians had come here."

"I understand. Thank you. I'll tell Elisabeth to keep her distance and stay among her own people."

Melchior smiles and replies, "Yes, well, I'm sure she will listen."

He goes out into the deep snow with his head down, deep in thought and occupied with squaring his conscience with the trouble he may have caused for his friends.

Elisabeth and Stoffel sit quietly together, each with their own thoughts. Finally, Stoffel asks her, "What is in the bundle?"

"Oh, I forgot about it. I don't know, a gift."

She unrolls the smoothly tanned leather. It is tough but quite pliable. Stoffel is curious and feels it in his fingers.

"It feels like heavy boot leather," he says. "What is that you have there?" he questions as he sees Elisabeth holding something in her hands.

"Mi'kmaq moccasins. Shoes, Indian shoes. See how beautifully decorated they are," she says, holding them out for Stoffel to see.

"They don't look very sturdy," he comments. "What's this?"

He points to a bark container that has rolled out onto the bed. Elisabeth retrieves it and takes a tentative sniff.

"I think it is grease, to rub into the moccasins and make them waterproof."

"There is enough leather here for several pairs of shoes, or a pairs of boots," says Stoffel. "It feels like good leather. I wonder what kind it is?"

"I don't know; it's too thick for a deer. Anyway, it is a very generous gift."

"I'm not sure I like Melchior introducing you to these people," Stoffel comments.

Elisabeth does not answer and Stoffel does not pursue it.

January drags into February and Elisabeth finds no opportunity to visit the Labrador household. She does not want to bring attention to them by openly visiting them, nor does she want to directly disobey her husband's instructions to be discreet and stay away from them. She has little time for contemplation, keeping her family warm, clothed and fed take most of the daylight hours, however, during the long minutes that it takes for the bedcovers to warm up and tease the chill out of her bones when she goes to bed, she sometimes thinks about the young girl and the baby and wonders how they are faring.

In the meantime, word of her skill as a midwife is spreading and an increasing number of requests for her presence at the arrival of a new Lunenburger follow tentative knocks on her door. Appolonia Schmeltzer who lives in the next section of homes produces a daughter in January, and their neighbours, Pieter and Sabrina Bubechoffer, joyfully welcome their first son, Conrad, in February.

Then, on February 25th, Margarete goes into labour. Elisabeth persuades Adam to go next door and wait with Stoffel and give her some room in the little cabin. Maria, despite her youth and independent ways, has a steady head in a crisis and when there are no other women in the household to assist, she goes with her mother. And so, it is Maria who sits with Elisabeth during the long night and day it takes Ferdinand Schauffner to arrive. There are moments when she fears her friend will slip away, but with the rising sun she senses a change in her. She believes that is the moment when Margarete decided to live.

"You are here my friend?" Margarete asks in a faint voice.

"I am here. It is taking long, but all is well. I will be here until your child is safely born."

"I am ready. I am ready to have this baby," she murmurs.

It is nearly time for supper when a final effort thrusts her baby boy into the world. He is feisty; no need to run and tell his father, young Ferdi announces his own arrival heartily. Adam soon comes running and joy banishes the worry on his brow.

As Elisabeth rises from the bedside, Margarete grabs her hand.

"Thank you, thank you my friend, I could not have done it without you. I'll owe you for the rest of my life. I am more grateful than I can say."

"You would have done so for me, you don't have to say anything."

Many births occur during that winter, increasing the population of Lunenburg by at least several dozen downy heads and demanding appetites. The men and older children cut and collect lumber and wood for fires, make temporary repairs to leaking roofs and draughty walls; the women cook what food they can find or have hoarded. When they have a few hours to spare, they meet in each other's cabins and talk among themselves while sewing, mending, or quilting any and every scrap of material into warm clothes and bedcovers.

Elisabeth remembers the intense conversation with Melchior Seiler about the expected war and listens keenly to people's conversations. Are they aware of the threat to their settlement that is brewing or are they as ignorant of the world outside Lunenburg as she is? The women are immersed in the care of their husbands and children, interested in the gossip of the community, and the men are concerned only with their own ever present problems. They have little interest in the politics and intrigue's of governments, or in the wildlife and plants of the forest except for the ones that can fill an empty stomach, or the fish in the sea, or in learning new ways; they want to establish their old ways on the new land. These settlers are farmers and tradesmen, born and bred for generations far from the ocean, used to the rhythm of land crops. The women think as their husbands think.

Elisabeth is frustrated with herself, and with them, for knowing so little and having so little power for action. With her healing and midwife skills she is in and out of many homes in Lunenburg, from poorest to wealthiest, German-speaking, French-speaking, occasionally an English-speaking one, but still she is trapped in a woman's world and not at liberty to discuss her ideas or ask questions. She is relieved when early March brings longer hours of daylight and a relief from the incessant cold and wind that has turned her home into a prison.

On her way to the privy, she stops for a moment in the watery light of the moon and reflects on her recent feelings of restlessness, *"Lord, is it selfish to want more than I have? I do not understand what it is I am feeling. There is so much to know and I know so little. I am ignorant and seem to have naught but questions. Forgive me, my Lord; I am not ungrateful for what I have, truly. Amen."*

6

The Acadians

Despite the sun, the early March air is bone numbing; the coldness of the North Atlantic seeps into Elisabeth's feet through the soles of her boots and insinuates chill fingers beneath her cloak. Since the cold weather began, worship has been held in people's homes. No one's house is large enough for everyone to meet together, so they have separated into groups of friends and neighbours, the host acting as lay pastor for the service. Sunday service today is at the home of Bernhard Herman.

It is only two blocks to the Herman's house. Elisabeth is ahead of the others as Catherine asked her to assist in last minute preparations; she carries drinking cups for her family for a welcome hot drink before service commences.

She knocks at the front door instead of the kitchen door as usual; she is an invited guest of the household this morning, not a guest of the maid. For a moment she considers the luxury of actually having two doors, of having enough rooms to make two doors necessary.

"In time, if it pleases God," she prays, *"in time.*

Catherine greets Elisabeth at the door, relieves her of her cloak and the cups, and hands them to a young girl who must be a newly hired maid. Elisabeth recognizes one of the young girls orphaned on the *Sally* but cannot recall her name.

"I remember you from the voyage but, I'm sorry, I forget your name. I'm glad to see you again," she greets the girl.

The girl smiles, bobs a curtsy and replies softly, "Thank you Ma'am, I am Juliana Margarete—"

Catharine interrupts her, "That will be all, Greta, a maid does not converse with the master's guests."

Elisabeth's eyebrows draw down; she wonders if the rebuke has also been meant for her, a reminder that guests do not talk with the servants. She refuses to be moved along into the parlour and again addresses the girl.

"Yes, now I remember. Your father was Philip. I was very sorry to learn that your parents did not survive the journey." She pauses, "Didn't you have a brother?"

The little maid looks covertly at Catherine but answers, "Yes Mistress, Daniel. He's still in the orphanage at Halifax."

"He's not here with you?"

"No Mistress, he's only 10; Master says that he's too young to be useful."

"And too young to be without his only family," comments Elisabeth. "You're young yourself. Thirteen?"

"I am 14 years old," Greta replies proudly, squaring her thin shoulders and lifting her chin, "old enough to work, and to look after my brother."

"Yes, I believe you are," answers Elisabeth.

Having made her point and satisfied her curiosity, Elisabeth smiles and nods her head at the little maid, then moves into the parlour with Catherine. Instead of being put to work in the kitchen as she had expected, Elisabeth is offered a seat beside a round table in the corner of the room and a warming cup to ease the chill of her fingers and toes. She sips and waits for Catherine to reveal why she has been invited to arrive early. Outwardly, her face is calm but, inwardly, Elisabeth is alternately amused and rankled at Catherine's boldness to comport herself as the mistress of the house.

"Surely," she thinks as she waits for Catherine to come to the reason for her early invitation, "they could have brought the little brother as well as the sister."

Bernhard Herman is not a mean man, rather, a man centered on his own affairs and not those of the household; he could have been persuaded to accept the young boy. And here is Catherine entertaining her in the parlour. Is this significant or merely a sign of the impending Sunday service?

Catherine begins, "Elisabeth, you know that I am your friend."

This being an exaggerated statement of their relationship, Elisabeth raises her eyebrows slightly but remains still, calmly placing the cup on the table and folding her hands on her lap as she waits for Catherine to continue.

"I have heard some distressing tales. I'm sure they're not true." Catherine leans forward and gives Elisabeth's hands a quick touch before continuing, "Anna Catharina tells me that a friend's mother saw you with a strange man and you went with him into the house of Old Labrador." Catherine leans forward and whispers, "I heard he is an Acadian spy. The man looks like a savage!" Sitting upright again, she continues, "I'm sure it was on an act of mercy—but what have you done?"

Of all the narrow minded—this is her affair, not theirs. Elisabeth remembers that Anna Catharina is one of the Herman daughters. She feels her lips compressing; however, before she can utter the rash words that come to her tongue, caution takes over. If Catherine knows of her visit to the Labrador home and the birth of the child there, so do others. How best to douse this pile of embers? She isn't worried about the rumour of her being with a strange man, that is easily quashed, but the exposure of Melchior's friend, Noel, and the story of Azelie could hurt many people. This is not a moment for a discourse on the dangers of gossip. She chooses the biggest weapon she has, the truth, at least part of the truth.

She forces her mouth into a relaxed smile and laughs lightly.

"Your teller of tales can only be referring to one event, and whoever it is should have looked more carefully, the "stranger" she saw was Pastor Seiler. Old Labrador had tanned a deer hide for him and he was on his way to collect it. I was on my way home from a night visit and so we walked together. I will admit to a curiosity to see the inside of their house."

"What were you doing out so early?" persists Catherine.

"A sad matter and a private one," answers Elisabeth, foreclosing on any further questions. Inside, she silently apologizes, *"God forgive me the partial lie."* It seems the wiser course and the only story she can think of quickly.

Catherine's curiosity is obviously not satisfied, but there is little more she can ask and remain within the bounds of good manners. Elisabeth is often out and about on errands of mercy; Melchior Seiler and Stoffel are good friends. It is reasonable that if he and Elisabeth should meet, he would walk her safely home. A knock sounds on the front door, heralding the arrival of the rest of the worshippers, and an end to their conversation, this time.

Eight families attend the service. Too many for the small parlour, they fill the family sitting room as well as the dining room, the children sit on their parents laps and on the stairs. Master Herman acts as pastor for the service, standing in the narrow central hallway. As the service closes, Melchior stands and asks if he might speak to the people. Bernhard agrees.

"I have come to make a request, to impose upon your generosity and Christian charity. There are several families of our congregation who have lost either a father or a mother, or both, and the older children are trying to carry on. They need help if they are to survive until the warmer weather," he tells them.

Melchior describes their plight and asks if any are able to help them. People offer wood, a hot meal, bed covers. Bernhard Herman nods his head in support of these ideas and stands up to make his contribution, telling the people; "I have three daughters and two female domestics, five women, in my household. I am sure they will delight in producing a patchwork bedcover or two for the poor families. You may count on me."

Elisabeth throws a quick glance at Catherine whose face has gone as white as bleached linen. She admires the grace with which she holds her head up at being called a female domestic in front of such a gathering and smiles in pleased acquiescence. She regrets her earlier pique at Catherine; it must be unnerving to be treated one minute as Bernhard's hostess and the next as his servant. She resolves to offer her assistance with the bedcovers. Also, Melchior will let her know which families are in need and she will take them a basin of pudding or pot of soup tomorrow.

The lingering days of winter begin and end in starless darkness. Occasionally, the moon provides a silver light over the harbour, forming shadowy sculptures among the ice pans that litter the shore. The branches of the tall spruce and balsam fir trees bow gracefully under their weight of snow while the sturdy maples thrust their bare arms skyward as though enticing the moon to dance.

Inside their single room, Elisabeth and Stoffel bend their heads towards the flickering light from the oil lamp. Stoffel is sewing yet another patch over the toe of a worn boot. He wears them out pushing the endless small rocks out of his way as he makes trails and drags his cut logs to the head of Back Harbour. When he has enough logs, he will transport them to the main wharf for shipment to Halifax. Elisabeth sews a strip of scavenged canvas to the bottom of Peter's britches; he has grown taller since the cold weather began, gangly and awkward, with his thoughts kept in his head. She looks up and smiles at her younger son. He smiles briefly back and returns to his carving. He is turning a piece of poplar into a puppy for Evie who sits at his side watching his hands intently. Maria and Gertrud are preparing the bread and meat pudding that will be reheated for their breakfast; baby Bettina is already asleep under her sheepskin. Elisabeth suppresses a worried sigh; they will be out of food well before the next harvest arrives, even before the spring bounty of forest and marsh becomes available.

A cold draught rolls across the floor as the deer hide is pushed aside and Christof enters the cabin. He and Christian Graff have been out checking their rabbit snares.

He shakes his head and says, "No luck, too much moonlight, or else they are getting more clever." He removes his cloak and crouches beside the last of the fire to warm himself. "We met Philip Schmeltzer, the husband of Christian's mother. He had caught only one rabbit himself by the way and he is a good trapper," he tells his mother.

Elisabeth smiles ruefully to herself. Christian Graff has reconciled with his mother but continues to refer to his stepfather as his mother's husband. Philip Schmeltzer is a good man; however, Christian remembers his own father and is determined to be faithful to his memory. No use explaining to him that a woman with a son to raise, and a future to secure, can do so better with a husband than without, and a good man was better than a mean one. Christian is dutiful but determined to make his own way as early as possible. He is probably right to do so; the family already has a new child of its own.

"However," Christof adds, "I have some news. Some of the men are talking about building a sawpit below the blockhouse, where the land slopes down to the water. We will receive more for squared timber than round. Also, we can cut some of our logs into timber for ourselves. Tomorrow morning a group of the men are going to erect the main platform. Anyone who has something to offer, spikes or hammer, some logs or timber or a digging tool is invited to help. I was thinking that I could donate two logs." Christof looks at his father, "What I really mean is that I could donate two of yours and then give you two of mine when I get out to the Mahone Bay land."

Christof as well as Stoffel had received a grant of 30 acres of farmland. Stoffel claimed the nearer one on the North West Range, which would allow him to walk back and forth easily to the town site, while Christof accepted the one farther away, on the western side of Mahone Bay. They are fortunate grants, well located and accessible, containing good timber trees and not requiring undue preparation before areas of them could be planted. Adam Schauffner received a grant much farther away, northeast of Mahone Bay, called Clearland. He has been unable to take up his land and helps his old friend Stoffel with his. Peter, now 11, will not be eligible for his own land for at least three more years.

Stoffel continues to work silently with his awl and leather thong until he completes the last knot, then he raises his head and says, "It is a fine idea, son, but you will give only one log and I will give the other. If they need more, we will think again. And tomorrow we will go and help with the construction although I think the ground is still frozen and not much will be accomplished."

Christof's thank you holds tones of relief and Elisabeth understands that he had already committed the logs before consulting his father. She suspects Stoffel knew it, too, and that was why he had made him wait for the answer. The lamp flickers erratically, warning them that it is nearly out of oil. Time for bed. Not only does it save fuel, it is warmer in bed. The men go out to the privy while the women make themselves ready for sleep and then the men do the same.

By the end of March, the snow is slumping into itself and the ice is rotting into puddles and no longer provides a safe bridge across the ponds and creeks. The saw pit is ready to be erected as soon as the ground thaws enough to dig the post holes and the men are preparing to start work on their land again; clearing the stumps of the trees they felled during the winter and upgrading the rough trails; some even have enough land ready to think of planting root vegetables or barley come warm weather.

Elisabeth and the girls have pieced together two bedcover tops for the needy families which are ready for quilting when they find backing and batting to complete them. Catherine and the Herman daughters have also made two tops ready for backing. To this point a quilt can be done alone but the finishing is much easier, and more social, when done in a group around a table or a frame. A timid knock on Elisabeth's door one noon announces the arrival of Catherine. As usual when she wants to talk with Elisabeth, she comes prepared with a ready excuse.

"Why doesn't she just say, I would like to speak with you?" wonders Elisabeth.

This time it is to ask Elisabeth if she and her daughters would like to join her and the Herman daughters for a quilting. It could be one afternoon soon and she would make them some hot drinks and sweet biscuits. Evie and the youngest Herman daughter, Henrietta, could look after Bettina while the others make a start at finishing the bedcovers. Elisabeth hesitates, she does not want any of the prying questions she was subject to the last time she was alone with Catherine. Of course, all the girls will be there and so the opportunity would be unlikely; in addition, it is a sound idea and she is tired of her own company. The winter is growing wearisome.

"Will any of the other ladies be coming?" she asks Catherine.

"Perhaps one or two others. We'd already be six around the table, there's not room for many more. Who would you like me to invite?" she asks.

Elisabeth smiles. "Anyone with a steady hand and a fast needle," she replies.

"Yes," agrees Catherine with a fleeting smile, "it is an occasion more for sewing than gossiping. The needy families will be saving the last of their wood for cooking and let the fires go out at night. Their houses will seem colder than ever."

"I took them some basins of pudding and stew a few times. In a couple of cases, I fear their problem is a lack of industry. Sadly, they don't seem to know how to help themselves. Now they're weakened with illness and hunger and their plight is even worse."

Catherine nods her head in agreement but reminds Elisabeth, "Some are working hard but have been struck with ill fortune."

"Indeed. You are right," Elisabeth concurs. "About the quilts. What can we use to make them warm?"

"Several of the women brought me some torn and worn bedcovers that can be patched together. I also have another idea that I want to discuss with you. I was wondering what happens to the military blankets when they are worn out and no longer useful for bedding, and if Captain Sutherland would give a few to us. We could turn them or stitch pieces together. They would make warm quilts. Most people are using any material they have for their own beds, there is little to spare."

"I have made two covers from pieces I collected from neighbours around the section but I have nothing to make them warm," says Elisabeth.

"Oh, you are very generous, as always. I heard that you have taken them food many times. How do you manage all this?" Catherine inquires with a hint of envy in her voice.

"Many hands make light work," Elisabeth explains. "My daughters as well as my neighbours helped and it was not a burden. They are very plain bedcovers, meant to keep someone warm, not to be a fancy piece. It will be a great help if we could find blankets or wool for filling. Even dry grass could be stuffed into a cover and tied in place." Elisabeth thinks for a minute and then adds, "The idea of using old military blankets is a good one, leave it with me and I will see if I can beg several for our use."

Victoria helped her with much of the sewing; however, she knows Catherine's views on Victoria and doesn't wish to bring her into the conversation. To Catherine's way of thinking, people from the American colonies are wild frontiersmen, and a red haired colonial mistress is incomprehensible and suspicious. It matters not if her lover is someone important; she disapproves wholly of Elisabeth's friendship with her. As do some of the other ladies.

As Catherine rises to take her leave, another knock comes at the door. This one brisk and confident. It is Victoria herself.

Victoria sees the quickly masked look of consternation that flashes over Elisabeth's face as she opens the door.

"You have company," she says, "I will come another time," and turns away.

"No," says Elisabeth, putting her hand on Victoria's arm and encouraging her to enter. "It is Catherine, come to ask whether I can help to finish the quilts for the church."

Although they know each other by sight, the two women have not been introduced nor ever spoken to each other; however, through their friendship with Elisabeth, they know quite a lot about each other. What they don't know, they speculate. Although both are loyal to Elisabeth, they have never wished to pursue a friendship between themselves. Introductions are acknowledged coolly and Catherine does not extend an invitation to Victoria to join in the finishing of the quilts despite Elisabeth's hints.

After Catherine's departure, Victoria apologizes to her friend for putting her in such a position, "I would not have come if I had known she were here."

Elisabeth tells Victoria, "Do not concern yourself; it was bound to happen at some time. Eventually, she will welcome you, as I do. I am happy to see you, you are always welcome."

"I try to like her for your sake but I think she takes advantage of you, you are always doing things for her. What does she do for you?" she asks in an exasperated voice.

"I know, she can be difficult and unpredictable, but she has no one else; she's scarcely older than the girls she looks after. The girls mostly do what they want and their father leaves all of their upbringing to her plus the running of the house." Elisabeth pauses, and then adds, "I think she's had very little guidance herself which is why she watches everyone so closely, to see how ladies act."

"That may be, but she's still only a maid who puts on airs above her station," replies Victoria in irritation.

"I confess that in weak moments I also think that, but I don't know the things that haunt her, and I try to be charitable. You must agree that she tries to better herself and does her work dutifully."

"Yes. That's true, Elisabeth. I apologize for my hasty words. Now let's talk about something happier. The quilt tops are very attractive. If I say so myself, we were quite successful in arranging the pieces into a pleasing design. Have you any thoughts on how we can finish them?"

"Actually, Catherine had an idea for that problem and I think it's a good one. Do you think that Patrick could arrange for us to have several of the old military blankets? There must be some that are worn through and could be pieced to make a warm batting. I doubt the soldiers turn their blankets but use them until they are threadbare. What happens to them then?" asks Elisabeth.

"I don't know," Victoria answers. "The government is very miserly with the soldiers and provides them with very little. The men mend their own uniforms, do their own laundry and repair their own boots." She turns her head away so that her eyes cannot meet Elisabeth's, "I don't think Patrick would listen to me on the matter, but he might listen to Melchior, he seems to like him and respect what he says. As it is for the church, he might listen to Reverend Moreau as well. Is he in favour of this project?"

"I think so; Melchior was going to talk to him about it. We had no word to stop our activities." Elisabeth wonders at Victoria's lack of enthusiasm.

"I can speak to Patrick about the work the women are doing to help the poor. The fact that the settlers are helping themselves will look good in his reports. Perhaps you could see whether Melchior would put the specific request to him; he might think I was trying to help some people over others," she explains. "Patrick will like the idea of the settlers helping each other in a way that does not require him to ask Halifax for something. He knows he will have to request more rations for the people soon, it's obvious that you can't survive on your present supplies until summer. Governor Lawrence is still determined that this town will be a success, so he will agree to the extension of rations as long as they are needed, and as long as he can convince the London Board of Trade they are a necessary and worthwhile investment."

Victoria stops for breath.

Elisabeth sorts through the information in Victoria's words while taking her wrap and preparing a warming cup of hot water and molasses. They are to receive rations again; that is welcome news. She is disturbed to realize once again that Victoria is unwilling to ask any favours of her lover; she doesn't understand whether this speaks of his relationship with his former commander, the present Governor Lawrence, or his relationship with Victoria. However, she realizes it isn't so different from many other women, thankful once again for Stoffel's patient understanding. She vows to show her appreciation for his acceptance of the demands of a healer's life. She often is away at mealtime or slipping out in the night to deliver a baby or see to a sick child.

"I am certain that Pastor Seiler would agree to present the request to Captain Sutherland," Elisabeth says. "He can justify the donation of old blankets quite easily in his accounting, I am sure. We only need a half dozen. I will ask him."

She places the cup in front of Victoria and seats herself on the bench opposite. During the winter, the bark on the blocks of wood which serve as seats has dried and Peter has been able to chip it away so that the roughness no longer catches at one's skirts. The rough timber of the table has smoothed under the onslaught of many scourings with sand. Elisabeth looks more closely at Victoria; she is not her usual ebullient self.

Forthright as usual, she asks, "Is something the matter, Victoria? You appear overly thoughtful today."

"I had supper with Patrick last evening. He invited me to his quarters. He won't visit me in town, but his rooms are separate from the men and sometimes we share meals there. I don't see him very often these days. A small number of the men have brought their wives to Lunenburg and housing them is a problem, some of them are living in lean-tos built onto the storage buildings. He refuses to let me live in such conditions, so I must live with the van der Hydes, but having my own place would be much more convenient for us and much cozier." She smiles wistfully.

Elisabeth sits quietly, not wanting to interrupt Victoria's hesitant beginning. She is worried about something, something she does not know how to broach. Let her speak it in her own time.

"Elisabeth, Patrick was asking me about you, asking questions about what you do when you go about the town, asking why you are in and out of so many houses, especially the Swiss families. He didn't seem happy when I told him that you spoke French."

Elisabeth draws in her breath in exasperation. First Catherine and now Victoria.

Victoria continues, "Now don't get upset, I admire what you can do, you help so many. I wish I could heal people like you do. It's just that the soldiers see enemies everywhere, especially the Acadians and the Indians and the French. When the war comes between the English and the French, they will think anyone who speaks French is a potential spy."

"Even the Swiss?" asked Elisabeth. "They brought them here themselves and they are Protestant as well."

"Some of them fled Lunenburg during the summer and fall, probably to go to Fortress Louisbourg with the French."

"Fortress Louisbourg? I've heard of that, a large French fort. I thought it was far from here."

"It is on Île Royale, an island off the northern end of Nova Scotia, beyond Halifax; it is only a few days by ship in good weather," explains Victoria. "I was there with Patrick for three years before we came to Halifax."

"Oh. Why were you at a French fort?"

"For a few years, between 1745 and 1749, it was English. It is French now, again."

Elisabeth decides not to pursue a subject she knows nothing about and returns to the question of the fleeing Swiss.

"I only know the families from the *Sally*, and they want only to have their land and raise their crops and their children. They know nothing of the conflict between the kings of England and France. Nor care."

"I know. That's what I told him. Those who wanted to leave have left, the rest consider themselves under the protection of the English and are loyal to the English king." She hesitates and adds, "He says that you are friendly with the Acadians and are sympathetic toward the Indians, the Mi'kmaq."

Elisabeth is stung and refutes the slur on her loyalty to the English, "No more than he; he meets with Cloverwater, the nephew of Old Labrador frequently. They are as close to Acadian or Indian as I have met. Even Colonel Lawrence befriended them when he was here. He was the person who encouraged the use of him as an informant." She quickly stands up and as abruptly sits down again. "People can be so exasperating," she adds. "Is he saying it is alright for him to befriend them but not me?"

Victoria raises her head and looks at Elisabeth, "I know about the birth of the Indian baby," she hesitates, "and so does Patrick."

Elisabeth looks a question at Victoria.

"Melchior told him."

Elisabeth is startled. Why would Melchior tell Captain Sutherland of the birth when he had cautioned her to be silent about it?

"Patrick is not certain that you delivered it, but he suspects. Patrick is an English military officer; his first loyalty is to his King and to the interests of his King, which is how he views everything. And so with Governor Lawrence."

Elisabeth understands that this is Patrick's prejudices talking, not Victoria's. Victoria is caught between her friend and her lover. The only thing she can do is reassure Victoria that all was an innocent act of mercy; Patrick knows more of Cloverwater and Labrador than she does.

"I know, Elisabeth, I know you are true and loyal. So does Patrick underneath. Let's talk about more pleasant things. I have wonderful news," she says as a rosy blush colours her freckled cheeks. "Patrick and I are going to have a baby."

Elisabeth rises quickly to embrace and kiss her friend, "Quelle bonne nouvelle! That is indeed wonderful news. I am very happy for you. How long have you known? What does Patrick say?"

Victoria gives a little laugh, "Slow down, one question at a time. In the late summer or early fall." She reaches for Elisabeth's hand, "I'm so glad that you'll be with me, only to you will I admit that I'm afraid of the road ahead. So many of the women disapprove of me, and I will not be able to stay in my position with the van der Hydes. Where will I live?"

"Surely Patrick will take care of you, see that you have proper shelter and provide for his child."

"Patrick was surprised when I told him. We've been together almost fourteen years and this is the first time I have become pregnant. I believed it was not possible for me to conceive. Soon I will be 30 years old." She turns her head away and a single sob escapes from behind the hand pressed over her mouth; without raising her head she looks at Elisabeth and confesses in a low voice, "I always thought that if I became pregnant, Patrick would marry me, but he did not mention it."

Elisabeth instantly squashes the harsh thoughts that sneak into her mind—Patrick is no different than many men. She begs God's forgiveness for her lack of charity.

Again Elisabeth takes her in her arms and comforts her as she would a child until the weeping subsides. No wonder she had been gloomy today. How could Patrick not want to marry this lovely intelligent woman who adores him? There is no other woman in his life. And he is not a young man with tens of years ahead of him.

"He says a soldier's life is too uncertain and it would be unfair to inflict it on a wife and children," reveals Victoria.

Elisabeth says nothing. To her mind it is unfair to inflict the burden of social condemnation and the rearing of an illegitimate child on a woman. A selfish attitude garbed in sanctimony is her conclusion. She has heard it before, the same sad story and the same sad tears poured out between the birthing pains of another child who will have to endure the stigma of illegitimacy.

"I thought he would marry me. He said he loved me."

Elisabeth sighs and strokes Victoria's shoulder.

"Mayhap he will change his mind when he holds his child in his arms," Elisabeth offers a hope to encourage her friend. "He does love you, in his way."

"I will pray for such, but he is a very stubborn man when he settles on something. He was shocked by the news, but I could see that his first reaction was pleasure. His face lit up and he smiled even to his eyes." Victoria straightens and dries her tears, "Then he quickly covered his pleasure and gave me the old 'I'm a soldier' speech again."

Patting Elisabeth's hand in thanks for her friendship and comfort, she stands up and walks slowly around the small room to regain her composure.

When she returns to her seat Victoria says firmly, "Whatever Patrick decides, my feelings for him will not change. I love him and I will love his child. With God's help, I will manage. I do not believe that Patrick will desert me, I know that he loves me, too."

"Yes," confirms Elisabeth, "I believe that he does. I have seen the way he looks at you; he is always aware that you are near."

Victoria smiles at this thought and seems more her usual happy self when she takes her leave.

When Maria returns from visiting her friend, Anna, Elisabeth sends her to fetch Gertrud and Evie from the Schauffner's where they have been entertaining Bettina and Margarete's infant son, Ferdinand, Ferdi for short. With the preparations for their supper complete, she leaves the girls in charge and goes to meet her husband and sons as they return from working on the North West Range farm, the home farm. How good that sounds, the home farm.

At the western end of town, a street leads up from the Harbour along the line of the western palisade and meets the ridge path, providing a sure place to encounter people walking to and from the town and the hinterland. Although there are hints of warmth in the late March sunlight, the ground is a mix of frozen earth and sloppy mud, so Elisabeth puts on her Holzpantoffel, wooden shoes, that Stoffel carved for her and her wool cloak. When Christof learns to tan rabbit skin so that it does not stink, she will try lining a cloak with rabbit fur next winter. She breathes deeply of the clear air and steps out purposefully for the meeting place. Her eyes stray to the buds filling on the twigs and search for any hint of green among the leaves and emerging undergrowth. Which are edible? Which healing? She will learn.

There is no sign of the men returning from where they have been cutting and hauling logs. She sits on a dry rocky outcrop to wait. She thinks about what they have accomplished. Working together, Stoffel, Christof, Peter and Adam have nearly an acre of land partially cleared. The stumps remain as do the large rocks. The earth is fertile. If they turn it up between the tree stumps, they should be able to plant potatoes this year. Extra potatoes can be sold for cash in Halifax. A sudden shadow rouses her from her reverie. Melchior has come silently along the path from town. She rises but he gestures her to retake her seat.

"How have you been keeping?" he inquires, "I've scarcely seen you these past weeks."

"Yet people seem to see us. How is that?" Elisabeth asks with a stern face.

"What do you mean? You sound angry, or upset; what has someone said to you?"

"Sutherland asked Victoria about the baby, actually he didn't ask her about the baby, he hinted that he knew an Indian baby had been delivered at the Labradors and hoped 'your friend' had not been involved. He is wary of the idea that I visit many homes and understand the French language. Although that is an exaggeration, I barely understand the Acadian way of speaking. She didn't know if he regarded me as trouble or was warning me to stay out of trouble."

Elisabeth looks up at Melchior and asks him bluntly, "Why did you tell him about the baby?"

"He already knew, from town gossip possibly. In this town, you know how a hint becomes a legend overnight. I satisfied his curiosity by telling him that it was only an unexpected birth to a visiting relative of Cloverwater's and that I had insisted on fetching you when difficulties arose."

"Why should he be asking Victoria about me? He knows that I am regarded as a healer by some folk and a midwife. Of course, I visit many homes."

"To be truthful, I think he is jealous of your friendship with Victoria and that is why he is alert to your comings and goings. I'm sure you have nothing to worry about, Elisabeth. He is yet somewhat insecure in his new post, perhaps, and overzealous."

"Catherine asked about the same thing."

"I am sure it is just your friends coming to your protection. Believe me, I am sorry for putting you in this spot. Just be discreet in your meetings with Anne."

"I am. I'm so discreet I never see her," she tells him in exasperation.

"I'm sorry. You should be good friends," he placates her. "The English see potential Acadian spies and enemies everywhere. Captain Sutherland is coming to rely on me to evaluate the information from Cloverwater which he sends to Governor Lawrence. He does not know that the information includes the news that Noel brings to me. Noel's visits are a secret; he would be in danger from the English for being Acadian. He has no 'special relationship' as the Labrador's have."

"Has Monsieur Rousse been back? What of the baby, and the young girl?"

"No, he won't come again until the summer; a muddy trail leaves too many tracks." Melchior paces a few steps away and back.

"Elisabeth," he says and stops.

Alerted by his suddenly sombre tone, she looks at him directly and awaits whatever bad news is coming.

"I'm afraid that I've been keeping something from you. I have sad news to tell you," he begins. With sorrow etched in his face he tells her, "Azelie took her own life."

Elisabeth drew in her breath in shock, "Suicide? No. Oh, the poor child. When?"

"A few days after the birth; she walked away, into the woods. It was no accident. They found her clothes neatly folded beside a deep freshwater spring, one that remains open even in winter."

Sorrow draws deep lines on Elisabeth's face. She doesn't know what to say, remembering the delicate little girl, the pain and shame she endured to have her son. Too little life; too much sorrow.

"I do not understand. How could she commit suicide? I assumed she was Catholic as, I thought, are the Labradors. And Noel, her grandfather. Suicide is a sin."

"To us, maybe not to her. She was part Mi'kmaq and had her way of thinking. It is my belief that she blamed herself for dishonouring her family and that her shame was too great to be endured in this world, and so she chose to join her ancestors in the spirit world."

"I do not understand these words. Do you mean that her suicide would restore honour to her family? What is this 'spirit world'; do you mean 'heaven'? However you say it, she took her own life, and that is wrong."

Melchior shakes his head. "She was both Catholic and pagan; she likely believed both in God's heaven and the spirit world of her mother's gods. 'Pagan' is not right, it is too strong a word; it evokes thoughts of witches and Satan. The Indians have their own beliefs about life and afterlife, gods and mortals. Many of them accept the God of the French priests; however, many also believe as their ancestors did."

Suicide is not something she had thought much about since the sad death of Thérèse in the camp at Halifax. That it should happen twice in a short span of time, both to young women giving birth, is heartbreaking. Neither has she known a pagan; the idea of a god other than God is unsettling. She follows her own line of thinking.

"I believe there is only one God. And our life is God's to give or take; if we take our life, we deny God his right and cannot enter Heaven. Yet Azelie was innocent of any wrong; she was a mere girl, the sin was committed by her brother. How can God not take her to Heaven?"

Melchior gives an exasperated laugh, "You ask awkward questions. I have no answer. Azelie followed the way of the Catholic religion and the way of her Indian people. To her way of believing, she has redeemed the honour of her family, and when she arrives in the spirit world she will join those ancestors who have died before her. She was not afraid to die, only afraid of her welcome in this world because of what her brother did to her. However, our prayers to our Lord for her safe journey cannot hurt."

Elisabeth is a staunch Lutheran, as her family has been for generations and, although she often questions God's intentions for her, she never questions her religion. In fact, she rarely thinks about religion in any abstract way. Everyone she knows at least professes to believe in God and they differ mostly in the manner of their worship or the interpretation of his word. Surely there is only one God, and one Heaven. Lamenting her ignorance and surprised once again at the things Melchior knows, she feels inept in the face of her naivety.

"How do you know so much about the Indians?" she queries him. "Through Noel, I suppose, and your travels. I, too, have journeyed far but do not seem to have learned so much. Are you telling me that she will go to her own heaven, that there is more than one heaven?"

Melchior gives Elisabeth a partly exasperated smile.

"You ask more questions than a theologian! She was sinned against, not a sinner. We'll pray she finds a welcome with her ancestors and also a place in God's heaven."

Another line of thinking returns to Elisabeth.

"She has been dead more than three months and you are just telling me now. That is unfair," she accuses him. "I am not some fainting woman to be protected from the truth. I thought you held me in greater respect than that."

She knows her chin is jutting out and her mouth is compressed into a thin line but she cannot do otherwise. She is overreacting to her grief. She refuses to look at him; her sorrow is too great, and she does not want him to see it.

"Elisabeth, look at me. Look at me."

Reluctantly, she obeys, but stands up so she can look at him more equally.

"I do hold you in great esteem; however, you still need protection from idle gossip. This is a small town and in winter people have time on their hands."

"But I already knew about the birth, what difference would this news have made?"

"You are compassionate, you would have wanted to visit Anne, and you would have wanted answers to too many questions. You must accept that this has happened. It is their tragedy, not ours. We cannot share in it. It was Azelies's choice to atone for her family's shame in this manner. We will never know what happened to the baby; he was passed to other people and will live out his own destiny. Noel will never know nor ever speak of him. He has been shamed by his grandson, but he loved Azelie, and the sorrow will never leave him."

Melchior holds her with a steady gaze and she knows that she must acquiesce.

"You are wiser than I in this matter. I know that I can sometimes rush in with good intentions and only make matters worse. I will accept what you say," she tells him. "Please, will you show me where she died?" Elisabeth asks him.

"Someday, not today, for here comes your family," he replies, raising his arm to wave at an approaching group. "Greetings, Stoffel, and to you Christof and Peter. Greetings, Adam. How went the work today?"

She sighs in frustration; there is too little time for following lines of thought. Endless hours are spent in discussing the weather, the fields and the lack of tools, while they work their way through the ever pressing chores of the day. At the end of the day, they are too tired for thinking. The men go ahead and Elisabeth follows with Peter.

"I went exploring on my own today, guess what I found?" Peter asks his mother. Answering himself, he excitedly tells her, "On the side of a forested ridge farther along than we are clearing now, I found a split in the rocky hillside that has a small waterfall. I wonder if it falls all winter? At the bottom is a deep pool. Maybe you can find lots of healing plants there; I'll show you when the weather is better. Wasn't that a lucky find?"

Elisabeth stumbles slightly. "Yes, that is lucky," she manages to reply. She rebukes herself for hasty conclusions, there is surely more than one deep spring in the surrounding woods; however, in her heart she knows this is Azelie's spring, and on their land. They are forever connected.

"One day, you can show it to me," she tells Peter.

As they go their own ways, she finds a moment to ask Melchior, "Is Azelie's spring on our land?"

"I don't know how you know, but, yes," he confirms.

The May sun warms the earth and frequent showers encourage new growth. Elisabeth is loathe to be indoors and longs to be out about the woods and shore, exploring the plant life that abounds everywhere. She had inspected the garden lot last week and with a few more days of warmth it will be dry enough to work. The lots higher up the slope are already being cultivated, but theirs is at the bottom and will be one of the last to dry, putting her a week behind some of the others. There are advantages though; when the summer dries out the garden plots, hers will be the last to suffer from any drought. Her small garden plot behind their cabin has drained well and is ready for working, even if the main vegetable garden is not.

On a warm morning, she sets the girls to digging out the undergrowth along the western edge of the property and clearing it of stones and roots. Some of the small beds are shaded and others in the sun. Many of the medicinal herbs like to put their roots down at the edge of a lightly wooded area and she is keen to grow a few of the most needed ones, feverfew where the sun will shine on it and the soil is rich, mint where it is shaded and damp, horehound where it is sunny and poor, and camomile the same as feverfew but with deeper soil. Many of the women brought seeds and they have been exchanging them among themselves. Others she intends to find here, either on her own or with help from Anne.

So it is not by happenstance that she chooses to explore south of town along the ridge and marsh beyond the barracks and the palisade, on the little southern peninsula guarding the entrance to the main harbour. This means that she has to cross behind the barracks and in front of the Labrador house. Soon she is out of the town. She avoids the farm lots laid out on the western side of the peninsula and stays to the woods and the marshes where the plants which she seeks are more likely to grow. As she goes, she crushes leaves and buds, smelling her fingers and seeking familiar odours and scents. Many of the evergreens are familiar to her: spruce, juniper, cedar, pine; their scent freshens the air. She gathers the corners of her apron to make a carrying pouch and collects some of the new spruce buds to sweeten the air of the house.

A man's voice speaks quietly from the shadow of a tall spruce, "Do not be startled, Madame Elisabeth. We saw you from the house as, perhaps, you hoped."

Elisabeth starts despite the warning but quickly recovers as she recognizes the soft voice.

"Monsieur Rousse, Madame Guidry, yes, I had hoped I might chance upon you again."

Anne chuckles as she reaches out and briefly holds Elisabeth's hand.

"We Acadians do not take our husband's name until he is dead, please God a long time yet, only then will I become the Widow Guidry. I am called Anne Muis d'Entremont after my father's name. I am not making fun of you, it just sounded peculiar. Anyway, you should call me Anne."

"And I am Elisabeth."

Anne opens her arms slightly and Elisabeth takes the chance and embraces the tiny woman. The women hug, trying to convey what their language barrier will not allow, the events of the January night, the trials of being a healer, their desire to be friends should God permit. They back away and smile.

Noel beams. "Anne would not come alone so I volunteered. I can see it has been worth the risk. What brings you to the woods today?"

"Medicinal herbs and edible plants. I know they must be here but they are not familiar to me."

"You have one of them in your apron. Spruce. The new tips, the inner bark and the gummy sap are medicinal and the roots can be made into thread or rope. The tips make a tea that prevents scurvy and acts as a tonic. It is also good for the stomach. The gum can be used as a poultice on sores or boils. It can also be made into beer," Anne explains.

Elisabeth eagerly follows her explanation.

"Wonderful, I was only going to freshen my house with its scent."

Anne laughs. "It is good for that, too. And so the cedar boughs, also."

Their stroll takes them along a ridge where Anne shows her the white pine and describes the making of a syrup for coughs and congestion and urinary trouble, of using the sticky gum for covering wounds and the straight wood for arrows; the ground hemlock that is both medicine and poison; the slim pliable alder stems that can be woven into collecting baskets and fish traps. She explains about the mussels and periwinkles that can be boiled and eaten, and how the men erect brush weirs to catch fish when the tide ebbs. Under the trees where it is damp and shady, she points out the curled shoots of the tête de violon or fiddlehead, the tétine de souris or slender glasswort, l'herbe de Saint Pierre or the samphire, and the patches beside the sweet water rivulets where the wild mint grows and higher up the ramps or wild leeks—all edible as vegetables or savoury flavourings.

As they come to the edge of the wood where the land changes into a stretch of marsh, a freshwater stream runs to the sea. Along its banks are tall grasses and Anne shows Elisabeth the young pods of bulrushes that can be cooked and the spring leaves of the sweet flag whose root is a powerful all-purpose medicine. Elisabeth sees a patch of similarly straight-leaved plants with a flower of deep blue.

"Oh how beautiful," she exclaims, "what a clear shade of blue. Is it the same plant?"

"No. That is blue flag, the fleur de luce, not sweet flag" smiles Anne. "The root, ground to a paste with a little water, makes a good poultice for bruises and sprains, but it can cause violent upset if swallowed. Let me collect some plants. You must mark their location when they are blooming so that you do not harvest the wrong one. Sit here a while and rest in the sun."

Elisabeth sits on a dry log just at the edge of the woods and tries to remember everything that she's been told. Noel sits beside her, choosing a piece of log hidden by a clump of sumac where he is less likely to be seen by a casual passerby. His caution reminds her of the risk he is taking; in the pleasure of the afternoon she had forgotten the dangers of their meeting. Noel is not known by the military at Lunenburg and, as an Acadian, he would be arrested if he were captured. Elisabeth realizes then what a risk he took to join her and Anne on the herb hunting excursion.

She turns her back slightly to look as though she is alone. Curiosity overcomes her good manners and she asks him if he has brought news for Melchior. He admits he has. She remains silent, not asking the question, but leaving it to him to tell her if he chooses. Noel asks her if she has heard of l'Abbé Le Loutre.

"Le loup?" she asks, "the wolf?"

Noel chuckles quietly and replies, "Oui, vraiment il était un loup, un loup noir, but no, Le Loutre is his name, he is a French Jesuit priest, l'Abbé Jean Louis Le Loutre, who came to Nova Scotia more than fifteen years ago to convert the savages. Well, he did that, but he is also an agent provocateur for the French government who stirs up the Indians against the English. He is more a soldier than a priest. He also does his best to keep the Acadians upset over the intentions of the

English. When he is seen in an area there is often an increase in Indian raids and Acadian hostility. At the moment he is staying close to his headquarters at the head of la baie de Fundy where he travels among the villages. Occasionally he comes as far as Piziquid and Grand Pré on le bassin de Minas, near Fort Edward."

"Is that far from here?" asks Elisabeth. "I don't know of these places. I have heard of Piziquid, Cloverwater's family lives there and he travels there."

"Yes. They are some distance from here but not so far from the French fort at Beauséjour."

"Where is that?"

He shifts on his log and says, "Let me explain. The Bay of Fundy is very wide and long, nearly cutting Nova Scotia from the mainland. A narrow piece of land joins Nova Scotia to the rest of the country and this is where Le Loutre has stationed himself, at Fort Beauséjour."

Elisabeth remembers the map she studied in Halifax and tries to recall those parts that had not been important to her then. At the time, she had been interested only in where her home would be built.

Noel continues. "The English want to control the coastline with their ships and keep the French bottled up on Île Royale, Île St. Jean and Quebec City. If Le Loutre and some others like him can be kept quiet, it may be possible for England and France to work out treaties of peace and we can all get on with our lives."

Elisabeth sighs in agreement, "Yes, that is what I want, to get on with my life, and my family's life."

They sit in companionable silence for a time, Elisabeth mulling over the new names and deciphering the information.

Noel takes their conversation in another direction, "You could have been a shaman had you been born an Indian," he comments.

"A 'shaman'?"

"A medicine woman, a shaman is one who heals or maybe can talk with the spirits, or do magic or see into the future."

"I know nothing of witchcraft," Elisabeth declares emphatically. "I am just a simple healer, a midwife not a witch. No magic or visions for me. I know a little about homely simples such as herb teas or ointments, and about birthing, that is all."

"Do not be alarmed, a shaman is not a witch as you fear them. They are respected people who have special powers. They are respected, and sometimes feared, but never harmed, nor do they harm others. My wife was a daughter of a shaman; she knew nearly all of the plants by name and what they could be used for. She sometimes had visions of the future; she saw the settlers coming, and knew that it meant the end of her people's way of life. She has been with her ancestors for a few years now."

Elisabeth now understands that being with one's ancestors means "has died".

"I'm sorry," she sympathizes, "but these are all things beyond my knowledge. Anne also told me that she fears our coming will mean the end of her way of living. Does she, and your wife, mean the Acadian way or the Indian way?"

"Both, because they are intertwined in Nova Scotia. There are many of you and few of us; in the end that will change everything." He sighs and tells her, "Sometimes my wife comes to me in dreams and so we continue together until it is my time to join her."

This conversation with Noel is taking many directions; Elisabeth is again conflicted by what she is hearing. It is as bad as talking with Melchior. No wonder he and Noel are friends, they understand each other's thoughts.

"But you are Roman Catholic, nein? You must believe that you will go to Heaven after you pass away."

"Yes, but I believe that it is all one place, the Roman Catholic God's Heaven, the Lutheran God's Heaven, the Indian spirit world, and all our loved ones are there in the spirit place, in a place of wisdom and contentment. And that we will eventually be reunited whether we are Catholic or Protestant, Indian or English, German or French. I do not know about the evil ones, where they will go, but there will be no evil ones in heaven."

Elisabeth has no comment to this extraordinary idea but she realizes that it is one that will haunt her.

"You sound like Melchior and you talk to me like Melchior. You say strange things to me and it teases my mind into thinking unfamiliar thoughts. I don't know if I like it or not."

Noel softly laughs again.

"That is a good thing, Elisabeth. Anyway, you welcome new thoughts or you would not ask so many questions. Many people do not want to think new thoughts."

Anne returns, bringing a basket woven of alder stems filled with plants and a handful of birch bark. She puts the basket down in front of Elisabeth, selects two plants and holds them out.

"In spring and summer it is easy to tell them apart, see how the sweet flag has longer, narrow leaves and the flower bud is hidden halfway along the plant, and the blue flag has shorter and wider leaves with the flower held up to the sun."

She demonstrates to Elisabeth how to distinguish the two plants. "But, when it is time to harvest the roots in the autumn, the blooms of the plants are gone and they look much the same. Mark them in spring so you will know them in the fall."

Handing Elisabeth the birchbark she tells her, "Regarde! If you turn the bark over, you can make marks on the soft brown inner side with a sharp twig. Perhaps you can make sketches of some of the plants and leaves to remember them by."

She has another small trailing plant in her basket, one with scattered small pinkish flowers and smooth round leaves opposite each other on a thin stem. She holds it up to Elisabeth.

"This is a most important one; this is partridge berry or squaw vine. Make a tea from the stems and give it to women in the last weeks before delivery and they will have an easy time. More, but not too much, if the delivery is slow. In men, it is good for the gout."

Elisabeth takes the piece of vine and studies it. As they sit in the warm sun, they discuss her drawings and make corrections. It is a wonderful afternoon, too soon over.

They walk back through the woods along the ridge where they part before descending the slope to the town. Noel takes his leave and tells her that he will be leaving that night and will only return if there is news to convey. In the winter, it is easier for him to come and go because of the long hours of darkness. The long summer days are more dangerous with the settler farmers about at all hours. He warns Elisabeth that the Indians are restless and to be careful on her wanderings, and warn her family to exercise caution in the woods.

Elisabeth thanks him, telling him that their lot is near to the town and not as exposed as some of the outlying farms; however, she will heed his warning. She and Anne embrace again as they say good-bye, not knowing when they will meet again.

When supper is over, the utensils cleaned up and the preparations for breakfast made, Elisabeth takes the little sketches on the birchbark pieces and studies them by the last of the sunlight. It appears to her that the Mi'kmaq Indians use mostly evergreen trees: spruce, pine, fir, hackmatack in their healing. This last is an odd looking tree, tall, skinny with short fine needle leaves that fall to the round in the winter, is unknown to her, however, Anne said it was most important to the local people. Its straight wood used for arrows, its roots for sewing hides and its bark for medicine.

The Acadians had brought some seeds from their homeland and planted them widely, some seeding themselves and becoming common in the surrounding open areas. Merlegueche had been an Acadian village, surely some of the seeds had taken root here and there; Elisabeth would look out for them. Anne has promised to give her seeds of the yarrow plant for bleeding wounds, women's complaints and loss of appetite. And for food, the young bulrush pods, water lily corms, leaves of the young dandelion, the shoots of the fern that look like the head of a violin, wild garlic and onion, seeds of the wild carrot for flavouring. And more to come, the bushes with berries for eating and leaves for drinks and tonics, the sapling alders to bend into containers. There is so much Anne can teach her.

As she sits musing over her drawings, Peter looks over her shoulder to see what holds her attention so intensely. He points to one and then another and says, "I've seen those in the woods. What are they?"

"Fiddleheads," replies his mother. "I made little pictures to remember them by. Some are food and some are for medicine."

"How do you know them?" he asks.

Trapped into further dissembling, she responds, "I know them from home and from talking to people here."

"Then why do you need pictures?"

"Enough of your questions; go and be useful to your father who is sharpening his axe for more work tomorrow."

Peter does not go away, but he changes the subject. "I can do better," he says of her drawings. "May I take them and try some of my own? I can burn some green branches into charcoal to draw with, or a sharp nail to make lines with. May I try?"

His mother raises an eyebrow at the strange request but hands over her pieces of bark. Two days later he shows her his results. They are accurate, clear and beautifully executed. She is delighted with her reference pictures and pleased at his skill and interest. He offers to make drawings for her of the plants and flowers and tree leaves he sees when he roams the woods. She accepts and takes a closer look at her younger son. He has always been different than his father and brother, never giving her any trouble, always doing what is asked, but never seeming to share the interests of the others. A bit of a dreamer she considers him but not in the way Evie is. Evie is slow to respond, away in her own world and has to be called back, and needs to have things repeated carefully. Peter catches on quickly and speeds through his tasks so he can get away out of the house. Exploring is his usual explanation for his wanderings.

"Can I go exploring with you one day, Mother?" he asks.

"Indeed, I would be glad of your company. I will tell you when I go again," she says and gives him a fond smile; not something there has been much time for in the last few years. He is 11, still boyishly slight and gangly, his dark eyes and hair similar only to Maria's. "My gypsy child" she thinks. "There's one in every generation."

Stoffel enters the house with Christof who has just marked his seventeenth birthday. They are discussing the work for the next day. With two 30-acre farms to clear, they will have more work than ever. Stoffel still owes money for their passage, and will continue to labour on public works from time to time, but most of their energy is given to their farms. The English have distributed seeds for potatoes, turnips, cabbage, barley, buckwheat, oats and flax along with tools for working the land. Stoffel and Christof each have a felling axe for chopping down trees, a broad axe for smoothing boards, a pit saw for squaring logs and cutting timber as well as wedges for splitting the logs. Elisabeth and Maria have taken charge of the three hoe heads, fitting them with long pieces of tree limb to work the vegetable garden. In the next shipment from Halifax they are to receive one scythe and two sickles for harvesting marsh grass and hay for livestock.

"The ground will be dry by next week," comments Stoffel. "Have you looked at the garden lot yet, Elisabeth, it must be near ready for working."

"Yes, I judge it five more sunny days before we can work it and ready it for planting. And five after that for the cabbage and turnip seeds, then five more for the potatoes. If it rains or turns cold, longer. Too soon and we will lose the crop. Be patient, my husband, have I ever lost you a crop by mistiming it?"

"Indeed, you have not," he apologizes and lays his hand on her shoulder. He turns to Peter, "This year you can help Adam and me with the limbing of the trees after they are cut. Christof and Christian want to work on the Mahone Bay land and they are old enough to take on men's work. If we do not show improvement of our grants, both farms, the house and the garden, the government will reclaim them. I think we may be able to plant potatoes between the stumps and rocks of the cleared farmland. There is much to do, all of us will need to work."

"Surely the English will not take back our land," exclaims Elisabeth. "You have worked endlessly; there cannot be any question of our industry."

"No, but we have come too far to take any chance. We will improve all our land so there is no doubt," Stoffel states, his uncertainty over the future harshening in his words.

"Anyway," Elisabeth tells him, "It is too much for one ten year old boy to plant and tend all of those potatoes; I and the girls will come and help when we can take time away from the vegetable garden. After the main planting is completed, the girls can easily tend the small garden by themselves. I will come to the farm as often as I can."

Later, when the fire has been banked for the night leaving just enough embers to start the morning fire, Elisabeth sits with her cloak wrapped over her chemise and petticoat in which she will sleep. On her feet she wears the beautiful moccasins which Anne gave her. She admires them in the firelight, warmed both by the remaining heat of the hearth and the friendship that made them. She would dearly like a rocking chair in this spot, a sturdy wood one on smooth rockers in which to rest and order her thoughts. She always does her best thinking in a rocking chair, even when encumbered with a sick or fretful child. Tonight her thoughts are jumbled.

She lets her thoughts drift back to memories of home that are becoming harder and harder to recall; it saddens her that they are slipping away. She concentrates on collecting her thoughts for her nightly prayers. This ordering of her mind helps her to accept when action is needed or when she can do nothing.

Resting her arms on her knees and clasping her hands, she opens her thoughts to some of the unsettling questions Noel has raised in her mind. She has been taught and still believes that there is only one Heaven and believers in Christ go there after death by the grace of God. Evildoers go to Hell. She has never considered whether there is a Roman Catholic Heaven and a Protestant Heaven, or an afterlife that is not Heaven. Noel spoke as though witchcraft was a part of religion, the Indian religion. That the Indians might have a religion of their own is a new idea. Can there be a religion that is not Christian? She grieves for Azelie and prays for her soul, for surely she has a soul, and for her son.

"Dear God," she prays, *"this is Anna Elisabeth."*

She still tells God who she is, afraid He might not recognize her among all the others who pray to Him.

"Please, bless my family and guide them in their lives, keep them safe from harm and disease and welcome them to Heaven when their time here is finished.

"As for me, help me stay strong in my faith so that I may also come to Heaven. Please, do not doubt my faith even though along the way I desire to understand the ways of others. For truly I believe Noel to be a good man, and the young girl unjustly wronged, and the baby an innocent. It seems unduly harsh for them to be denied life after death, but if they have their own afterlife, then there is more than one Heaven. These are things I do not understand. Perhaps that is faith, to accept your teachings even though I do not understand. Please, help me to recognize the truth and walk in your grace. Amen."

7

GIFT FROM GOD

June, 1754–August, 1754

As she inspects the garden, a runnel of sweat trickles out from under Elisabeth's bonnet, runs behind her ear and under her chin to join the others making their way between her breasts and into the band of her petticoat. She has loosened the ties at the waist of her skirt, dressed in her coolest chemise, even removed her apron and kerchief and placed them on a dry tussock of grass, but still she is hot and uncomfortable. She has fashioned a brim for her bonnet to protect her face from the worst of the sun. Her feet are bare in the hot garden earth.

"Moderation, Lord, moderation. Last year rain, this year sun, a little of each would be received gratefully."

The seeds are planted and the carrots are a haze of green. The turnip, cabbage and potato are putting up their third set of leaves. She remembers last June with its rain and damp and cold. This year it has been hot since the middle of last month and not one day of rain. If it does not rain soon, the seedlings will dry in the ground. She is thankful now for the low land of which she had complained; some women are already carrying water to their tiny plants.

When the last row has been carefully examined, she returns to the side of the old elm and sits down in its shade. No wind stirs the leaves. No seagull cry disturbs the shimmering air. She has brought a wooden bucket of water and some cold molasses pudding. The past six weeks have been a haze of spring chores: finishing the quilts and cleaning the house; washing and airing all of their covers and clothes in the fresh air and sunshine; standing in line to receive food rations, and then seeds and then tools; and, day after day, preparing the ground and sowing the seeds, here and on their farm land.

"I'm not complaining, Lord," she apologizes mentally, *"I am grateful for the rations and the implements. It is only that I would welcome a day of rest."*

She smiles with pleasure as she remembers the cow Stoffel received in the livestock distribution, not many families received a cow. He also received a share in a sheep. Adam received six sheep, a pig and a share of a goat. Sight of a woolly sheep turns Elisabeth's thoughts to spinning and weaving. She and Margarete have already been planning the loom to be built before next winter. The livestock are turned out onto the common land outside the palisade. Stoffel has marked their animals with a half crop and ha'penny, cut with a knife into each ear. She had blindfolded the animals and held their heads to keep them quiet. Her thoughts become exasperated as she considers the lack of a bull to breed with the cows. The town's lone bull, unfortunately, ran off into the woods where he continues to evade capture, maybe a ripening heifer would entice him to return.

She looks around the garden. There are a few people hoeing weeds farther up the slope, but no one that she recognizes. Sighing with pleasure at the rare solitary moment of rest, she opens the cloth around her pudding and takes a dipper of water from the bucket. She does not feel overly uncomfortable as long as she sits still here in the shade; altogether, it is a pleasant place for thinking. She has a fondness for this old tree, and the shelter it offers.

Biting into the pudding reminds her to be thankful for the rations they have again received. The never-ending sameness of the food and the scarcity of fresh produce are a problem. She has harvested some of the wild plants that Anne had shown her; however, collecting them takes time. She doesn't like to send the girls out into the woods by themselves and the men have no time to spend looking for greens. Now that the garden is planted, the girls can maintain it and she will take a few hours to look for wild food. She smiles as she remembers the wild roots and leaves she sometimes finds on her doorstep, tangible evidence that Anne would be a closer friend if political alliances permitted. And one day, a clump of the blue flag with the fat roots packed in mud. She planted them where she dumps the laundry water; maybe it will be wet enough.

"Ah, Elisabeth, here you are, taking your leisure beneath a shady tree." Elisabeth starts as she hears a voice speak from behind the tree.

Startled out of her reverie and not immediately recognizing the woman's voice, Elisabeth scrambles hastily to her feet and brushes the loose dirt from her skirt. Chagrined to have been caught at rest and apparently lazing away a hot afternoon, she rises, hoping her bare feet are not noticeable. It is the Misses von Helger and Jammer, ladies active in the church and community, inseparable, always consulting with a look and then nodding their heads in unison like flotsam bobbing on a ripple. They are good hearted and well meaning, but inveterate speculators over rumour and gossip.

"Good afternoon, ladies. It is indeed a peaceful afternoon for the contemplation of God's handiwork and blessings," Elisabeth greets them.

They look at each other, nod and answer, "Amen to that."

"We were thinking," begins one, "yes, we were thinking," interrupts the other. They chuckle at themselves and one motions to the other to continue. "We were thinking, in ten days we will have been here one year, a year since we stepped ashore. Should we not give thanks and mark the occasion with a small celebration? We have been going around, talking to people, asking what they think, so to speak, about a Landing Commemoration Day."

"I remember the day well, I bore my daughter Sophie Elisabeth on that day," responds Elisabeth.

"Oh, my goodness." "What a travail." "A little Lunenburger born. Maybe our first." They stumble over their sentences, not sure that this was a proper thing to be told. It is not often they are taken completely by surprise.

Elisabeth takes pity on their consternation, and answers their first question.

"The men have been working hard for a number of weeks now. It might do the town good for everyone to rejoice for a day and give thanks for our continued survival. Reverend Moreau was speaking of completing the basic structure of the church this summer. With many hands it could be done in a day, followed by a service and sharing of food."

The ladies beam.

"Had you thought of a day for the thanks giving?" she asks them.

141

"We heard that service this Sunday is to be on the church site, if the weather holds fine. Oh, what a pleasure it will be to worship together again," they exclaim with their hands clasped. "A plan could be announced then, if the Reverend Moreau agrees with the idea."

"I think it's a fine idea. How have other people responded?" asks Elisabeth.

"Most people seem to feel it's a good idea. If it's announced in church, we think many of the families would take part," they reply.

"I'll talk to my husband and my sons. I believe they would come." She smiles at the two eager ladies as they leave. "It has been pleasant speaking with you, and now, I must continue with my work: a large family is a responsibility as well as a blessing. Good day to you, ladies."

"Good bye, blessings on you," they call as they depart.

The two women make their farewells. It is time for her to go home as well. With a final look at her garden, she puts on her wooden clogs, pours the last of the water over a row of seeded cabbage, collects her hoe and bucket, and turns for home still thinking of the past year.

Following a long, hungry winter with too many deaths from lung fever, fluxes and accidents, everyone is working hard to plant crops. Many of the men are not used to swinging the heavy felling axes and sometimes a mistake becomes a fatal lesson. The broad-headed axes have caused a few missing toes and one or two of the men have a missing limb from a gash too deep to heal. Stoffel, because he has the skills of a butcher, has had to remove a leg from two of the settlers. A grim task and not one he was thanked for; the men preferring to die rather then become a burden to themselves and their families. Elisabeth thinks that a day to build a proper place of worship, mingle with friends, thank God for their survival and ask his blessing for the trials ahead would be welcome. She determines to encourage Stoffel to speak of it among his friends.

Instead of walking home through the town, she takes the trail to the new sawpit. She excuses her choice of the longer route by reasoning that her men need to know if it is ready for use. Secretly, she admits that she misses her meanders in the woods and, on thin grounds, is making an opportunity for a leisurely walk. The pit is completed and already in use. There are four men at work; some of the skilled sawyers in town are cutting lumber for more buildings, grunting as they pull the pit saw through the green timber. It takes a pair of men to work the long two-handled flexible saw; one man down in the pit, the other on scaffolding built a man's height over the pit. The man below is covered in sawdust, straining on the down pull and taking a breath only when the man on the scaffold hauls the long blade upward. Two pairs of men work side-by-side in the pit.

When they see her, they take the opportunity to stop and wave.

"Good afternoon, Frau Baltzer. How grows your garden?"

"It does very well, thank you. Would you like a cool drink?"

Nearby, a freshwater stream still runs to the harbour, so Elisabeth fills her bucket and offers it to the men. Four times she fills the bucket; they drink a portion and pour the rest over their heads. Refreshed, they return to work.

"That was most welcome." "Many thanks to you." "Come back in an hour," one jokes.

There are also makeshift sawpits cobbled together on each farm. The farmers and their sons take turns in the pit and, when they can, they hire strong backs to help; so much labour to make one piece of lumber, and so many pieces of lumber needed to build a town.

Her path takes her along the top of the ridge, above most of the houses and in front of the eastern blockhouse. There are soldiers leaning on the parapets and looking out of the rifle embrasures; others are hacking at the spring growth that clutters the land around the blockhouse. A group of four men is setting out to patrol the headland beyond the garden lots. Most look up and quickly return to their tasks, some greet her with a touch to their caps and a few call out "Guten Tag, Mistress." She gives them a nod and walks on. She is still not comfortable around them, a rough mix of men and boys who talk and joke in English.

She thinks about the idea of celebrating a year in this place. Is it a happy time or not? There is satisfaction in having survived, firstly, the voyage across the ocean upon which she never wants to set foot again, and then, the terrible winter in Halifax with cold and hunger and death as constant companions, and finally, the year here. Can it be a year? Little Bettina is a sturdy infant, learning to walk and needing a constant vigilant eye on her. Her birthday is in two days time, on Sunday, which means that a year ago tomorrow their ship dropped anchor in Lunenburg Harbour and she saw this place for the first time.

She stops for a moment and gazes out over the town site. Houses are set out in neat rows, ships drift at anchor in the harbour, garden lots are sprouting new crops, timber is piled waiting for shipment to Halifax and barrels of rations, boxes of tools, military supplies, bricks, coal and iron for the forge are stored in sheds along the waterfront. Families in every section have or are expecting new babies and young children fill the church services with whispers and movement. They are better off than they were a year ago. Yes, there are things to celebrate as well as memories to dust off and pack away.

She steps off the path and walks around her house to the door which Stoffel has built into the wall away from the path, so that it gives easy access to their home garden. It also gives her a sense of protection from the north where there are no houses and no barrier against enemies sneaking up the wooded hillside from Back Harbour. An illusion, but comforting. Peter is desultorily clearing back a clump of young alders which are resisting his attempts to cut them with an axe.

"You'll need to swing it harder than that, they're young and withy. Better you try one of the sickles," she chides him gently. It is obvious that he is keeping an eye out for her return. "Were you waiting for me?"

"Yes, mother." He gives her an assessing look. Is this a good time to ask for a boon?

She knows the look; he has a request and he is uncertain of her response. Her children have their own ways of asking: Christof always asks after dinner and chooses to ask her and Stoffel together; Maria throws decisions in their faces on the way out of the door, usually before church; the younger ones have yet to show their colours. Peter approaches her first and prefers to find her alone and relaxed—and he offers up a gift for her in advance.

"I have a present for you," he says, reaching under a shady branch and retrieving a bundle wrapped in wet leaves. "A fresh fish, Jacques calls it 'la morue' ". He flashes her a smile of pure pleasure, "I caught it myself."

He shoves it close to her face so she can see it easily. All she can see is two glassy dead eyes and fat slimy lips hovering inches from her nose.

"Ohh," she gasps, and inadvertently takes a step backwards. Unfortunately, she steps into the bucket which she had set down on the earth. With her foot lodged in the bucket, she loses her balance and collapses with a thud onto the ground.

"Ahhhhhh," she grunts.

"Mother!" Peter calls out in anxiety.

She is too winded to speak. Peter does not know whether to help or flee.

Stunned, and in no little discomfort, she simply lies back and closes her eyes, waiting for the shock to pass. Peter, thinking he has killed his mother, screams for help. Two of his sisters, who have been at a neighbour's house watching over their infant, arrive and start crying, along with the infant. At Peter's scream, Adam Kohl rushes up from his property below and Pieter Bubechoffer arrives from where he has been digging a water catchment just down the hill in front of their properties.

"She's only in a faint," a voice says, "Fetch some water."

Elisabeth sits up in time to receive a full bucket of water in the face. Her bonnet wilts over her forehead, her bodice clings to her breasts and the rest of the water seeps down into her skirts, but her eyes are open.

"She's alive." "Oh, mother." "I thought I'd killed her." "There, I told you she'd just fainted."

"Are you all right, gnädige Frau?" asks Herr Kohl. "Do you need help?"

"I seem to be fine. Thank you all, but I am truly all right. Please, just let me sit here for a minute. Danke. Dankeschön. Thank you. Go back to your chores. I am fine."

The neighbours drift away and courteously hold their laughter until they are out of earshot, almost. A frightening moment has turned out well. A false alarm.

Peter is on his knees with his arms around his mother. He is speechless with aftershock and remorse. She is just speechless. She and her children sit on the earth and clasp each other until their heartbeats slow. Startled and angry and embarrassed, she fights both tears and laughter. Dignity and training reign.

"I must change my clothes," she murmurs and starts to rise. Her daughters help her. She looks at Peter who is still on his knees at her feet, "Is the fish for supper?"

"Yes," he replies in a soft voice, not daring to look at her. "Jacques showed me how to cook them."

"Then you had best get it ready. We will have it tonight. It will make a welcome change from salt beef."

At the door she turns back to him, "It is all right, Peter, I am not hurt, nor angry at you. In an hour, come to me, we will discuss thinking before acting."

He looks at her in relief. In an hour, he hopes his mother will see the humour in the chain of events, although he doubts that he will ever laugh at it. It scared half a lifetime out of him. Whatever lecture she gave him, this time he would accept it without excuses. For a moment he thought that he had killed her.

His fish is a success, mostly because his mother has smothered it in crisp fried pork fat and mashed it with softened hard bread. Unfortunately, it has meant that he must reveal to his father that he has been fishing with Jacques Bizette instead of helping his mother with the garden, his mother having thought that he was with his father and his father having thought that he was with his mother.

"I was there when you needed me, when you were doing fine without me I helped Jacques. His sons are working their own farms and he is alone. Besides, I love the water and the shore and the wind and the waves, they are like freedom. He wants to build a fish trap out beyond the vegetable gardens."

"How do you trap a fish, by its tail?" jokes his brother.

"No. You build a barrier across a narrow deep opening where the shore curves inward. The fish swim in at high tide and then we put the trap door down and when the tide goes out we pick up the fish in baskets. What we need is netting, but we don't have any so we use brush wood for now," explains Peter seriously.

His family looks at him as though he were a stranger.

"And how does Jacques know this?" asks his father.

"He travelled to Bretonne, in France. He asked me if I could help him next week now that the garden in planted and you are finished planting potatoes at the farm." He looks at his mother, "I said I would ask."

Stoffel muses, "I don't know this Jacques, only to pass on the path and nod. He is one of the Montbéliard Swiss and speaks no German. What kind of a man is he?"

"He lives next to the Berghaus, at the end of this section. He lost his three daughters, but he has a wife and a grown son, maybe two. I have spoken to him in passing, he seems reasonable," offers Elisabeth.

"I would speak with him about this. I don't suppose he speaks German?" says Stoffel. He looks at Elisabeth.

"No, but I will make an occasion to have a conversation with him," she offers.

Then she remembers the Misses Helger and Jammer.

"This afternoon, two of the church women spoke to me about a commemoration celebration to mark our first year in Lunenburg. They said that the service this Sunday is to be on the church site and, if he agrees, Reverend Moreau will announce it then. I think it is a good idea. It would be good for people to have a day of rest together. The men can raise the remaining walls and roof of the church."

"I thought it was to be a day of rest," comments Stoffel.

"Building our church will bring rest to the soul," she retorts. "And, you may remember, Sunday will be Bettina's first birthday," she adds.

They all look in surprise at the baby, who opens her eyes wide and purses her lips in preparation for a howl at the intense inspection.

Landing Commemoration Day is announced for Monday, July 1st, following a service of Thanksgiving and Remembrance on Sunday, June 30th. Christof won't be there. He and Christian Graff are moving out to the Mahone Bay lot on Sunday where they plan to clear a house site and erect a small Hutt, clear a garden area and put it to buckwheat, as well as choose and mark trees for felling the following winter. An ambitious plan for two young men.

Adam needs to work on his own farm this summer in order to retain his claim to it. Unluckily, it is in Clearland, beyond Mahone Bay, a hard day's trek by land and open to Acadian or Indian attack. He will not be able to return home each day which will leave his wife alone.

Elisabeth and Margarete have made their own plans. When Adam is away, Maria will stay with Margarete overnight. In return, Margarete will help Elisabeth's daughters to take care of both the houses freeing Elisabeth to work beside Stoffel on their farm. Stoffel will not want her to labour at the farm site but, like her children, Elisabeth, too, has a strategy for making announcements that might not be well received.

For supper she prepares a pudding with fresh strawberries—tiny, dark red, sweet and delicious. She beats the softened hard bread into a fluffy mixture with molasses and one egg begged from Catherine, adds the berries and cooks it in the spyder. She puts chopped dandelion greens into the pease pudding, making sure it is well cooked and beaten to a soft mass before she serves it with a piece of smoked pork, soaked, sliced and cooked by draping it over the hearth spit. When Stoffel has finished, she places a cup of cold watered rum in front of him, resumes her seat and addresses them.

"I've been thinking," she starts. Stoffel looks up; this conversation opener doesn't always bode well. "With Christof gone to the Mahone Bay farm, with Adam needed to work his own land, and maybe Peter working some of the time with Jacques," she holds up her hand to stop interruptions, "we will be short handed on our own farm land." She looks at Stoffel who is impatient to break into her speech. "Maria is old enough to run the household for a week at a time, and Margarete is next door as is Sabina Bubechoffer. I have decided to come with you to the farm; I will work beside you this summer," she tells Stoffel. "We can come home at the end of the day and check that everything is going well, or we can remain at the farm, in the small Hutt you built to shelter from the rain, when there is much to do. Beside," she pauses, "beside, we are blessed with land near enough to the town for someone to come for us if we are needed."

Her arguments are all on the table; her offensive manoeuvre delivered.

Stoffel splutters, Christof is startled into silence at the idea of his mother working as a farm labourer. Maria is of two minds, she loves the idea of being in charge, but aware that it means less freedom to catch a few minutes with her friends, not that there is much leisure time; her mother keeps her busy.

"It takes a lot of strength to swing an axe." "You'll cut off your foot." "How can you drag a log?"

She has anticipated the argument about her nor being strong enough to lift the stones and branches, or to heft the tools. She points to a tub of dirty bedding soaking in soap and water beside the door.

"Come," she says, "this is the washing waiting for tomorrow to be pounded out, rinsed and hung to dry. It needs to be carried out to the washing bench. I lift and carry that nearly every day, then again with rinse water maybe twice, all the way from the brook opposite."

Peter innocently adds his argument to his mother's. "I cannot lift it. It is too heavy for me and I work all day at the farm."

Christof rises and takes up his mother's challenge. He doesn't actually grunt, but he widens his stance and tightens his grip. He looks at his father and admits, "It is not a light load." Elisabeth smiles, reminding herself to remove the large flat stone she has placed in the bottom.

Stoffel lays out his real reason, "What will the neighbours think, my wife working at farm labour like a serf's woman?"

Elisabeth laughs, knowing she has won.

"I work all day at the garden lot. They will think nothing of it; many of the women are doing so. The work needs many hands and I have strong ones that are not needed at home all the time. The work I do every day is hard and this summer I am needed to build our farm. Our daughters are capable and responsible; it is time they took up their duties as women, not children."

When their father looks at them, they nod their heads, even Evie. They all laugh when Bettina bobs her head, too.

"I would like to try, after the Landing Commemoration Day activities. What do you say?"

He stares at the hearth for a few moments and then nods his head, "We can try it for a time."

As Elisabeth stands up to start the evening chores, she lays her hand briefly and gently on Stoffel's shoulder as she passes.

The weather on the day of the first anniversary holds hot and clear. The women bring baskets and bowls of food for their families. The boys run and play tag while the girls play pretend house with their rag dolls. The church is raised and roofed. It smells of freshly sawn lumber. The wooden shutters are fastened open, but can be closed against inclement weather; when there is money enough, they will put in glass windows. The men gather in small groups and talk and plan their summer work between stints of laboring on the church. Everyone is relaxed and the older boys and girls take the opportunity to look each other over; some wander off casually to find a little privacy for conversation and a stolen moment of discreet hand holding. Elisabeth sees Maria stroll slowly away with Johannes Bauer. Later, just as she about to stroll in the same direction, they return, smiling sideways at each other.

"So the winds still blows in that direction," she thinks to herself.

After the final blessing, Stoffel and Adam leave to put a final edge on their tools and Maria offers to prepare the evening meal with the help of her sisters. Elisabeth carries Bettina over the rough ground as she makes her way to the home of Jacques Bizette. Catherine Bizette has some absinthe growing in her garden and Elisabeth intends to ask the favour of some seeds in the fall and lead the way to speaking to Jacques about Peter helping him with this fish idea. She finds Catherine and Jacques alone. Catherine is pleased to find someone interested in her effort to grow some of the medicinal plants she brought from home. She and Elisabeth spend a few minutes exchanging ideas and information on the use of absinthe as a cure for worms in children.

Jacques compliments her on her son. He confirms his determination to design and build a fish trap to supplement their diet of meat and tries to explain it to her with stones and sticks. She likes the man and his enthusiasm, and offers to seek permission for Peter to help him when he is not needed at home. She is bewildered by Peter's interest in the sea but believes that knowledge is never wasted; she will give him her blessing.

Taking advantage of not being needed at home immediately, she turns downhill towards the waterfront. She rarely walks along here. It is usually bustling with activity and strangers but, today, it is quiet although there are two ships at the wharf being loaded on the high tide. She smiles. The sea is becoming a factor in her life despite her loathing of it. It determines the weather; the fog rolls in and out with the tides; the winds come off it or are stilled by it. It determines where you can walk along the shore, whether to pass by one path or another. All their goods come and go by sea at the whim of the wind and weather. Their timber goes out by sea and the ship returns with their payment. To come here or to leave here, one must go by sea. She puts Bettina down where she stands hanging onto her mother's skirts.

She hears Melchior's familiar voice.

"Good day to you, Elisabeth," he says. "I am relieved to find you so easily; I wanted to see you before I leave."

"Leave? Not just another little expedition?" The idea had not occurred to her; she has become accustomed to Melchior being here, being here even if she doesn't see him for days, even a week at a time. "I, we will miss you," she answers, "and you will be dearly missed at service."

"Oh, I'm not leaving permanently; however, I will be gone for several months. If all goes as planned, I should return before the fall harvest. There are some visits I must make, people I need to see. Peter tells me you are going to work the farm with Stoffel this summer and that he is going to catch fish with le Vieux Bizette. You will have a busy few months."

"It seems you know things almost before I have decided them," she remarks.

He is looking into her eyes and his lips curve into a smile as he admits, "I make it a point to know what you are doing, Elisabeth."

Before she can respond, he gestures to a ship that has nearly completed its loading. "I am returning to Halifax on the *Ladysmith* and will take ship from there to Boston. I will return overland to Yarmouth, Maine. While I'm there I hope to see Noel and learn his news before taking a small boat across the Bay of Fundy and, thence, overland to Halifax again."

"A journey, as you said," replies Elisabeth meanwhile thinking with a certain anxiousness, "A lot could happen to a person on such a journey."

"I will return. Take care, Elisabeth; I won't be here to keep you out of trouble," he jokes. "I gave Stoffel my rifle to use while I am gone, make sure it is always with you, ready to fire, when you are on the farm. It wouldn't hurt if you learned to shoot it yourself. It has a hearty recoil; so make a pad for your shoulder or you will have a bruise."

"My father taught me to shoot," she assures him, "but I will take care. Thank you."

As he turns to leave she calls out, "Take care yourself; come back safely. Fare thee well, Melchior." They raise hands to each other.

The work on the farm is hard and hot, even the sea breezes do not reach this far inland. And there are hundreds of small flies that buzz and bite. She wears a kerchief over her head and ears, a long sleeved chemise under her skirt and an old pair of boots donated by Jacques Bizette. Her face is sunburned, her hands and legs are scratched from evergreen needles and slapping branches. Her neck and hairline are ringed with the bites of mosquitoes, black flies, deer flies and midges. Instead of walking home each evening, they decide to stay in the little farm *Hutt* built of spruce poles with hemlock branches for roofing. They walk home on Saturday evening. On Sunday evening, they haul their food for the week back to the *Hutt* on a pole sledge. Elisabeth has cleared space for a small stone hearth on which she prepares their meals and heats water to wash her hands and face at night. Azelie's spring, for such she has called it, yields fresh water in abundance and gives Elisabeth an excuse for a moment of peace and prayer.

"Lord, it is I, Anna Elisabeth. We are working daily to prosper and live as You would have us live. I thank You for the continued health of my children and our progress here. Bless our family back home and take care of them. Watch over those who are absent, dear Lord. Help me to walk in your way and live by your teachings. Thank You for our many blessings. Amen."

Despite her determination, by early August, she has had enough. By happy coincidence, the fish have stopped running and Peter is able to return to work on the farm. It has been a dry summer and the garden needs hand-watering every week. Their poor cow is looking thin and hippy from lack of water. The sheep are no better. The stream running through the common is nearly dry and has become a series of evaporating mud puddles. She is needed elsewhere.

After Sunday supper, Elisabeth and Stoffel discuss what they need to do for the garden and the animals; a number of livestock need regular water, but how to get it to them. It is Peter who suggests using the spring.

Elisabeth makes a noise of exasperation because she had not thought of this earlier. "Of course, Peter, we must be able to use it somehow." She pauses. "It is too far to carry buckets of water."

"We can bring the animals to the water," exclaims Stoffel. "We can build a pen large enough for our cow and sheep and for Adam's sheep and his pig."

"Margarete was complaining that the pig has gone feral over the summer and is impossible to corner safely," interjects Gertrud. "They want her to have piglets."

"Okay, not the pig, then," says Stoffel. "I will go and talk with Adam before he leaves for his farm in the morning."

He comes back to announce that Adam will stay home for this week and help build a pen for their animals as well as help move them onto the farm land.

"I think he's glad of an excuse not to have to be so far away. He always worries about Margarete."

Elisabeth helps round up the animals and move them onto their new pasture.

Two weeks later, by mid-August, the animals are settled into the new pen and slightly improved in health. It means a number of daily trips to and from the spring to fill the trough but it should save them.

The vegetable garden is suffering from the heat and drought as well. The low land of their garden lot has retained enough moisture to prevent the crop from dying; however, Elisabeth carries buckets of water to the garden each day—one day the carrots and turnips, one day the cabbage and potatoes and one day the buckwheat and, then, start over again.

Adam is preparing to return to Clearland when news of an Indian attack reaches the town. A farmer, his wife and all their children have been massacred and scalped. He was killed with an arrow and scalped with an axe, she was hit in the throat and scalped, and the children were just scalped. Their buildings were fired but did not burn, so the bodies were found by a military patrol. Their farm was in Clearland, at the farther edges of the section where Adam is clearing land. His farm is an hour's walk nearer the shore but it is enough to panic Margarete into hysterics. Adam decides that he will not return to the farm, at least for the present, and will help Stoffel on his farm.

Stoffel reassures Elisabeth that Christof is much closer to the town, a day's walk from where the attack took place, on land surrounded by other farms where people are working daily. She accepts that in her head but doubles her prayers for her son's safety.

The end of August brings a short lull between the hard summer work and the harvest. By Thursday, Elisabeth feels the need of a few hours of leisure. There are no chores pressing and the older children are about their own duties. She has been looking after Bettina as well as Ferdi Schauffner while mending torn shirts and patching a bedcover. She collects the children and takes them over to Margarete who has been turning out her house and restuffing their bed ticking with dried marsh grass and tansy. Margarete welcomes Elisabeth's assistance to put her furniture back indoors and agrees to take the two youngsters for the rest of the afternoon.

Patrick Sutherland has found new quarters for Victoria over the chandler's store on the harbour front. Elisabeth decides to visit, partly to see her quarters and partly to check on Victoria whose baby is due next month. She takes a route that allows her to pass by the church with its freshly whitewashed walls and its cedar-shingled roof. As she turns toward the waterfront she feels a slight breeze, almost an illusion. Tilting her face upward, she closes her eyes. The sensation is repeated, a slight movement of air caresses her face. She scans the horizon and there, off to the west, is a low bank of clouds on the horizon. Rain or false alarm? An hour or two will tell. She stands still for a moment, yes, the breeze continues.

She locates the chandler's shop across the road from the larger of the two wharves. Barrels of rope, piles of canvas, various metal pieces and bits of apparel are visible through the open shutters. There is a set of stairs leading to the second floor. There is no railing so she stays close to the wall. Entering an open door, she finds herself in a room full of canvas and rope and something that permeates the air with the smell of creosote and tar. The smell makes her dizzy; she backs out on to the landing again and puts her handkerchief over her nose. Looking around, she locates another door beyond the open one. This one is closed and she knocks on it. It is opened by Victoria who silently welcomes her in. With the door closed the smell is not as strong, but it still taints the air.

"I was thinking of you, Elisabeth, and wishing you were here. You must be clairvoyant," says Victoria softly.

"What is the matter? Here I expected to find you bubbling with plans for improving your new home and I find you pale and sad. Are you ailing?"

"Perhaps. I have not felt well for a day or so."

Not wanting to criticize the rooms Patrick had found for his mistress, Elisabeth bites back any comment on the smell and the lack of light. Leaving the door open would allow for more air to pass through the little window at the back of the rooms, but it would also let in more of the smell. There are two rooms that she can see, this one and a smaller one beyond. They are new and clean; she can see a bed and a washstand in the small room; this room contains a table and two chairs, a rough sideboard and a military fire pot set on bricks. The fire pot is essentially an iron bucket lined with clay in which a fire can be built with wood or coal.

"I am so pleased at Patrick finding me a place to live with the baby, but I cannot become accustomed to the smell. At first it was faint and bearable, but then chandler Beckt brought in a supply of tar to repair the boats over the winter. He is afraid it will be stolen from the shed beside the boat repair slip, so he keeps it next door," says Victoria in a low voice.

"Have you told Patrick?"

"No, I haven't seen him since the tar was moved next door."

Victoria looks pale and there are beads of sweat on her forehead.

"You need some fresh air. Come outside and walk a little with me," suggests Elisabeth. "Perhaps that will help you feel better."

Elisabeth helps Victoria go down a few stairs but she sits on a step. "I can't go any farther," she whispers in a strained voice. The air is a little fresher, still the odours and noise of the waterfront cannot be avoided.

"Stay here a moment, I'll be back shortly," advises Elisabeth.

She goes up the stairs and closes the door to the storage room and opens Victoria's door. Inside she opens the two little windows and takes one of the chairs out on to the little landing. The air is fresher here and a little breeze is moving. She helps Victoria to sit on the chair and fetches a cup of water from the sideboard for her. Victoria takes a few sips and then straightens her back with a deep groan.

"I feel ill," she whispers.

Her friend takes a closer look and reaches her own conclusion.

"What you feel are the beginnings of labour, your baby is starting his journey into the world," corrects Elisabeth. "Let's get you inside."

She takes Victoria into the bedroom and helps her undress, leaving on her chemise and drawers that have a convenience, or long opening, from front to back. Elisabeth has not seen such a garment and surmises that it must be an English thing. Laying some cloths over the mattress she puts Victoria to bed and covers her lightly. She lays her hands gently on Victoria's stomach, feeling for the contractions. There are pulsing ripples under her fingers. A quick look shows no sign of the baby yet.

"I must go home to get the things we will need; nothing will happen for a while, just lie here and know that I will be back as soon as possible."

Victoria holds out her hand which Elisabeth clasps briefly.

"I am afraid," she murmurs.

"I will return as swiftly as I can," Elisabeth reassures her.

The rapid trip up the steep hill makes Elisabeth pant and gasp slightly for breath. The sight of her unaccustomed speed brings a few of the women to their doors with concern on their faces; someone is in need, usually another woman in pain with a complicated birth. As she returns down the hill, one calls out, "Do you need help?" Elisabeth waves her hand in negation and realizes that if it had been anybody but Victoria, she would have been glad of help. She sighs; Victoria has chosen such a complicated path for herself. Hastening past the smithy, she sees a man she recognizes, Captain Zouberbuhler, discussing some piece of ironwork with Herr Jammer. She approaches him.

"Guten Tag, Captain Zouberbuhler, may I speak with you?"

He excuses himself from the smithy and steps into the sunshine with her.

"Guten Tag, Frau Baltzer. How are things with you?"

"Quite well, thank you, Captain Zouberbuhler; however, I find myself with a delicate problem. I do not speak English and am in urgent need of sending a message to Captain Sutherland. You are a friend of the Captain; could I impose on you to send him an urgent message?"

Sebastien Zouberbuhler looks at her with a resigned smile, "I never meet you but what you have a request, Frau Baltzer. I might be able to help you; however, Captain Sutherland is a busy man, you know."

"Indeed, I know," she says. "If you can send someone to find him, just say that he is needed at chandler Beckt's shop, and that I sent the message."

"Ah," he says, his face clearing in comprehension "I understand; it is Victoria's time. I will send the message."

"You are kind. Thank you for your help," says Elisabeth turning to hurry on her way. It was as she thought, the top men in the town all knew each other's business and were aware of Victoria's relationship with Patrick and of her advanced pregnancy. Let Captain Sutherland be annoyed or not, his place was at Victoria's side this day.

She stops for a moment on the landing to look over the harbour and slow her breathing. The clouds have thickened up and they appear to be moving closer as the tide rises; the breeze has stiffened a little and there are little white caps on the water. She props the door open with the chair to freshen the stuffy rooms and goes in to help her friend through whatever lies ahead. By her reckoning, this baby is three to four weeks ahead of its time and Victoria is old at twenty-nine to be having her first baby.

Victoria has twisted the blankets about her legs and is lying with her arms flung wide, her head thrown back and her skin grey. It is much too early for her to look that exhausted.

"How long have you been feeling ill?" asks Elisabeth.

"Yesterday, no, the day before, in the night. I thought it was some stew that was too old," she answers. "But I have not needed the chamber pot over much."

"Did your waters break?" queries Elisabeth.

Victoria shakes her head and replies that she does not know. Feeling that she would know if it had happened, Elisabeth reassures her. She sees the chamber pot hidden under the washstand and lifts the lid. No blood. Good. There is only a little water in the jug on the sideboard in the larger room; she needs more water and some hot water to clean her few instruments and wash her hands. She looks askance at the fire bucket and a few sticks of wood along with some lumps of coal. She finds a pot in which to boil some water; that will have to do. She wonders at Patrick's ignorance, or lack of interest, in the things required to run a home.

Victoria moans from the bed. Elisabeth goes to her side and wipes her forehead with a damp cloth. When her friend falls into a light sleep, Elisabeth goes down the stairs to the chandler's and steps inside where she finds a young lad weighing out nails into wooden boxes.

"You, you there with the nails, where is your employer?" she demands in her best no nonsense voice.

The boy jumps and drops some of the nails.

"I don't know Misses, he went out."

"Are you here alone?"

"No, there's Max in the back."

"Who is Max?" she asks.

"Max lifts the heavy things."

"When is he coming back?" she asks.

"Who?"

"Your employer, Herr Beckt" she explains becoming more irritated by the minute.

"He'll be right back; he just went for a p---"

"I'll wait," she interrupts before the explanation becomes more vivid. At that moment a large red-faced man comes into the shop wiping his hands on his apron.

Elisabeth turns to him. "I hope you are the chandler, I have urgent need of a bucket of fresh water."

He looks at her in confusion and answers, "Ja, I am Herr Beckt, the chandler. We have several buckets for different uses but I do not sell water."

"You do not understand," she continues. "I need a bucket full of fresh clean water, now. The person living in your back room is—." She gestures, how to say these things to a strange man. Then she says, "I am a midwife."

The chandler's face clears as he understands her needs. He grabs a large bucket from a small stack at the end of the counter and hands it to the lad who is gaping at the conversation.

"Fetch the lady a bucket of fresh water, mind you don't spill any, I want it full." As the boy hesitates, the chandler cuffs him on the back of the head and sends him off with an admonition to hurry.

"I'll bring it to the door," the man offers.

"I cannot pay you," she says.

"Do not worry, the bucket can still be sold after you return it."

"You are most kind, I am grateful for your help."

Returning upstairs, she starts a small fire in the fire bucket and puts the remaining water on to heat, using only enough to wash her hands. She looks in on Victoria who is still moaning quietly with each contraction but is easier now that she is not alone. Elisabeth fears that she has been in labour for over a day now, nearer two days than one. The contractions are not strong enough to move the birth ahead. She brews a cup of buckwheat tea, letting it steep until it is lukewarm before she strains it and helps Victoria sip it slowly. It will ease some of the pains. She remembers that none of her family know where she has gone, perhaps a neighbour saw her rapid journey and will tell them she is okay, just on a call. She cannot worry about that now.

"Elisabeth," Victoria calls out.

"I'm here," she answers

"The pains are worse."

"That is a good sign; they will become stronger right up until the baby is born. It means your body is pushing him into the world. I'll bring you another drink."

This time she makes a cup of partridgeberry tea to help strengthen the contractions and speed delivery.

Victoria manages a small smile, "You always say 'him'."

'I think of him as 'him', a boy or a girl, we will soon know."

A sudden rolling boom of noise makes both women start and cry out. Elisabeth goes to the door and looks out. The sky has become dark and the wind is picking up, sending strong gusts that sway the trees and roll the ships in the harbour. The chandler has left the bucket of water on the stairs. She picks it up and concentrates on the work ahead.

Closing the door behind her, she goes back to Victoria's bedside.

"It is thunder. It is going to rain at last, now that it is almost too late for the gardens, still it is welcome. The streams are running dry. "

The next clap coincides with Victoria's scream as she arches her back and thrusts her hands at her belly. She pants when the contraction is over.

"That was different than all the rest," she gasps.

"Your baby is ready to come into the world," Elisabeth comforts her. "It will not be long now."

"Thorold if it is a boy, Thora, if it is a girl," Victoria tells her, "for the thunder announcing his arrival.

Elisabeth is glad to see her able to converse, an improvement over the pallid wraith that met her at the door.

The storm reaches shore, with pelting rain and rolling thunder. The waves surge and crash onto the shore and against the wharf. Bolts of lightning throw flares of brilliance into the little bedroom. The wind makes the lantern flicker constantly, causing shadows to dance and slide over the walls and ceiling. The storm surging outside paces the drama unfolding inside. As her pains increase, Victoria rallies from her earlier lethargy and participates in the birth, dutifully following Elisabeth's instructions; at one stage, after a vicious contraction, she calls out in anger.

"Where is Patrick? He should be here."

Elisabeth couldn't agree more. The waters break and pour over Elisabeth's hands as she makes a place for the baby to arrive. She throws the wet cloths onto the floor and reaches for dry ones just as the outer door slams open with a gust of wind and Patrick enters. He comes into the small room and demands to know what is happening, standing in the light from the lantern on the washstand. Furious, Elisabeth tells him to get out and wait in the other room.

"Your child is being born, you are in the light," she shouts at him, pointing emphatically with a finger at the other room.

He turns in the doorway.

"I'm sorry," he apologizes, "I mean, is everything all right?"

His English words are only sound to her.

"Go and wait, it will be only a few minutes now. You missed all the hours when you could have helped," she tells him emphatically, waving him briskly into the other room.

Victoria seems unaware of his arrival, her concentration wholly engaged with the birth of her child. The baby is now anxious to arrive and needs only a few more strong pushes to slide out onto the clean cloths where Elisabeth wipes him off and cuts his lifeline to his mother. She looks between his legs and confirms his gender; he is indeed a boy. She wraps him snugly and hands him to Victoria.

"Thorold, I think you said," she tells her. "Patrick is waiting in the other room," she adds. Victoria smiles in happiness.

While Victoria counts her son's fingers and toes, Elisabeth cleans up the bloody bed and readies her for a visit from Patrick. The baby is tiny and very quiet as it lies in his mother's arms; his colour is not as pink as she would like and his quietness worrying.

"Are you ready to see Patrick now?" she asks her friend.

"Oh, yes, we are ready."

Elisabeth goes out into the other room and gestures for Patrick to go into the bedroom. She removes his heavy wet cloak from the chair and spreads it out to dry near the little heat that is emanating from the brazier.

"Don't bother," he says, "I can dry it back at my quarters."

Elisabeth raises her eyebrows in question, not understanding his English words. He takes the cloak and returns it to its former heap on the back of the chair. Rebuked, she repeats her gesture for him to go into the bedroom. He reluctantly enters the room while Elisabeth rehangs his cloak to dry. She wonders what her friend sees in this limply pompous man.

Victoria, happily smiling, holds out the small bundle to him. He ignores the baby and gets down on his knees at the side of the bed and takes one of Victoria's hands and kisses it. They begin to talk but Patrick refuses to hold his son. Elisabeth cannot understand his words, but can see that they are not making Victoria happy. This is not what her patient needs. In a few minutes she goes into the room, takes the baby from Victoria's arms and retreats into the main room. With warm water she carefully washes him and wraps him again in clean cloths, one extra between his legs. He wakes and looks at her intently, opening and closing his fists and moving his legs. Patrick comes in as she finishes.

She holds his son out to him and says, "Thorold, his name is Thorold."

Patrick reaches for his cloak and Elisabeth's patience with this insensitive man snaps. She has never thought he treated Victoria properly and this is the last straw.

"Nein," she says, "No. You sit down and hold your son that Victoria has struggled three long days to bring into the world. " She gestures vehemently and points to a chair.

Patrick has no idea what she is saying but her tone is clear. His displeasure is plain; however, this is not a soldier he can rebuke and put in his place, so he sits down. When he does, Elisabeth places the baby into his arms and steps back. He gives her a stony look but holds on to the infant.

"Thorold," she repeats, pointing at the baby.

"Thorold," he repeats softly.

He takes a look at the small face in the bundle of cloths. They gaze at each other without expression.

Elisabeth has a message for Patrick. How to make this man understand?

She points again to the baby, "Er ist Frügeboren, zu klein; il est très petit," she gestures with her hands, "prématuré. He needs better housing, warmth, fresh air; Victoria must be well to feed him properly." She sighs in frustration. She points to the wall separating the rooms from the storeroom and puts two fingers over her nose.

"Phew. Not good for Victoria or the baby, l'air est malsain; die Luft hier drinnen ist ungesund—es stinkt." She makes a bad smell face and gestures around the room.

Patrick looks at her expressionlessly, stands and hands back the baby who has gone to sleep. He leaves, saying something to her she cannot understand. She does know it certainly is not "thank you" for helping my beloved mistress and baby through this dangerous travail.

Victoria has fallen asleep. Elisabeth makes a nest of bedcovers beside her and pushes the chairs next to the bed to protect it from slipping onto the floor. Thorold is also sleeping and does not wake as she places him next to his mother. She gently shakes Victoria awake and tells her she will be back early in the morning. She has no idea what time it is; however, the storm has passed and the air has cooled although the wind still blows gently. The stars are twinkling in a clear sky and the moon has crossed into the west so it is late, maybe already tomorrow. She is tired and takes a shortcut through Adam Kohl's property into her own backyard. Stoffel is sitting on a stump beside the back door waiting for her.

She sits on the ground beside him; he removes her bonnet and loosens her hair, the long braids uncurling over her shoulders.

"I knew it was important for you to be away so long. Maria said she thought it was Victoria's time. Was it difficult?" he asks.

"Yes. It was Victoria and, yes, it was difficult. They are alive, she is well, but I do not know about the baby. A boy. A tiny little boy. Too young and too small. And a father who refuses him."

Stoffel kisses the top of her head.

"If anyone can keep him in this world, it is you. Beyond that, it is God's will. Come to bed now, it is tomorrow already," he says, raising her to her feet and opening the door.

Her prayers that night are for her friend and the tiny life that she holds in her arms.

"Dear Father in heaven, it is Anna Elisabeth again. Thank You for your blessings this day. Thank You for the safe delivery of Victoria's little boy, watch over him this night and give him strength to stay with us. Please, don't take him into your arms too soon. Amen."

8

AMONG FRIENDS

August, 1754–October, 1754

Elisabeth finishes her breakfast and goes to visit Victoria. She does not want to meet Patrick, uneasy about his reception of her, but knowing that it is inevitable. Victoria is sitting in a chair, holding her baby and talking softly to him, "—handsome little man, with hair like your Mother's and your father's brow—" A ray of sunlight falls over the infant's face and he turns his head into his mother's bosom at its brightness. Victoria looks up when she hears the footsteps on the stairway.

"Good morning, Elisabeth, dearest of friends," she greets her. "Thank you, thank you, for your help yesterday. How you knew that I needed you, I don't understand; but just as I thought I would have to call out to someone on the street, there you were. Bless you, my friend."

"I'm glad I could be here and most relieved that I arrived when I did, but you did most of the work. The early labour went on for a long time and you didn't realize your baby was starting to come, that's why you were so tired and afraid. And alone. Next time, send for me earlier," she answers with a smile.

"Next time? Oh, no. I doubt there will be another time. I consider Thorold a gift from God, one wonderful unexpected gift. He is so good, he never complains.

"Is he suckling?"

"Yes. He is very gentle. A gentleman like his father."

Elisabeth bites her tongue. Victoria is her friend and she loves this contrary man.

"You'll never imagine who came by this morning on his way to talk with Patrick. Sebastian Zouberbuhler. He is very kind and thoughtful.

Look what he brought me—us," Victoria says, pointing to a carved wooden cradle on the floor. "He borrowed it from his neighbour lady for Thorold. She also gave him a fleece. See? There's a sheepskin on the bottom. He also carried up some more wood and coal for the fire bucket, and a bucket of fresh water from the stream. When I thanked him for his kindness and wondered how he knew, he said you had mentioned it to him yesterday."

"Yes," she admits, keeping her tone casual, "he asked why I was hurrying so and I told him. It looks as though you have a friend there, too," says Elisabeth getting up to admire the cradle. "Captain Zouberbuhler can be surprisingly kind."

"Have you eaten today?" she asks Victoria, changing the subject before she probes any further. Let her continue to think Patrick came of his own accord.

"Not yet, I don't want to put him down," she admitted, nuzzling her face into Thorold's blankets.

"I brought you some broth. Why don't you eat it while it's still warm? You must take care for yourself now that you have somebody who depends on you for everything. Here, let me hold him."

Elisabeth changes places with Victoria who places the baby in her arms and then touches her hair, feeling the tangles in the red curls.

"You are right, what if Patrick saw me like this?"

She looks at her baby and strokes his cheek with her finger murmuring, "We are three, now we are three for me to love."

While Victoria sips the soup and heats water to wash herself, Elisabeth examines the baby. He waves his arms and kicks his legs as she unwraps him; his soaker cloths are wet and he makes little sucking noises with his mouth when she strokes his cheek. To her experienced hands, he hefts more like a plucked chicken than a suckling pig, but then, he is an early arrival by three to four weeks. She swaddles him up again and looks at him. He is pink and white, like a painted angel in a church fresco, not red like a lusty bawling infant. Perhaps she is looking for something that isn't there; however, she feels he will need constant vigilance.

She hands him back to Victoria, reminding her that an early baby needs lots of nourishment and quiet handling, so she should eat well herself and rest whenever she becomes tired or Thorold is not demanding her attention.

"You should rest now, so that you are both ready for Patrick's visit this evening," says Elisabeth, taking her leave. "I'll come and see you tomorrow."

"Oh, yes, I'm sure he will come this evening."

The rain has washed the sky of its summer dust and a heaven of azure spreads to the horizon. Here and there brilliant puffs of pure white cloud drift lazily. The air has lost its enervating humidity and fills the town with a vigour that has been missing since mid-spring. Even the seagulls are displaying their acrobatic skills with more artistry.

Elisabeth walks the length of the waterfront and up the hill toward the vegetable gardens. She visits the garden nearly every day now, judging when to start the harvest. The tops of the potatoes have turned yellow and started to wilt. In a few weeks they will be brown and ready to dig up. The turnip and cabbage might put on a bit of growth yet, the dry summer has probably made the turnips woody and unpleasant to eat but the carrots are ready to pull. Catherine is doing the same inspection on the Herman's plot and the two women halt to talk over their plans for preserving the harvest.

"Put the carrots down in barrels of sand, buried feet first and not touching; they will last until spring," she advises to Catherine.

"And the potatoes? How do you keep yours from rotting?"

"I plan to keep them between layers of clean straw, in the dark; they must not freeze or get too cold or they'll turn black."

They discuss coating turnips in tallow melted down from the hoarded ends of candles. And the making of sauerkraut. Pieter Bubechoffer has fashioned a cabbage slicer and, when they are harvested, she and Sabina Bubechoffer and other nearby women will gather and spend a day slicing and preparing the sauerkraut.

"Has anyone started a gristmill yet?" asks Catherine. "How will we grind our barley and buckwheat?"

"I have been wondering the same thing," replies Elisabeth. "Do you have much grain?"

"Enough to see us through to the new year if I am careful, no more," she admits.

"Yes, we are about the same, enough for a few months. I haven't heard of a mill starting up; we had so little grain last winter, I could grind it with a stone pestle. If you hear of anyone setting up mill stones, will you let me know?"

"Of course. Well, I must go, take care, Elisabeth."

As she makes her way back up the hill to her home, Elisabeth wonders to herself how many times she has made this trek; from the house to the garden, down the hill and up the hill; this town is made of hills and she is either going up or going down. Hills and trees and the sea. Her thoughts move on.

Tonight they will have to decide what to do with their livestock. Transferring the cow to their farm has kept her alive but she is not thriving. There is no sign of her being in calf. Is it worth the effort of sheltering and feeding her through the winter? The sheep were returned to the common to breed with the ram in early September. Adam salvaged one pregnant ewe but the other five will be slaughtered and their wooly hides kept for use against the cold. Stoffel's shared sheep is also pregnant but in a poor state of health, and Elisabeth is not hopeful she will survive. Without doubt, they are better prepared for this winter than the last. She is optimistic that the English will authorize rations for them again if they run out of food before the next season. Governor Lawrence seems sincere in his desire to have Lunenburg succeed; she suspects that he may look upon it as part of his preparations for war with France.

The sound of hammering wakes her from her reverie. It sounds as though it emanates from her house, curiosity spurs her steps. Their house is built into the side of a small slope, so that the upper end is dug slightly into the hill and the lower end is raised with the earth dug out of the upper. Her husband and sons appear to be building a structure onto the lower end of the house. Its roof is lower than the roof of the house and it has no windows and no chimney.

"What are you doing?" she calls to them.

"Building a byre," answers Christof.

"So, we are keeping the cow, ja?"

The animal in question stands lop eared and uncaring at the edge of the path, tethered to a tree with a rope. She has one leg at half cock and her nose to the earth, either smelling the grass or having a sleep. Evie stands at her head with her arms around her neck.

Her husband comes up to her.

"Sometimes decisions are taken out of our hands in such a way that there is no discussion."

Elisabeth looks quizzically at him.

Stoffel pulls her over to admire the finer points of their construction and explains.

"Evie heard Christof and me talking about the cow, considering whether to keep her or slaughter her, and asked what we meant. When we explained that the cow looked unhealthy and it might be better to use her as food, she looked at me in horror and shouted 'No'. She flung her arms around the poor cow and said, 'There's nothing wrong with her. She's like me, just slower than others. She'll be a good cow when she grows up. You can't kill her because she looks funny. I'll take care of her, you'll see.' She was adamant and very upset; there was no talking her out of it. Every time we came near the cow she started to scream."

Before going to admire the cow with Evie, Elisabeth smiles at her husband of twenty-four years, "You're a good man, Johannes Christoffel Baltzer, and a good father to our children." She adds, looking at the byre, "Make it large enough for the sheep as well."

Victoria's baby continues to live and has learned to suckle. He is still quiet, lying silently wherever he is put down until his mother picks him up. On Sunday, Elisabeth goes to church to give thanks for his safe birth along with her usual prayers and requests for God's continued safekeeping. Her head is bowed and she is busy with her thoughts when she hears Melchior's voice begin the prayer. She looks up quickly to confirm what her ears have told her. Although he has been gone nearly two months, she has not realized how much she missed his presence until now. Elisabeth is not surprised to find that Stoffel has invited him for the Sunday meal.

After they are finished eating, the three of them retire to the sunny bench beside the herb garden. He tells them what he has told Sutherland, that there are more Indians in the area, that Abbé Le Loutre has been made Vicar General of Nova Scotia and has more power over the French and Indian population than ever. In fact, Le Loutre has spent the summer travelling along the coast of the Bay of Fundy raising the feelings of the Acadians and Mi'kmaq against the English. The complement of English soldiers at Fort Edward near Piziquid and at Fort York has been increased and there seems to be no mood to sue for peace treaties between the two sides. When he spoke with Captain Sutherland, the Captain reported Governor Lawrence more reluctant to consider peace an option than previously.

"The military solution seems to be the popular one with the government in Halifax," Melchior says in a despondent voice. He turns to Stoffel.

"Let's change the topic. I hear your wife took on the Captain and administered a lecture the other day."

"What is this? I have not been told of this. Elisabeth?" replies Stoffel looking at her, a puzzled frown on his face.

Elisabeth does not answer, wanting first to be sure of what Melchior spoke.

"Yes, I think the Captain was a little offended to be tasked so severely," Melchior went on in a teasing tone. "He thinks she told him that he needed a bath, that he stank."

"Er stört mich. He annoys me," answered Elisabeth with asperity. "I was trying to tell him that the air in Victoria's room smells of tar and creosote, much too strong for an infant."

"He is the Captain; you can't tell him he stinks," utters Stoffel in astonishment.

Melchior laughs while Elisabeth's pique with the Captain gets the better of her tongue.

"He is an impossible person. I hold him responsible for the Indian massacre at Clearland. There are many soldiers in Lunenburg, he could have them patrolling the outlying farmlands. That might discourage the Indians from coming too near. And where was he when Victoria was having his baby? He came just as it was nearly over. And, and he would not hold his own son. Besides the rooms which he has for her are not fit for a baby. The smell from the tar and creosote is nauseating. He is not caring for her properly—"

She is still in mid speech when both men stop her, neither one understanding the half of what she said.

"Slow down, tell it slowly."

"Calm yourself, Elisabeth. I think he understood your message."

Stoffel agrees with the need for more patrols while Melchior picks up on her concern for Victoria's infant son. Alarmed to realize that Elisabeth has had an argument with the most important man in the town, Stoffel puts his hands on his head and groans.

"Elisabeth, sometimes you go too far. You forget you're just an ordinary person and he's in charge of the town. What have you done?"

Melchior puts a hand on Stoffel's shoulder.

"No, no, do not worry. He was not angry, just astonished and bemused. He put it down to a woman's usual behaviour in a crisis. I will talk to him and explain your concerns over the baby though; he is not an unfeeling man, but he is a soldier first and always. He has lived a soldier's life for nearly twenty-five years, he does not know anything else. Do not be too hard on him." He looks at Elisabeth, "I think Victoria understands and accepts that."

Elisabeth nods her head in acknowledgement of his words; again she has rushed in without considering that someone else may view a situation differently than she does. Stoffel stands up to end the afternoon and walk Melchior to the pathway. They wave farewell to him and return to their house.

"Has your big heart gotten you into trouble again?" he asks her tenderly. "Never mind, it will work itself out. Tomorrow is another day; it will bring troubles of its own. "

"Thank you, husband," she tells him quietly. *"Dear Lord, I love this man, keep him safe."*

The carrots are harvested, waiting to be topped and brushed off and stored. Half of the potatoes are dug, resting on the earth for their skins to dry off and harden before being put into alder baskets and stored on the rafters of the new cow byre. Storing the crop would be easier if she had a proper root cellar; however, Christof has contrived a makeshift one in the angle of the byre and the house. *"By next year maybe, with your continued blessing, dear Lord."*

She is standing with her back to the town, gazing at her garden, satisfied it has produced all it could in this dry, hot summer. In many ways she misses the ease of her former life, going to the market for vegetables and fruit, shopping at the bakery for meat pies on washday and choosing meat from their own butchery. And buying shoes if they need them, or an extra bucket, or beeswax candles for holidays. Here, staying fed and clothed and warm is a daily challenge. "Nevertheless," she thinks, as she has so often before, "there is satisfaction in surviving by one's wits and skills, in living where hard work pays off and an honest man can better himself." That was one of the reasons they had come here, at home it no longer seemed that hard work was enough to ensure a family's future. She digs her hoe into the side of the potato hill, releasing its crop of white tubers.

"Guten Tag, Frau Baltzer, Elisabeth," calls out Catherine from up the hill, "I was looking for you, one of your girls said you might be here."

She looks up and greets her.

"Good day, Fräulein—" With surprise, Elisabeth realizes she does not know Catherine's family name, only thinks of her as "with the Hermans". Had she ever asked? She couldn't remember.

"Good day to you, Fräulein Catherine. Yes, I am here, my world is very small these days, my garden and my house. It is a busy time."

Catherine walks slowly, the rocky hillside is difficult for her to negotiate because of the thick sole and heel on her shoe. Whether a birth defect or an accident caused the shorter leg, Elisabeth does not know and she is reluctant to ask. There is much she does not know about Catherine. She is carrying a small bundle which she hands to Elisabeth.

"It is only tallow ends, for the turnips; we had more than we needed," she explains. "I left some things at your house, if you can use them. Just some worn dresses and shirts.

As Elisabeth starts to protest, Catherine raises one hand to hush her and ask her to wait.

"It is nothing, I want to give them to you, in return for your friendship to me, from the beginning. And—I want to talk to you; I really must speak with you, Elisabeth, my friend."

She hesitates.

"I have a confession to make to you, a secret that I have kept to myself longer than I should except that I didn't know how to tell you."

Elisabeth is startled and not a little alarmed. What is coming?

"I remember when I saw you on the beach, in Halifax that awful day we landed. You gave me courage to carry on, to do what I needed to do. You were organizing your family and your trunks, looking so calm and sure. Your husband was ill as I remember and you were so patient with him and the children. I just felt if I could be that strong, then my little bit of family would be alright. Because if they were not, then what would become of me? I didn't know who you were then, that you were married to a Baltzer from Bracht, in Hesse. Elisabeth, I'm relieved to finally tell you; you and I are related, at least by marriage."

"Related? But how?" Elisabeth exclaims in astonishment. She is rarely taken completely by surprise, but this is complete.

"My grandfather was a descendent of Jacob Baltzer of Bracht. Although he left Bracht with his mother as a young boy and never returned, he told me about the family. Jacob Baltzer was great-grandfather to my father and to your husband. So, your Christoffel and my father are distant cousins. My name is properly Louise Katarina Baltzer."

Elisabeth is at a loss for words and a bit doubtful of her story.

"Are you sure? Of course you're sure. Who was your father, what was his name?" asks Elisabeth, trying to recall all of Stoffel's relatives and understand who this girl could be. Realizing that she is questioning her sharply, Elisabeth softens her tone. "You have completely surprised me. I don't know what to say. We are related and you never introduced yourself?"

"No. I didn't want to impose. My father was Heinrich Martin Baltzer of Oberlahnstein, my grandfather was Martin Jacob Baltzer who came from Bracht with his mother, Roswitha Baltzer, a widow, related to Jacob Baltzer, your husband's great-grandfather."

"Well, Stoffel's great-grandfather was named Jacob, and he was from Bracht," confirmed Elisabeth. "I do not remember any woman called Roswitha, though. I'll talk to Stoffel, perhaps we can find out who your great-grandmother was."

"I don't need to know who she was," Catherine goes on, "I only wanted to tell you because I have some happy news to share with you." She places her hand tentatively on Elisabeth's arm. "Herr Herman, Bernhard, has asked me to marry him. And I said yes."

"Oh, Catherine," she declares. "That is happy news, I'm very happy for you. I think it's what you really wanted to happen.

Catherine smiles contentedly.

"Yes, I am happy. I've wanted to tell you for a long time that we are related but I didn't know how; it seemed presumptuous of me. You are one of the older respected women of the town and I'm only a young servant woman."

Elisabeth understands Catherine's thinking and hopes, now that she will be the wife, not housekeeper, of a moderately wealthy man, she will be more respected by the other women. Catherine is already well regarded within the church and often admired for the character with which she carries out her duties as mistress of the house despite being the housekeeper. Elisabeth is sorry that Catherine has felt ashamed of her position.

"I wonder if you would stand with me, as my family, I have no other," asks Catherine. "I would be grateful and proud if you would recognize me as a relation."

"Yes, of course we will."

There is no other answer. The relationship may be false or true, it does not matter.

"I am honoured to be asked to stand with you," surprised and happy to realize that it is the truth. Catherine is the type of strong willed woman that the new country needs.

"The marriage will be soon, on the 17th, at the house. Bernhard's oldest daughter is to marry in a few weeks and Bernhard wants to have our nuptials out of the way before then."

She looks down at her folded hands.

"Bernhard feels it will be more seemly if I am his wife rather than his housekeeper," she says in a soft voice and returns her eyes to Elisabeth's face. "I think he does have a fondness for me, though."

Elisabeth puts a reassuring hand on Catherine's.

"How could he not? Fondness and respect for the capable way you manage his domestic affairs is a good enough start, it portends a good marriage." Elisabeth can't resist the urge to add a motherly admonition, "He is a number of years older than you; it would not be wise to expect the ardour of a young man."

Catherine blushes.

"I have learned to keep my expectations within reason; I will be grateful for whatever I receive. This is more than I expected already. And I have you for a friend and now a relative, I am satisfied," she replies.

They embrace before Catherine leaves and Elisabeth returns to her potato harvest. As she turns up the potatoes, she ponders the conversation. This news has come out of nowhere. And for it to be Catherine, the one woman she finds not only perplexing, but frequently irritating, is ironic. All questions aside, she doesn't think Catherine has made it up from whole cloth, there were too many details. "*Who is this young woman?*" She poses the question to God, for only he knows. As she thinks about it, she recalls that Catherine has been a recurrent part of her life since the early days in Halifax, asking questions, small favours, bringing gifts and just conversing. Many of the days when Elisabeth passed the Herman house on the way to and from the garden lots, Catherine would be there with a reason for a conversation or an invitation for a visit; when the women gather after service, she often finds Catherine beside her.

Elisabeth thinks about the names Catherine mentioned, certainly the men's names are common enough in the Baltzer family: Martin, Christian, Heinrich, but they are common in many family lines. Roswitha she has never heard used in any of the family stories. It sounds like a Romanische name, and, in every generation, among the robust blond children, there are a few dark ones; she has two herself. Catherine's slenderness and dark looks are no indication of lineage.

When she retells the tale to Stoffel that evening, he dismisses her concerns over Catherine's parentage, saying it has no relevance now; if she is a Baltzer, she is a Baltzer and probably a relation. Anyway, she is soon to become a Herman so it is of no matter. Sometime later he looks up from where he is rubbing the dried earth off the carrots while Elisabeth inserts them into the sand.

"I think I remember my father telling me about an uncle that was rather a rogue and not welcome at great-grandfather Jacob's home. The rumour was that he stole a mistress from his father. They both disappeared. I recall her name as being unusual."

"A pregnant maid might well take her master's name," comments Elisabeth. "I think we will keep that story for ourselves," she adds.

"Yes. It is old history," he agrees.

Catherine's full skirt is of deep mauve with a double band of black ribbon decorating the bottom. The long-sleeved jacket has a single band around the neck and front with a row of tiny black buttons down the front and on the sleeves. Bernhard has given her new shoes for the occasion, made of soft leather dyed to match the dress, the high tops closing with tiny buttons that took many minutes to fasten even with the special hook. The dress is English in style and reveals nothing of her ancestry or homeland. Elisabeth wonders whose choice it had been.

She has brought Catherine a spray of autumn wildflowers to carry and an embroidered handkerchief as a gift. The purplish blue of the michaelmas daisies and the yellow of the goldenrod brighten the sombre colour of the dress. Catherine looks happy and very young as she enters the room in her wedding finery and Elisabeth remembers that she is only sixteen years old.

Elisabeth still hears Catherine's last words as they waited in the hallway, half prayer, half avowal, "I know he will grow to love me; I will be his partner in everything. He will love me."

"Please, God, make it so, at least a little bit," prays Elisabeth as they walk slowly to stand in front of Reverend Moreau.

October passes quickly with days spent in completing the harvest, in patching their quilted vests and petticoats, lining footwear with sheepskin and making sauerkraut. There is also the wedding of Bernhard Herman's daughter, Anna Catherine, to Franz Demone, and the birth of Susanna Elisabeth Berghaus both of which Elisabeth attend. Christof continues to work on his land at Mahone Bay and comes home only for Sunday service meanwhile Peter has taken over most of his work around home. Stoffel and Adam have kept a few of the healthiest sheep and slaughtered the rest. The cow is improving under the tender ministrations of Evie who takes her on a rope each day for a walk along the path and brings her buckets of water from the stream.

Elisabeth has harvested seeds from some of the wild herbs to plant next spring in her own garden, picked nuts from the hazel bushes, dried some of the blueberries and huckleberries, and made syrup from the juicy blackberries and raspberries. She has also dried leaves from the raspberry bush and the soft green tips of the spruce tree as well as collected some of the gum that oozes from its bark; and dried some of the sweet flag roots.

She has even accepted a gift of salted and dried fish from Monsieur Bizette.

"My share of the catch," Peter tells her proudly.

Stoffel and Christof have successfully hunted two deer which they butchered, brined and smoke dried. Stoffel made a few rings of sausage from the offal mixed with salt and dried wild chives. It will be a long winter, but they are pleased with their preparations.

The leaves on the trees have finished their fall display of colour and fallen to the ground leaving the evergreens to dominate the landscape amid the stark black limbs of the maples and birch. In the woods, the last of the woodland flowers are drooping to the ground and the squirrels are frantically burying the fallen nuts and fruits. The beaver are reinforcing their dams and the porcupines are round and roly-poly with winter fat.

Elisabeth and Victoria visit each other most weeks. Baby Thorold continues to worry Elisabeth; he's too quiet and small for a healthy baby. Today Elisabeth is refreshing their bedding rolls with dried marsh grass and cedar tips. The girls have emptied them of the old grass and aired the covers in the cold sunshine. Now she is refilling them and sewing them shut for the winter. Her skirts are covered with detritus when Victoria enters the yard with her son in her arms.

Without preamble she reveals what is on her mind. "Elisabeth, I'm worried about Tory; I think he should be growing faster, he never makes a fuss; he's content just to lie there. At first I was so enthralled with him I wasn't seeing him clearly. That's why you come to look at him so often, isn't it? What are you not telling me?"

Elisabeth stands up and shakes the bits of grass and cedar off her skirt. She is glad Victoria broached this topic; she has been wondering how to tell her friend of her concerns over the infant.

"Come. Let's have a cup of hot buckwheat tea. We will talk." She leads the way into her house.

Buckwheat grows wild hereabouts, perhaps from seeds the Acadians planted, and she has collected a store of it for restorative drinks, the wild ones having greater medicinal power.

They sit at the table with their cups of hot drink; Thorold lies on the bed in a nest made from an old quilt. He sucks on a piece of clean rag, twisted and tied into a teat and dipped into the hot drink. Elisabeth hesitates before telling Victoria about her vague fears; she has no definite indication that the baby is not perfectly healthy, or will not grow into a strong vigorous boy. After all, it may be just that he was born too soon and is taking more time to mature.

"I also want to tell you some good news," begins Victoria before Elisabeth can start. "Patrick has found Tory and me a house. It is near the west end of town, on Montague Street. It was vacated by one of the settlers; he is having it fixed for us. It has a proper hearth and even a wooden floor."

Elisabeth is delighted for her.

"That's very good news. I'm happy for you and it's very thoughtful of Patrick to organize it, especially the fixing up. It will be much healthier for you both than the chandler's rooms. Just what Thorold needs. Do you know where on Montague Street?"

Elisabeth recalls a small, well constructed house in the middle of a section of Montague Street, and it had been empty for some months now. It must be that one.

"No, but it may be near Old Labrador's place." She leans forward, "We must talk about Tory now. What is wrong with him? I was talking with one of the English women and when I showed her the baby, she said, 'Oh, you poor thing. I'm so sorry.' What did she mean?"

The words of the thoughtless woman anger Elisabeth. She had no reason to upset a new mother with such talk when there was no cause for it.

"She was talking foolishly. Forget her words, yet it is true that we should talk about Thorold. Don't be alarmed. I am probably making too much of little things. I have seen many babies and Thorold is different than most. He seems just fine, but I have some small concerns. He is too good, he never cries; he rarely tries to roll over and he is still very small. By now he should be catching up with babies born on time."

Victoria gasps in distress at her words.

"Please, calm yourself. Do not be alarmed," Elisabeth tells her. "He is fine, but he does not seem to thrive as I would expect. He is very pale. I think that is what the woman saw, but your skin is also very pale so it likely means nothing. I have no improvements to suggest in the way you care for him, you are doing everything properly. You surround him with your love."

"But you have been worried about him, haven't you?"

Elisabeth puts her hand on her friend's arm and admits that that is so.

Tears start to Victoria's eyes. She goes over to the bed and picks up her son, holding him protectively against her breast.

"Nothing is going to happen to him, promise me."

"We will all do our best but is in God's hands." Elisabeth pauses. "I do have one suggestion though, if you are willing."

"What?"

"We could go and consult with Anne. She is a healer who learned her skills here and may be more effective than I am. She understands both the Acadian way and the Mi'kmaq way. Your baby was born here and local ways may be better for him."

"I don't know. Patrick would not approve," she says in hesitation. "Yet I will do whatever I must. When can we go?"

"If your house is where I think it must be, then you are practically neighbours. It will do no harm to wait a week or two. If you are neighbours, you will meet by chance in any event."

"I don't want to visit her alone, can't you come with me?"

"Why would you be afraid of her?" asks Elisabeth. "You can speak French with her as well as I can, better. And you understand her as well as I do."

Even as Elisabeth speaks, she realizes that it is Patrick's reaction that Victoria fears, and she needs Elisabeth as a buffer. Elisabeth is willing to take the blame; however, the less Patrick knows, the easier it would be.

"I will go with you," Elisabeth promises. "If you need help to move, let me know and I will bring the boys along to carry furniture and buckets. I am eager to see your new home."

The first early snow of the season has fallen before Victoria moves into her little house. Captain Sutherland organizes some of his soldiers to carry her things the short distance uphill from the rooms over the chandler's to Montague Street.

At an intimate meal the evening before, Patrick had told her, "If you can find a reason to be out tomorrow morning, when you return you will find that your belongings have been moved to your house."

"Oh, thank you, thank you, Patrick," Victoria told him. "You are so good to me and Thorold. These rooms have been wonderful but a house of our own will be much healthier for him." She had looked up at the man she loves and suggested hopefully, "You will be able to visit us often there. I noticed that it is some little distance from its neighbours."

Patrick had hesitated before he responded.

"I hope it can be so," he finally said.

Victoria had knelt at his feet with her head on his knee while he stroked her hair which she had let loose over her shoulders. The flares of light from the brazier sparked highlights the hue of burnished copper from it as it twined around his fingers.

"I hope it can be so," he repeated.

Victoria hugs these words to her heart as she climbs uphill to Elisabeth's house. She hopes she is home; she has nowhere else to go on this cold morning. She is in luck, Elisabeth is there. She and Margarete are teaching the girls how to make boiled-wool leggings from the ends of the shearings. The small room is crowded with people and babies, steamy from the hot wet wool and noisy with laughter and the pounding of wooden beaters.

Elisabeth is laughing.

"I only saw this done once and I had forgotten how much wool it takes, I think we will be lucky to get even one pair of warm leggings."

Three wet mats of wool are hanging over sticks propped a little distance from the fire; Gertrud and Evie are rolling another one with a smooth log to remove as much water as they can into a bucket filled with hot water and more raw wool. Baby Bettina is happily banging another small pile of wool with a stick and laughing when it sprays into her face. It is a scene of happy confusion. Elisabeth offers Victoria a hot drink and a seat on the edge of the bed.

As she sits down herself, Elisabeth raises her cup in a toast.

"To laughter," she says. "There has been little enough of that," she adds as she wipes her brow with her apron.

Victoria understands little of the rapid German flowing around her, but she is content to be part of the group of women. Margarete is a tiny person, spending most of her time keeping her son, Ferdi, and lively Bettina out of trouble. Elisabeth is the energy of the group, talking, explaining, making people smile and laugh. Margarete glances often at Victoria, trying to convey acceptance and friendship in a smile. She holds Thorold for a time, talking to him and making him smile. In too short a time the morning passes and Margarete leaves. Before she goes home she gives Victoria a quick hug. It is the first time since Victoria arrived in Lunenburg that someone has made such a gesture of friendship toward her, apart from Elisabeth, of course, and she feels a welcome sense of belonging.

"Her three children died on the voyage across the sea," Elisabeth explains quickly. "It was a long time before she could smile again. Stoffel and her husband, Adam, are old friends."

"How dreadful for her. She seems a very nice person, kind, I am glad to know her," says Victoria. "I came because I am moving into my house today. Patrick has organized for my things to be moved this morning; I was hoping you could come with me, maybe after your meal."

"Of course," replies Elisabeth. "You will eat with us first, and then I will come." As Victoria starts to leave, Elisabeth pushes her back gently, "No, no. You can eat with us. There is plenty of food."

Stoffel and the boys have been working close by and they come in with a rush of cold air and stamping of feet. The jovial chatter stops while they devour their bowls of hot soup, potatoes and meat followed by egg pudding and hot rum. When they are done, Stoffel lies on the bed for his mid-day nap while the rest of them enjoy a quiet conversation. Maria asks to hold baby Thorold who has had his own meal by now. Gertrud and Evie cluster around her and play with him, rubbing his feet and tickling his fingers. He gurgles in contentment while Victoria looks on in happiness.

A short time later the two women make their way along the top of the town and down the hill to the lower streets. In the morning sun, the snow has mostly disappeared from the pathways.

"I want us to come on it from the west, that's how Patrick will come to it from his quarters," says Victoria.

There are a few people in the streets. Some nod their heads and a few greet them, others, mostly women alone, walk past with the merest of acknowledgements. The military men give them a casual salute, mindful of Victoria's tenuous status and her man's very tangible one.

The one-room house sits well back on the treed lot, protected from the winds and public view by tall evergreens and several maples. An uncleared lot separates it from the Labrador's. Two piles of stones mark the beginning of the gravel path that leads to the front, and only, door. Smoke spirals lazily from the chimney and Elisabeth's opinion of Patrick inches up a notch when a banked fire in the hearth greets them. The smoke draws well despite the shuttered window opening. There has been some attempt to arrange the few furnishings, the table, the two chairs and the cradle beside the sleeping bench. The small items are still in their buckets and piles, but they quickly put that to rights. In a few minutes, the room is cozy with the fire burning briskly and pots and dishes in their places.

"It is small but very well built, you will be warm and comfortable here," comments Elisabeth, taking a seat in one of the chairs.

"It is my first home," remarks Victoria. "I went from my father's home to soldier's quarters or maid's rooms. This is mine, mine and Tory's and Patrick's. This has been a remarkable day. I spent the morning with friends and now I have returned to my own home. I never dared to dream of such a thing since I left Georgia. Tonight my prayers will be heartfelt and true."

Elisabeth is pleased for her young friend. Her own life has held many moments of joy as well as crushing grief, but she has never had to bear them alone as Victoria has. She has had many friends over her years and cannot imagine how it would be to have no family around. Not a state she wishes to experience. She admires Victoria's courage and steadfast love for Patrick.

"I am very happy for you," she tells Victoria. "However, if you still wish to consult with Anne about Thorold, there may not be a better time. They are only a short walk away through the woods."

Victoria bends her head to kiss her son on the forehead and stare into his face.

"Yes, I would like to do that," she whispers.

"It is best not to wait after the decision is made," Elisabeth quotes from her store of homely wisdom. "We can go through the woods, across the uncleared lot, it is not far. There was smoke coming from the chimney so I think she is at home."

It is colder now that the sun has started to dip toward the western hills of the town and here under the trees some snow remains. The Guidry-Labrador house is larger than most of those in the town but still it has only one storey; however, it has two hearths, one at each end. It is like two houses built end-to-end with a wide front porch, reflecting a time when a large extended family lived here. Elisabeth remembers that there is also a back door and several sheds behind the house. She knocks on the door. A young boy opens the door and stares at them without speaking.

Elisabeth smiles and says in French, "Je m'appelle Madame Baltzer, a friend of Madame Muis d'Entremont. Est-elle à la maison? Is she at home?" she asks in careful French. The little boy continues to stare silently at them until Anne herself arrives at the door and welcomes them inside.

"I'm sorry; he is from a village and has come to be made well. His family will come back for him in a few days. His name is Godefoy."

She turns to the boy and asks him to greet the guests politely. He ducks his head and mutters, "Bonjour." After another quick glance he disappears into another part of the house.

Anne offers them chairs which are covered in hide with bearskin pelt on the seat for comfort and warmth. A fire burns in the hearth and the odour of venison stew fills the room. Victoria looks around, the house is snugger and better furnished than most of the houses in Lunenburg. After Anne prepares a cup of hot spruce tea for them, she sits down and looks at them with inquiry. Elisabeth introduces Victoria as a new neighbour.

"Welcome, bienvenue. I am happy to have you next door. I recognize you, and your little son, and am very happy to meet you." She turns to Elisabeth and says, "I expect my husband will be back soon, he has been away on one of his little trips for a few days. It has been very quiet, I am very glad to have company." She looks at the bundle in Victoria's arms and asks, "How is your baby son growing?"

Victoria looks at Elisabeth who nods her head in encouragement.

"I have come for your advice," begins Victoria, "Maybe I am just overly concerned, but I am worried. He doesn't seem like other babies."

"Ooh," Anne murmurs softly, gently stroking the baby's cheek. "When was he born?" she asks.

"August 22nd, thirteen weeks ago."

Anne smiles and holds out her arms.

"May I hold him?" she asks Victoria who passes her precious bundle over carefully, as though any slight jar will damage him.

The women try to start a conversation, but their anxiety is too great and stillness settles on the room as the Acadian woman plays gently with Thorold. She unwinds his swaddling cloths and smoothes her hands over his limbs, tickling his feet to make him kick and letting him hold her finger. She puts a tube of rolled birch bark to his chest and listens intently. He looks very small without his wrappings.

She points to his loin cloth which has become soiled.

"We use something better, dried grass and moss in a soft leather cloth. The grass can be buried back in the woods. The moss can be washed, dried and used again like the leather. I will give you some. Few children come here now that the English soldiers are everywhere. I do not need it. I will show you. Do you mind?"

Victoria nods acquiescence and watches intently as Anne packs a soft piece of leather with dried moss and covers it with a circle of dried grass and re-wraps him.

"He is very beautiful," she tells Victoria. She lifts the baby to her shoulder and cuddles him, closing her eyes and murmuring in his ear.

As she hands him back she tells Victoria, "He is as he should be. The Mi'kmaq would say that he has an old soul and no one knows how long old souls will stay in this world before returning to their home in the Spirit World."

"You mean he is going to die?" Victoria's tears burst to the surface as she clutches Thorold to her.

"In his own time, as we all will. Your son is not going to die today, nor tomorrow; not until his reason for coming into the world is fulfilled. We are all going to die. If we are born, we will die, but some lifetimes are shorter than others."

"I do not understand," exclaims Victoria. Elisabeth rises and puts her hands on Victoria's shoulders to comfort her.

"I see nothing wrong with him except what you see and the only explanation I have is the Indian one," Anne tells them. "He does not appear completely connected with this world, as though he remains partly in the Spirit World. They believe that a baby comes from the Spirit World and its soul wanders back to the Spirit World while it sleeps. An Indian mother constantly talks to her baby, asking it to remain here, telling it that this is a wonderful place full of surprises and beauty, that the baby is precious and loved and needed in this world. She tells it stories to make it want to stay. They would say that your baby has not come entirely into this world of people and continues to wander back to the Spirit World."

Victoria and Elisabeth are bewildered, and frightened, by such a magical explanation and don't know what to say. It is obvious that Anne believes this explanation.

Elisabeth proffers a hesitant question.

"Are you are saying that it is in God's hands and we can only pray for his help?"

Victoria is quietly sobbing and rocking her baby in distress.

"In a way, but not exactly," Anne explains. "To take it as God's will implies that we can do nothing to change the situation. The Mi'kmaq believe that one should try everything possible to entice his spirit to remain in this world and that we may succeed. They believe there is a constant and active communication between the world of people and the world of spirits, that there is movement between the worlds.

Sometimes an ancient spirit returns as a new baby, especially if he has something to tell us, or teach us. It is up to the people to understand the lesson. Needless to say, the priests do not agree with this. They would say that it is in God's hands alone."

"I don't understand," Elisabeth says.

"I do," says Victoria suddenly. "He is a gift from God and like Jesus he may be here for a short time. It is the loving of him and the caring for him that is important. He is a special blessing and I am grateful. This is a good time; I will enjoy it and not expect it to last forever."

"Perhaps that is the teaching," sighs Anne softly, "that good things do not last forever."

A stamping of feet and voices calling out greetings interrupts them.

Anne jumps up with a happy smile on her face.

"C'est Paul qui arrive. Non, non. Stay there. For once let us act as neighbours. You must eat with us and meet my husband properly."

Three men come into the room, their cheeks red from the cold outside. They are rubbing their hands to rid themselves of the cold numbness in their fingers. Two are slender with dark straight hair and dark eyes, the other is familiar and his eyes light up at the sight of Elisabeth. Melchior has returned with Paul. Anne releases herself from the hugs of the two other men and makes the introductions.

"Madame Baltzer, Mademoiselle Downing, I would like to present my husband, Paul Guidry, and his nephew, Jean Deschamps. Monsieur Seiler, of course, you already know."

The ladies return the introductions, receiving courtly bows and a hand kiss as though they were in a salon in the old country. It seems so normal, thinks Elisabeth. It is the first time she has seen the half-breed men at close quarters. So this is Paul Guidry, called Old Labrador. He is a small man, like a sapling compared to her Stoffel, and dark, his eyes quickly assessing her and Victoria, wondering why they are here. His nephew looks like him but is taller, his hair not so black and his eyes not so piercing. This is Cloverwater, the agent the English use to collect information about the Indians. Is this why they have been away? Has Melchior been with them?

Melchior greets the women. When Victoria presents her son to him, his face creases with happy lines and he takes the little bundle gently into his hands.

"Welcome to the world, little man. May God bless you and keep you safe." He hands him back to Victoria, saying, "He is wonderful, a joy for you and Patrick, I am sure."

He greets Elisabeth with cordiality, as a friend of the family would; however, he contrives to be seated next to her.

"And how have you been? Getting into any trouble while I have been gone?" he murmurs into her ear as he shuffles in his seat.

"I am well, thank you, and the family also. And you? Any adventures on your journey?"

"None to speak of," he answers. "It is good to see you again, Elisabeth."

"And you, also," she replies. "Your absence was noted by many."

"And by you?"

"By us all."

The young boy who opened the door sneaks back into the room and attaches himself to Jean Deschamps' side. Elisabeth sees now that he must be related to him, perhaps another nephew; however, by his looks more Indian than Acadian with his burnished skin. She looks around the cozy room, Acadian, Indian, English, German, the new world and the old world in harmony. This is Melchior's vision and for a time they talk and share a meal forgetting about the clouds of war gathering over the ocean.

Anne serves them a stew of venison and vegetables, potatoes and ploys, which are buckwheat pancakes, with a sweet syrup for dessert.

"What is this delicious syrup?" she asks Anne.

"The sap of the sugar maple, tapped in spring and boiled down," Anne explains. "I'll ask Paul to demonstrate one day."

"That would be most welcome. It is delicious," Elisabeth repeats.

Soon after they are finished, Victoria makes her excuses for departure. Elisabeth is aware, too, that she has a family at home who by now are wondering where she is and beginning to worry. Melchior and Elisabeth walk Victoria through the woods to her front door and he accompanies Elisabeth until she is safely at her path. They exchange few words, understanding that conversation must wait another time. Some things he must tell Sutherland first; others, he must not say at all.

A tangle of thoughts weigh heavily on Elisabeth's mind, and the long dark night seems endless. Stoffel had been angry with worry by the time she returned home and she had been less then truthful with her explanation. *"Lord, was it wrong not to tell Stoffel of our visit with the Labradors?"* She feels ashamed that she doubts Stoffel would understand, let alone approve, of her visit. She hates the feeling of secrecy, the need for secrecy, yet caution prevents her from speaking of the return of the three men and what they might have been doing. She loves Stoffel and would trust her life to him, but he prefers others to tease apart the strands of political and religious thought, of right and wrong; he sees the world more clearly than she does. He would not have paid a visit to the Labradors; he more readily accepts the community strictures about what is and what is not acceptable behaviour. What information have the men brought back from their journey? If the news they brought were good, Melchior would have said so.

Her thoughts turn to Victoria. Anne's ideas have left her mind unsettled, but Victoria seems happier after their visit than before. In fact, during the meal, Victoria serenely showed off her son, allowing Old Labrador to sing rollicking Acadian chansons while doing a little dance around the room with him. Thorold enjoyed it, too, waving his baby hands and mouthing along. Again, she is amazed at her friend's ability to accept a situation and not waste energy railing against it. Elisabeth sighs. Her body shows the march of years, but her mind is still that of the restless young woman she had been nearly three decades ago. *"Dear Lord, will I ever grow up?"*

She hears her mother's voice saying, "Accept things as they are, my Anna Elisabeth, you will be much happier."

She doubts she will ever know the truth or falsity of that statement. She had always believed that with age would come certainty, the ability to recognize truth when she heard it, and the grace to bend to the wisdom of others.

"Forgive me, Lord, I grow more questioning with the passing years, and less accepting of ideas that I do not understand, and strictures I do not agree with. When teachings do not make living easier, or death less frightening, I feel it unworthy of your love not to ask why, not to seek understanding. The fault is mine, in my lack of understanding. Is it not my duty to grow in understanding? Please, forgive me, Heavenly Father, I do not question You; I only seek to understand. Amen.

9

TIME AND TIDE

December, 1754–February, 1755

Come December, the snow falls in earnest. Down it comes, in huge flakes, covering the rocks and trees and drifting in rills along the waterfront and over the garden beds. Elisabeth eyes the wet puddle in front of the door with distaste. A wooden shovel stays permanently by the door to move away the accumulation. Every morning Peter beats his way into the animal byre through snow up to his knees. Evie has tied together a broom of slender twigs to brush the snow off the shoulders and boots of people coming into the house. When it melts, it makes the dirt floor muddy and impossible to sweep clean.

"Stoffel, is there nothing we can do to get rid of this puddle?" Elisabeth asks one morning. "It is never dry. Everyone walks in it and spreads the mud everywhere, even where it is dry."

In response, for the next eight days, Stoffel, Adam and Christof work at the saw pit to make planks for the floors of both houses which they lay across timber stringers. The puddle is still there, but it is now under the planks. Stoffel has learned a lot about building a snug house since coming to Nova Scotia; perhaps in the spring, with more time and warmer weather, they can make their one room Hutt larger and snugger.

"Then I will have room for a loom. The girls are old enough to start weaving and we will be out of clothes by then. Thankful as I am for Catherine's donations, it will be a relief to be making our own cloth again," Elisabeth tells her husband. "We will have more sheep to shear next year and harvest to trade for wool if we have insufficient."

"Whoa, hold on," chides Stoffel, "you have ideas faster than I can saw wood. One step at a time, dear wife."

Their second winter is not as arduous as the first. The settlers are more prepared for the cold, they have more food although they will need government rations again before spring arrives; they have caulked the chinks in their timber houses more securely and have cut enough fire wood to last through the cold weather. The men have learned how to wrap their feet in fur hides and protect their fingers and ears from freezing. A few have made raindrop shapes of wood and rawhide to strap on their feet when walking over the deep snow in an adaptation of the soldiers' snowshoes, a design they had copied from the Indians. They are adapting old ways and learning new ones.

Building the animal byre onto the end of the house has made it warmer, a benefit which they appreciate despite the aroma of animal that seeps through the chinks and into their living quarters. In December, Stoffel receives two more sheep in an unexpected livestock distribution; this time they are sole owners. Evie's cow, as it would always be known, is thriving on her constant care and attention. Elisabeth never has to remind her to feed the animal, as soon as the cow begins to low, Evie is out to the byre. It is too soon to be sure but it is possible that the new ewes are pregnant; however, if the cow is pregnant, it will be a miracle.

Her hands continue to run the stitches through the stockings she is mending yet again. When will she have time to spin yarn and knit their warm winter leggings?

Her mind turns to Victoria and Thorold. The baby is slowly growing and gives his mother less cause for worry and his father has taken to visiting most evenings. In January, Patrick gave Victoria a simple one-treadle floor loom that weaves cloth in narrow strips. Elisabeth is overjoyed; weaving is as familiar to her as walking. The friends card and spin enough yarn to string the loom and produce a narrow length of cloth. It is a joy to hear the thump of the treadle.

Victoria is a skilled seamstress and embroiderer; Elisabeth an accomplished weaver. There are a few wealthy families in Lunenburg with daughters whom they wish to show off, and matrons who would relish a finely embroidered head bonnet, shawl, wrist pocket or handkerchief. She suggests to Elisabeth that they work together, start a small trade.

Elisabeth is excited by the idea, nonetheless she needs to consider it carefully before making such a commitment, and after all she still has a large household to run and many demands on her time.

Victoria reminds her, "But I have lots of time. Remember, a general store is opening on Montague Street. We could bring in supplies from Halifax through the store," she elaborates excitedly, "and sell our things through the store."

Elisabeth speculates, if Stoffel could expand his sausage trade and she could work as a weaver with wool and flax, it would mean she and Stoffel could work their trades in the winter and farm in the summer until their trade is large enough to allow them to hire tenant farmers for their land. This was the way it had worked in the old country.

"I will think on it over night. I confess I am excited by the idea and would enjoy the opportunity to earn money."

She is still pondering the prospect the following morning. With her mind on her plans, she doesn't hear Maria stop brushing the scouring sand from the table where she has been preparing vegetables and look at her mother.

"I have prepared enough for mid-day and to start the soup," she tells her mother. She pauses, "Is there something else I can do?"

"You are a great help to me, Maria," Elisabeth says as she looks up at her oldest daughter. "Our life here would have been much harder without you to share in the work of the house and the care of the other girls. We are doing well because we all work together."

Maria puts a hot cup in front of her mother.

"Thank you, Mama," she says, her cheeks flushing red at the rare compliment. In a rush she addresses her mother. "I want to talk to you, without the others here."

"Oh? Is something the matter?"

"Oh, no, it's not about me. It's about my friend, Anna," she continues. "She's in trouble, serious trouble. She is going to have a baby." Maria always rushes to the point, no beating around the bush for her.

Her mother draws in her breath and puts her hand to her throat. "Is she sure? When is it due?" asks the practical side of Elisabeth while saying an inner prayer of thanks that it is not her Maria.

"She thinks the baby is due soon, but she doesn't really know. Her brother found out last month, just before Christmas. He confined her to her room and the kitchen that's why we haven't seen her for so long."

Maria taps the table lightly with her fingers in agitation, then says in an angry spurt, "He beat her, with a willow stick that he cut for the purpose. It made her bleed and she thinks that he and his wife wanted her to lose the baby."

"How do you know these things?" asks her mother in shock.

"I sneak in through the kitchen when they go to prayer meeting. Oh, Mama, she says they will do harm to the baby when it comes, she is so afraid."

"Surely not. They are good Christians and that would be murder. She is just overwrought because of her situation," her mother reassures her. "Where is the father of the child in all of this?"

Maria takes a deep breath. "Next door. He is Tobias Wirth."

"Our neighbour? Well, he is a widower with a young son and he is not so much older than her, only ten years or so. They can marry easily."

"He lost one of the sons left to his care," Maria reminds her mother. "Besides, he is nearer twenty years older, she is only sixteen and he near thirty-four. She is afraid to tell him, he has such a temper."

"This is a pickle, but what can we do?" asks Elisabeth. "Why are you telling me this?"

"I went to Tobias and told him about the child. He was angry and slammed the table with his fist so hard that I ran away. He said rude things about her, and about me. " Maria looks at her mother seriously, "I don't think she should marry him even if he wanted her. He would not be nice to live with. And, his son is too rough when he plays with the younger children, too."

"Maria," her mother exclaims, "you went alone? To a man's house? Your father will be very angry at you for going and with him when he hears he was rude to you. You have more loyalty than good sense, child."

"I had to do something to help my friend. I don't know what else to do. Maybe I could speak to her brother."

"Nein, no," interrupts Elisabeth, "do not even consider that idea. It is a family matter and they would be rightly very angry with us for interfering."

"I sometimes wonder if they like her at all. They treat her more like a maid than a close relative."

"Don't ask too many questions. If people want you to know their stories, they will tell you. Some things are best kept private."

"Mama," Maria asks as Elisabeth starts to leave the table, "would they really kill her baby?"

"No. It has happened, of course, but I do not believe anyone here would do such a thing. Let me think about what you have told me; we will speak tomorrow."

In winter, the last meal of the day is taken early because dark falls quickly and dusk lasts only half an hour. Afterwards they sit by the hearth and doze, or tell tales about the old country, or gossip about their day. The women spin if they have the wool, or mend and sew by the firelight. Two nights a week there is prayer meeting at one house or another, usually attended by the men. Once a month the women hold their own Bible meetings during the afternoon to which they bring hand work so their fingers can be busy while they listen to one of them, or occasionally a lay pastor, read from the Bible.

The afternoon following Maria's confession to her mother, the meeting is at Elisabeth's house. Her neighbours, Sabina Bubechoffer, Gerdruth Berghaus, Appolonia Schmeltzer, Margarete Schauffner, Barbara Kohl as well as Catherine Herman and Melchior Seiler, who is acting as pastor for the occasion, arrive and seat themselves about the room. Melchior sits by the hearth where he can toast himself. Soon everyone has a welcome cup and with the door remaining closed the room warms up. Elisabeth has spread her best bedcovers on the sleeping benches and the steamed biscuits are wrapped in an ironed linen cloth edged with fine embroidery and lace. The women wear their second best Sunday clothes. Some of the seats have no backs, but that does not matter, the women sit straight, their spines not touching a chair back and their feet tucked demurely under their skirts. This may be the wilderness, but they know how to comport themselves properly.

Elisabeth, as hostess, does not have to wear the unrelieved dark colours of the others and has put a blue apron with yellow and red ribbons sewn along the bottom over her dark blue skirt. The white house cap which covers the braid secured on top of her head is of finely woven linen with brightly coloured flowers embroidered on the rim. She is not a vain woman, but her Stoffel was a respected tradesman and she is entitled to wear blue and decorate her clothes with bright colours, declaring her social position. The message of her Tracht, her regional dress, is a subtle, unspoken reminder that she is not a peasant woman and, as such, is allowed certain freedoms in her social life, her friends.

When Melchior stands up the hum of conversation stops and the women settle themselves to work and listen. He smiles at them, enjoying their warm smiles in return. He is an unusual man in that he is comfortable with women and women are comfortable around him. His wife had been a fine woman, one of intellect and inner strength, who had taught him respect and appreciation for all women. These are strong women, who toil beside their husbands and sons, who bear babies every two years and never miss a season in the gardens, who rarely complain and who watch over each other in good times and bad. They are the hope and future of the new colonies.

"Today, I would like us to consider a familiar story, that of Mary Magdalene, the sinful woman who anointed the feet of Jesus at the home of a Pharisee from Luke, Chapter 7," he announces.

He tells them the story and encourages them to talk and question their own capacity for forgiveness, the full meaning of charity and Christian love. At the end of the hour he leads them in prayer, asking them to pray in their hearts for God's help in increasing their understanding of the true meaning of charity and love and, thus, walk in God's grace. Elisabeth prays earnestly, but has a stray thought regarding what Melchior has seen or heard that makes him choose this particular text. She redoubles her prayers as she wonders if he is referring to Victoria, or to Anna Herman, or has he something larger on his mind.

The Bible meeting leaves Elisabeth in a pensive state of mind. She is quiet during their evening meal, not noticing that Maria is throwing frequent thoughtful looks at her father; however she becomes alert when Maria asks him about Tobias Wirth.

"Do you know Tobias very well?" she asks her father. "What kind of man is he?"

Stoffel puts down his spoon and regards his oldest daughter. "What kind of question is this, 'what kind of man is he'? Why are you asking?"

"I want to know if he is a kind man, a man who would treat his family and his children well."

"What are you asking?" he demands. "What have you to do with Tobias Wirth?"

"Maria," admonishes her mother, "this is not a well chosen time, we are at table.

"It is all right, Mama, I am just asking." She turns to her father, "I have nothing to do with him, Father, in fact, I don't really like him very much, but I have a friend who does."

"Then what kind of man he is, is no concern of yours. A young lady does not think about men, especially widowers with a young son to raise. You should not have time for such thoughts; I will see that your mother keeps you busier."

"Papa," she says in her placating tone, "truly I do not think of him at all, but my friend asked me to find out about him. She is of marriageable age. Please, do not be angry with me, I did not mean to be unseemly."

Stoffel harrumphs into his soup and ignores her for a minute. Then he says, "I would not permit you to marry him."

Fortunately, Peter is bored with this conversation and interrupts with an explanation of how Monsieur Bizette is showing him how to carve patterns on pieces of flat wood; how to use these patterns to decorate wood spoon handles, chair backs and hearth lintels. Only Elisabeth and Maria are aware of the significance in Stoffel's assessment of their neighbour.

The two women are up early in the morning, subtly hurrying the men about their day so that they can talk together. The younger girls know enough not to repeat anything they hear and pull on their capes to walk to the privy and then tend to the animals in the byre. Before they open the door, Maria stops them with an anxious "Mama", and faces Elisabeth.

"Anna is in the byre," she announces staunchly.

"In the byre? Anna? With the animals?"

"Yes. Since before dawn. I think she is in labour."

"Maria, you will be the death of me," exclaims her mother. "Go and fetch her. Your father will have to know," she adds. "After you fetch Anna, go and fetch your father here. He is with Herr Berghaus, they are repairing his byre roof which collapsed under the snow."

"Mama, Papa will be angry," begins Maria.

"Yes. Now, go and fetch Anna."

Anna is wrapped in a quilt made of old wool coats and scraps of men's britches. She is warm enough except for her feet, but she reeks of cow; she must have been sleeping huddled next to it. Elisabeth seats the girl next to the hearth and shoos Maria out to find her father.

"Gertrud, make Anna a hot drink, and then go and tend to your morning duties, I hear Evie's cow stamping in her stall. Please, ask Margarete if she can take Bettina for a few hours, also. If not, then maybe Sabina."

She removes the quilt from Anna's shoulders and tsk's in exasperation; she is unkempt, in her nightclothes and wearing only her house shoes. She needs a wash from head to feet.

"Had you no means of keeping clean, child? Even your hair is unbrushed."

Anna sleeps in a loft built over half the main room where her brother and wife sleep. She puts her hand to her hair and then lets it fall to her lap.

"They locked me into the house and forbade me to come into the main room until I told them who the father was, but I would not, so I was only allowed down to wash once a week. They passed my food in a bowl and cup up to me and took me to the privy in the morning and the evening."

Gertrud brings the hot drink and then supervises Evie and Bettina as they wrap up for going outdoors. One of the essential chores is emptying the chamber pot into the pit of the privy, and cleaning it out with snow. All the girls rotate the hated chore and make just audible noises of annoyance at anyone who gets up in the night to use it. Unless they are very ill, the men are expected to go outside at all times and in all weather. In the fine weather, the girls use the privy at night, too, accompanying each other through the dark. Bettina is just learning to use the chamber pot and manages on her own in the daytime, but she enjoys waking up her sisters to help her use it during the night. It is of no use to take her to the privy during the winter, she refuses to use it, day or night.

There is time for Elisabeth to take Maria's wooden comb and straighten some of the tangles in Anna's hair and then braid it into two strands before the stomping of feet announces the arrival of Stoffel and Maria. It is obvious that Maria has tried to explain something of the situation to him.

"What is this my daughter tells me about Tobias? Elisabeth, what is this story, and why does it involve my family?"

"It is because your daughter is a good woman who stays by when her friends get into trouble and tries to help. It is not a simple thing to explain. Please, sit down and let her tell you, from the beginning," she urges Stoffel.

He glares at Anna, but does not speak to her. She is not family, she is her brother's problem, not his, but she has involved his daughter and now his wife, so he cannot ignore it; a man protects his family, and guards their honour.

"Why is she here?" her asks his wife. "She must go back to her own home. It is not right that I let her hide in my house. Philip will be rightly angry at such presumption." He turns on his daughter, "Did you bring her here?"

"No, Papa. Please, let me explain it all to you."

Her father sits down at the table and glares at her, but keeps silent and gestures her to speak. Meanwhile, Elisabeth helps Anna to lie on the bed where she washes her face and hands, and judges the girl's condition.

When Maria finishes her tale, her father says, "We must go for her brother. It is up to him to deal with Tobias, not me. She has made her bed, she must lie in it."

At his words, Anna raises up on the bed and shouts, "No, no I will run into the woods and live with the Indians rather than go home. They want to kill my baby; they want to kill my baby." She lies back with a wail and heavy weeping. "Tobias does not know. I did not tell him. I tried to bring it up, but he just got angry."

"If you brought it up at all, then he does know, even if you did not say it outright," says Stoffel. "A man who knows as many women as Tobias, is not blind to the condition of women. He is pretending he does not know. Where does he think you have been these past months?"

Anna starts to cry, "I don't know," she wails. She suddenly screams out loud and clutches at the bedclothes, "My belly hurts." She falls back on the bed and lies moaning and weeping.

Elisabeth stands up from where she has been bent over the bed, trying to hold the girl still, and announces, "One thing is certain, this baby will be born today. Maria, I need you here to help. Stoffel, her brother must be told where she is, but, if they are going to rant and get in the way, I don't want them here. I can't stop her sister-in-law from coming, but her brother can wait until the child is delivered."

195

At this Anna wails and pleads, "I don't want her here and he hates me; he's only my half brother anyway, my real father is dead, he died when I was a baby. I don't want this baby. I thought Tobias loved me. What am I going to do?" she sobs.

"You are going to calm down and have this baby safely. Then, Anna, you will do what you must, because today you become a mother," states Elisabeth resolutely ignoring Anna's tangled family web.

Her calm, firm manner steadies the frightened girl. Stoffel tells her that he cannot lie to her brother and will be obliged to tell him the name of the baby's father if he asks.

"No," Anna sobs.

"Be calm, girl, have your child in peace, I will see no one bothers you today," Stoffel tells her before going out into the cold again.

Reassured by the warmth and attention, Anna falls asleep for a time. Elisabeth prepares a cup of crushed dried raspberry leaves to make her a hot drink when she awakes and readies the things she will need when the birth is at hand. She and her daughter sit quietly by the hearth, busy with their own thoughts, but relishing this shared moment. At fifteen, Maria is on the threshold of womanhood, confident in most things, knowledgeable about managing a home and family, eager to step into her adult role. It seems that Johannes Bauer is willing to wait for her to grow up, but after she turns sixteen in May coming, he will not wait much longer; all of Stoffel's blustering will not stop the inevitable.

"What are you thinking about so seriously?" she interrupts her musing to ask her daughter.

"About when it is time for me to start having my own family, about having my first child, about the fear, and the pain, and the joy. About how frightening it must be not to have a husband in the next room, waiting, eager to greet the child and know that I am safely delivered. Poor Anna," she whispers, "I tried to tell her it was wrong, she refused to change her ways."

"You are a good friend to her, but some people have to make their own mistakes. Don't blame yourself."

Anna sleeps for several hours, exhausted from the cold and terror of spending the night in the cow byre. When she wakes the pains are increasing, but there is nothing to do except wait for the baby to leave the womb. As the three sit talking, Gertrud arrives to say all of them will stay over at the Schauffner's until the baby comes. Elisabeth wraps a pan of dried berry pudding in a cloth and puts the vegetables Maria had prepared into a bowl and sends it back with her; Margarete is not used to feeding her three hungry men as well as Adam.

Another knock sounds quietly at the door. Maria opens it to find Melchior outside.

"I know what is transpiring. Is there anything I can do to help?" he asks, "Anyone I can fetch?"

Maria looks at her mother. "All is quiet for the moment," she answers. "Kind thoughts and prayers for guidance would be well received, if you are so inclined," she adds.

"I have been doing so already," he answers. Maria waves him inside the door before all the heat escapes. He says, "I should tell you that her brother is looking for Tobias Wirth with heat in his eyes. Stoffel has gone with him to keep the peace and persuade them to reason. Frau Herman was determined to bring Anna home, but Frau Schmeltzer persuaded her to let Anna stay in your mother's capable hands. However, Elisabeth Herman is a determined woman and will no doubt be along this afternoon. How long do you think it will take, for the baby to arrive?"

Elisabeth looks at her patient and shakes her head, "It will be sometime yet, not until the evening at least."

"Don't worry about your family, many have offered food and a place to sleep. They will be well cared for while you are busy here."

Just as Melchior leaves another visitor arrives at the door. It is Catherine, now Frau Herman, with her maid, Greta, carrying several pots and pans of food.

"I have brought you something to eat and my hands to help you," she says as she removes her wrap and outdoor shoes. A third person squeezes in the door, a young boy with his arms full of bedclothes. Catherine introduces him. "This is Daniel, Greta's brother that my husband has brought from the orphanage in Halifax so they may be together."

Elisabeth smiles at them both. "I knew Bernhard would see the right of keeping brother and sister together. It is good to see you together again. Welcome to Lunenburg, Daniel."

He bobs his head at her and smiles shyly. He is a cute lad; Elisabeth spies mischief sparkling in his eyes.

Catherine sends Greta and her brother home and sets about putting the food on the table. "I have brought some cold mutton, hot potato and turnip soup and steamed pudding with molasses-rum sauce. Do you think our patient could eat something?"

Elisabeth notes the use of "our patient" and smiles, sure that Catherine will explain in a moment. "Perhaps some of the soup with hot water in it," she says.

Surprise still shows on Maria's face at Catherine's new manner, but she politely asks no questions of the women. She is unsure how to address Catherine now that she is the wife of Bernhard Herman. Can she still call her Catherine? Or is she Frau Herman?

Catherine turns to her and says, "I wonder if your mother told you that we are related? I am a relation of your father's, through his great grandfather Jacob, so it not close, but this far from our old homes, it does not matter. I would be pleased to have you call me Aunt Catherine," she tells her.

"Oh, thank you, Ah-aunt Catherine."

"I like that," she tells Maria; "it means we are family." She explains to them, "You didn't think I would leave you to see this through alone, did you?"

"See what through, Catherine?" asks Elisabeth. "It appears it will be an uncomplicated delivery. What is going on?" Elisabeth has understood that it is not just the birth that brings her here in a show of solidarity.

Catherine takes Elisabeth by the hand and faces her. "Elisabeth Herman is understandably upset with Anna having a baby out of wedlock, but, she is attempting to blame others instead of the way she raised her. She was telling Frau Schmeltzer, Appolonia Schmeltzer, that it was the influence of your Maria that caused this shameful predicament."

"She said what?" demands Maria. "I tried to stop Anna from her wanton behaviour," she protests.

"I believe you," said Catherine turning to Maria. "I have told her and others of the women so, most emphatically, in front of her. That should put an end to it. People know you are an obedient daughter and would not encourage such wanton behaviour."

Turning to Elisabeth, she continues, "We're family, Elisabeth, besides, I'm not just a housemaid anymore." She goes on. "My husband is a respected man, and a Herman as well; it had a very calming effect on Elisabeth Herman. Melchior Seiler helped, too. He talked to Anna's brother about his Christian duty, and of how Jesus forgave sinners. He is a very reassuring and persuasive man. Your Stoffel has gone with him to find Tobias Wirth."

During this conversation, Anna lies wide eyed on the bed, hardly daring to breathe. At the mention of Tobias' name, she says in a small voice, "Tobias doesn't want to see me anymore. He didn't come once after they locked me in the house."

"They knew he was paying you court?" asks Elisabeth. "They allowed him to visit you at home?"

The girl looks at the wall. "Maybe he came to see my brother, but," she says looking at Maria, "he always had a word and a smile for me."

Maria kneels at the bedside and holds her friend's hand in sympathy.

"It will be all right, he must love you else he would not have bedded you. Father will find him and straighten it all out. You'll see. He will be here and demand to be your husband. First your darling baby must be born. Don't cry, my mother is the best mid-wife in Lunenburg, you and the baby are safe here."

The moon is well up in a cloudy dark sky by the time Isaac Alexander Herman makes his debut with red-faced squalling and thrusting limbs.

"He is a good sized baby. You did well, Anna," Elisabeth tells her. "There is no need to tell the neighbours, I am sure they heard him greet the world. Elisabeth and Philip will be here in a few hours, as soon as it is dawn. Have some rest; you will need your strength tomorrow, today."

Elisabeth tucks the baby in with his mother and the three women lie down together on a straw pallet beside the hearth. Exhausted, they are asleep in seconds. They, too, will need their wits to face to morning.

The single room is clean and neat when Elisabeth Herman arrives to take her wayward niece home. The baby is swaddled and has taken his first mouthfuls of nourishment. The four women are just finishing their first meal of the day when she knocks on the door.

After a brevity of thanks for Elisabeth, she takes her niece to task. "Well, this is a shameful pickle you have put us in, young woman. Philip is rightfully outraged with your Tobias and his refusal to do the right thing. By the time Philip finishes with him, however, he will have changed his tune. What were you thinking? Or were you just going about in your usual headstrong way? What have you to say for yourself?"

The girl clutches her baby and starts to cry again. "I don't know, Aunt Elisabeth. I thought Tobias loved me and wanted to marry me."

"He is a none too charming ruffian, he is, and not to be trusted, but he will marry you; he needs a mother for his remaining son and, no doubt, someone to keep his house in order. So dry your tears, girl, it's time to come back home and sleep in the bed you made for yourself."

Her aunt puts a pile of clothes on the bed. "Here, dress yourself."

Maria helps her friend to dress and keeps her arms about her as she prepares to leave with her aunt. "Take care; I'll come and see you."

"I don't think she will be seeing anyone for some time yet," says her aunt bluntly, "not until this mess is settled."

Elisabeth bridles at her tone and suggests firmly, "A young mother should not be cut off from her friends; it can lead to a decline. Maria could come and walk with them. It will do her good."

"Yes, and I will visit her as well," adds Catherine, "as a member, albeit distant, of the family, I want to lend you my support in this trying situation."

Through primly narrowed lips Frau Herman answers only, "We will talk it over, Philip and I."

Anna leaves with her baby. There is nothing left to say. Catherine goes home. Elisabeth heats water to wash the dirty bedclothes.

Before Maria goes to collect her sisters, her mother tells her, "We have done what we can for now. Let things settle for a few days."

Her daughter nods her head.

Maria is allowed to see her friend only once, but Catherine has been admitted regularly and reports that Anna and Isaac Alexander are doing well. She also tells them that wedding discussions are underway. It is three Sundays before they hear anything and then, on February 8th, the announcement of the forthcoming wedding between Anna Anna Herman and Tobias Wirth is made during Sunday service.

"I don't know whether to rejoice or not;" says Maria, "however, if she is to marry Tobias, then I want to be there with her," she tells her mother.

"And so you should be. Come, let us go to the Herman's and offer our felicitations. I'll go with you. They will not be so rude as to turn us away."

Anna marries Tobias on a blustery, sunny day, interspersed with whirling snow squalls. Maria accompanies her friend as she stands before the pastor with Tobias. Melchior, Elisabeth and Catherine attend the wedding along with some of Anna's friends. Tobias' five year old son, Georg, stands with a handful of his Wirth relatives. Baby Alexander is not there; Greta, Catherine's maid, is tending him at Tobias' house, allowing Anna to enjoy her wedding freer from censure and curious scrutiny. Considering the babies she has delivered in this new town, Elisabeth wonders at the hypocrisy of people over hurried marriages and pre-term infants.

Accompanied by their friends, she and Tobias walk to their home where guests are offered a slice of cake, which has been baked in a Deutsch oven on the hearth, and a cup of toddy. Anna is flushed with happiness and proudly shows off her son. Elisabeth is happy to see Tobias acting like a proud bridegroom, beaming with delight at his young wife and being the genial host, even taking his baby son into his arms and raising a toast to him. Stoffel, Adam and Bernhard arrive and toast the new couple, adding their stamp of approval to the union.

Perhaps all will end successfully, *"Please, God, let it be so,"* prays Elisabeth. It is obvious that Catherine has taken Anna under her protection, showing social courage in the face of disapproval from Anna's relatives. Elisabeth is relieved that the young wife will have at least one more defender in the town, one who understands both loneliness and lack of approval.

"Lord, bless this house," she asks God as she leaves.

10

RETURN TO THE SPIRIT WORLD

April, 1755–June, 1755

For the last few minutes there has been thumping sounds and voices coming from the byre. The April sun must be raising the spirits of her younger daughters who are cleaning out the byre and feeding the animals. She smiles, high spirited children are healthy children.

Evie, her always phlegmatic Evie, bursts through the door calling out to her mother, "Mama, Mama, there's something wrong with Lieblingsblume. She is dying."

Her voice rises to a high pitch on the last statement and tears start down her face. The bony hipped cow has become "Darling Flower" and no one dares to laugh at such a lovely name for such an unlovely creature.

"I'm coming, Evie, don't cry, I'm sure this is not so. Let me have a look at her. Come, we'll go and see what is the matter."

In her heart Elisabeth is afraid it might indeed be so. The cow had been poorly in the fall and, although she had improved over the winter, she never looked robust and healthy. She hadn't looked in the byre for a few weeks, but Stoffel had assured her that the cow was fine, even getting fat right along with the pregnant sheep.

The cow is lowing mournfully, her nose tucked into a corner of the stall and her back legs splayed. Elisabeth looks at the frightened faces of her daughters and starts to laugh.

They look at her in confusion, "Mama, what is funny? Poor Lieblingsblume is sick."

She opens her arms and hugs them, "No, no, meine Leiblinge. She is not sick; she is going to have a baby, a baby calf."

The runaway bull must have come home from time to time. She could not believe it, but here is their, or rather Evie's, cow about to give birth. Their very own "miracle birth."

"Now we are going to be busy, a calf and soon two little lambs," she exclaims. "We are indeed fortunate. Thank you, God, for this blessing." She turns to the staring girls and tells them, "In a few days, we will have milk for drinking and for cooking. Won't that be wonderful?"

"Can't we help her?" asks Evie. "She is crying."

Indeed the cow was making mournful noises and grunting. Her mother assures her that cows need little help to birth their calves; the noises are because she is working to push her baby out into their welcoming arms. They may sit quietly, watching, and come for her when they see the calf begin to emerge from its mother or if there seems to be difficulty. It's been a long time since Elisabeth saw a cow give birth, but she remembers her mother's instructions and is sure she can manage, provided the cow does her part. After a time, she goes to sit with her girls and watches over the staining cow with them.

By mid-afternoon a healthy young heifer is standing on shaky legs beside her mother and, butting her in the belly. Elisabeth helps to clean up the dirty straw, and then takes the girls into the fresh air to leave the new family alone. The girls are excited and awed. Life and death are everyday occurrences, but this is the first calf birth they have watched. They are alternately talkative and speechless.

"She did well, didn't she Mama?" asks Evie.

"She did very well," her mother assures her.

Stoffel is proud of the news and brags, "We have the only pregnant cow in Lunenburg, or rather, had. Now we have the only cow mother. This is a good omen. This will be a fine year."

He lifts his cup and they all shout, "Prosit!", cheers. Moments of celebration are scarce and they relish this one. The pregnant ewes are not quite so fortunate. One gives birth to twins, but they do not survive and the other delivers a young ram. He is healthy, but will do nothing to increase the size of the flock and will end up gracing the table. There are enough rams penned apart from the flock of ewes to impregnate them in the late fall. The dead twins had been ewes.

Winter snow runs away with the advent of spring showers and swelling buds. The men are impatient to get on the land again; sections of the fields were cleared last year and can be readied quickly for planting. In addition to food rations, the English have again provided some vegetable seeds and seed potatoes, along with barley and buckwheat. In April, the settlers repair trails, fences and farm sheds, erect farm buildings; by May, they will be ready to plant their fields. Their need for ready money is still urgent. They require additional tools, clothing and footwear, their living conditions need improving with furniture, dishes, bedding, and their houses with bricks and mortar. A good harvest which can be sold to the Halifax or Boston merchants or the military is vital. Everyone prays the summer of 1755 brings moderate weather with neither floods nor drought.

After a morning of showers, an afternoon sun entices Elisabeth outdoors for a walk around the edge of the woods that back the village. There is a haze of green if she looks closely along the line of trees and bushes, the leaves will start to burst with a few days of warm weather. As always, this season lifts her spirits and confirms her faith in a benevolent God. She lifts her face to the warmth and sends a prayer of gratitude heavenward. Things that seemed impossible in the dark of winter become practical with the birth of a new season. She encounters le Vieux Bizette on the path and accepts his invitation to visit with him and his wife.

A nook formed by the main house and an attached shed traps a patch of warm sunshine and they sit on wood and reed chairs in enjoyment and peace. Jacques eventually turns the conversation to increased tension between the English and French, more specifically, between the English military in the form of Governor Lawrence and the Acadians.

"I fear that the hostility is increasing," he comments.

Elisabeth knows this is true, Victoria has reported enough of Patrick's worries to confirm this. Governor Lawrence is more and more convinced that the Acadians cannot be trusted to remain neutral in the coming war, a war as yet undeclared, but already being fought in North America. Melchior tells her that many of the Indian villages are already being emptied as the Mi'kmaq glide away to New Brunswick, Île St. Jean and Île Royale, away from the English forts and closer to the French forts. Elisabeth wonders about his source of information.

He smiles broadly as he chides her saying, "You are not the only one who talks with Old Labrador. After all, we live closer to him than you do."

"You are right," she admits, "it was unheeding of me to assume I was the only one. There are many rumours. It is difficult to know what to take seriously and what to ignore."

"I expect you hear quite a lot from your friend Mlle. Downing, la jolie Victoria," he says, "I see her often taking walks along the streets with her baby. She seems a gentlewoman."

Elisabeth monitors the tone of his voice. She is used to censure in regards to her friendship with Victoria, sometimes because she is English, but most often because of her unmarried relationship with Captain Sutherland.

"We admire her courage," says Mme. Bizette.

"If not her judgment," adds Jacques.

"We do talk sometimes of the political situation and the threat of war and what it means for us in Lunenburg," Elisabeth acknowledges. "I think we are safe here. The English need the town for ship timbers and the food we grow. There is no fort here, only a couple of blockhouses, so there is no reason for the French to attack this close to Halifax. The English ships would be upon them before they could escape to Fortress Louisbourg."

"What if they turn against all French, including us Montbéliards?" asks Jacques.

"But the English brought you here, and gave you land, and rations. Why would they turn on you?" she asks in surprise, never having thought of the possibility. "No, no, I have not heard even a rumour of this, from anyone," she says. "I am sure you are safe here."

"Some of the families have moved to Île Royale to be near Fortress Louisbourg."

"And some have returned."

"Are you aware that a few are leaving now, afraid of the English. They do not feel welcome in an English land. If the French lose the war, this will be an English colony and they will be regarded as French, not Swiss; if the French win, they will have shown their loyalty to France. They feel it is the best choice for them to be allowed to farm and raise their families in peace," Jacques explains.

"I wasn't aware of that," says Elisabeth. "I thought they had just moved to their farms and, thus, I didn't see them anymore. Sutherland would not be happy to learn this."

"Are you going to tell him?"

"No. Nor Victoria either. It would not be fair to her, but eventually he will know, if he doesn't already." She pauses while she considers a new thought. "Are you thinking of going? Is that why you are telling me this?"

"Oui. Et non." Jacques strokes his greying beard. "Nous y pensons de ça depuis quelques temps. En tout cas, I think we will move out to our farm this summer. Our little house there is finished, and we have sons to help work it. I will miss fishing in the harbour, and my small boat."

"You will have little protection there from the Acadians, or any marauding Indians. You would be safer here, with the rest of us," she tries to persuade him.

"We are still thinking about it, but I wanted you to know." He pauses a moment, then continues. "Your Peter is a fine young fellow. I don't want him to think that I don't want to work with him again, but he is strong now and you will need him yourself; he shouldn't plan to fish with me this summer," explains Jacques. "I can't promise to be here."

"I'll tell him, but I'm sure he will be visiting you, he enjoys your company. Like you, he seems to love the sea and the boats, and the fish," she says. "I understand what you are saying; however, I think Lunenburg is a safer place to be until it is all over." She thinks a moment then tells him, "Peter would never reveal your departure, if you chose to go. Nor would I."

They enjoy the sun for a few minutes. "I, too, have concerns over the outcome of any war," she tells them. "If the French were to win, I don't know what it would mean for us Germans. We don't belong in either the English or the French camp. We know what is going on only by rumour and what the few Englishers who speak German tell us."

"But you, of all people, must know what is going on. You have a foot in all camps," Jacques reminds her, "and you speak with many of the people, French and German, even English. Not knowing is worse than knowing and some people think you know more than you tell. Forgive me, I have no intent to offend you, but I am being blunt."

"But I know almost nothing," she replies in astonishment. "Do you think I am withholding information from you? Because you are French? Never. Nor do I believe Captain Sutherland is either. Truthfully, I think no one knows what will happen until it happens, maybe not even Governor Lawrence."

Considering Jacques' comments as she walks back to her house, Elisabeth reviews what she knows about the situation between the English and the Acadians and the Indians. Her understanding is limited to the things that Melchior has told her and the stories that Stoffel brings from his conversations with the other German men. Well, she also has the insights that Victoria reveals. Maybe she has failed to put together what she does know, she chides herself.

The evidence of her own eyes tells her that there are more soldiers in town than usual, more ships needing masts and spars, more requests for fresh produce from the fall harvest. There are more stores opening and more merchants from Halifax starting businesses in competition with the settlers. The English incomers have more money than the settlers with which to set up their shops, making it difficult for the settlers to establish themselves; however, the town is starting to bustle with commerce, farming and town life.

"Is this the result of the town growing, or are they preparations for war?" she wonders.

Armies had marched back and forth across Hesse for decades, destroying farm land, ruining shopkeepers with taxes and taking boys from their mother's side for the Hessian Regiments. They had had enough of war, it was one of the reasons they had left for the new world. Everyone knows that England and France are fighting for control of the resources and trade opportunities in their overseas colonies, and for control of the settlers who take up land there. She has not thought too much about what a war might mean for Lunenburg and their future. She needs a better understanding; she needs to talk with Melchior. She needs to know more about her new country, especially Nova Scotia, this rocky wild intriguing place that is now her home.

Spring inches its way towards summer. Here and there, in warm sunny niches, the sweet smelling trailing arbutus is beginning to bloom, it delicate pink flower peeking shyly from its nest of old leaves and dry grass, harbingers of the blooms to come as May passes into June.

Elisabeth and Victoria spend the afternoon seeking out the first blooms and leaves, locating the places where the edible and medicinal roots will soon be ready for digging, and the green leaves of the wood sorrel and dandelion will appear. Victoria carries Thorold wrapped in a wool blanket, Bettina needs carrying only on the return home. Nearly three years old, she is sturdy on her feet and chatters away, investigating every interesting stick, puddle and rotting nut along the path. She holds up her treasures for Thorold to see and exchanges serious baby talk with him. It is an exceptional and peaceful afternoon, a promise of renewed vitality and a symbol of God's generosity to his people.

"I am so excited," Victoria tells her happily. "By next winter we will have more orders than we can fill, won't that be wonderful?"

They had taken a sample of their handiwork along to Master Kaulbach, the owner of the new general store. At first reluctant to offer such frivolous items, he had finally agreed to display them in a glass fronted case along with the information card which said, "Custom Embroidered Ladies Finery and Handloomed Shawls, Mayflower Cottage, Montague Street." Patrick had neatly written the card for them at Victoria's request and painted a sign for the entrance to Victoria's house. Today she has brought the exciting news that an embroidered edging for a little girl's petticoat has been ordered and another woman had expressed an interest in a woven shawl. The future looks optimistic and they revel in the moment.

The following morning, as Elisabeth is preparing for the day, an English soldier appears at their door. Stoffel, at first alarmed that they are in trouble over some misunderstood happening, soon grasps that he wants Elisabeth to come with him.

"Don't worry, mama, it is only another baby," says Maria. "Maybe he has a wife."

Meanwhile Stoffel looks at the young fellow in his English soldier's uniform and scowls in annoyance; his breakfast is being interrupted yet again. "Do babies ever arrive after breakfast and before bedtime?" he asks the world in general.

"No, Papa. Never," replies Maria, fetching her mother's needs and continuing to put the hot food on the table and keeping Bettina quiet with a hard biscuit to chew on.

The soldier is nervously trying to hurry her with impatient gestures and bumbling efforts at helping her with her cloak and bundle. Among his words, Elisabeth finally understands "Captain Sutherland."

She quickly looks at him and asks, "Captain Sutherland sent you? Victoria?"

"Yes, yes, Frau Baltzer, Miss Victoria."

A final stamp puts her foot into her boot and she hurriedly ties the laces, fumbling in her sudden anxiety.

"Oh, Stoffel, what has happened? We had such a good time yesterday. Tory was fine, he was so alert, so aware, and happy. We were all so happy."

"Don't fret until you know. Hurry now and go to her. We will be fine. May God take care of you. We will pray, all of us," admonishes Stoffel.

The young soldier carries her bundle and occasionally takes her elbow as she stumbles a little on the ruts and stones still evident after the spring rains. It is a drizzly morning, not raining, not sunny, the sky milky silver with a hesitant sun shimmering behind a veil of clouds. She walks as fast as she can, breathing rapidly with fear and exertion. When they reach the path to Victoria's house, she pauses long enough for three slow breaths and strives for composure. The house is silent and no smoke rises from the chimney. The soldier hands her the bundle, but does not enter the house. She looks at him in fear as he urgently gestures her to go in. Inside the house it is dim, no lamp burns and the window coverings are drawn as for night.

"Victoria," she calls out quietly. "Victoria, it is Elisabeth. Qu'est-ce qui se passe? What is it?"

Her eyes and ears become attuned to the house and she finds her friend huddled on the floor between her sleeping cot and the baby's cradle. She is keening softly and rocking to and fro. The sound of a boot scrape on the floor startles her and she whirls towards the noise with a gasp.

"I don't mean to frighten you, I am sorry."

She recognizes the voice of Patrick Sutherland.

"My son is dead," he says, "ist tot."

She guesses the truth before his effort at speaking German to her. Her hand confirms the dire news; there is neither breath nor heartbeat in the tiny frame. Elisabeth falls to her knees beside Victoria and takes her in her arms, cradling her and the baby she will not let go of, not yet. After some time she persuades Victoria to her feet and moves her to a chair, nearer the hearth. With her hand she gestures for Patrick to light the hearth and the lamp. He has been sitting, slumped forward over the table, his head held in his hands, but he now straightens and does as she asks. Reluctantly, the fire lights and begins to warm the room while the lamp allows her to see. Patrick is dressed, but his usually neat person is dishevelled and his face unshaven, his hair falling about his neck instead of tidily clubbed into a tail. He reaches out a hand to Victoria, but she shies away from him so he drops it and returns to his seat at the end of the table.

Elisabeth looks for the things to make a hot drink, some rum and molasses. She puts the water to boil and sets the cups out and goes back to Victoria, talking to her in low tones, repeating her name, trying to bring her back to herself, back to this world that she cannot face now that her son is no longer in it. Patrick makes the hot drinks, some for all of them, and hands it to Elisabeth. Victoria makes no move to accept the drink. Elisabeth has no words for him, so she takes his hand a moment and looks at him in sympathy. He tries to smile, struggling, he manages a brief, "Danke, thank you". He slowly finishes his drink and then puts on his great coat to leave. He bends over Victoria and kisses the top of her head. With his hand he caresses the body of his son, then turns and departs.

Reluctantly and with much persuasion, Victoria lets Elisabeth take the baby's body from her so she can place him in his cradle. His mother hasn't spoken yet and Elisabeth has no idea what transpired. Thorold appears just to be sleeping. Gently, she asks, "Can you tell me what happened?"

Finally, Victoria heaves a deep sigh and says, "Nothing. Nothing at all. We passed a wonderful evening, we three. Patrick even stayed the night. We were like a family. " She stopped talking for a time and then continued, "I awoke at five o'clock as usual to feed Thorold. I know the hour because I heard the night watch blow reveille in the barracks to wake the soldiers. Usually, he is awake and waiting for me. This morning, I couldn't wake him up."

Her voice breaks and she begins to sob, cries that take her breath and make her gasp for air, cries that echo the unbelieving rage and emptiness of all mothers who lose their children; cries that Elisabeth can feel for she, too, has endured the sorrow of children dead before they are old. There is nothing to do. She puts her arms around Victoria and waits.

A death for which there is no explanation, a cradle death. He simply stopped breathing. Some would say God called him back to Heaven, too good for this world of sin, an angel come to earth for a time. The local natives would say he had gone back to the Spirit World to be with his ancestors, his mission accomplished whether understood by people or not. Either way, it is a test of faith and a test of a mother's will to live. It is the hardest work a healer does.

Within a few hours, the news will spread around the village. Reverend Moreau, Melchior, and some of the women who know Victoria will come to the sad little house, offering their solace and help. They will bring soup, bread, sweets if they have them, a flask of rum, food for the body as a restorative for the soul. They will clean the house, answer the door and accept the messages of sympathy for Victoria, prepare hot drinks for those welcomed inside, even wash the little body and prepare him for eternal sleep if Victoria cannot.

Elisabeth helps Victoria to wash herself and put on day clothes then she asks, "Shall I make Thorold ready?"

"We will do it together," she responds with a sob. "We saw him into this world; we will see him prepared to leave it."

She removes a long, delicately embroidered gown from her trunk. The white is yellowed faintly with age, but the fine cotton is tucked and pleated with dainty stitches, the front has two rows of lace from the waist to the hem which is finished with several more inches of finely tatted lace. The ribbons on the matching bonnet have blue forget-me-nots. Tenderly they remove his soiled swaddling clothes, wash him and put on the gown in which he had been baptized. Too big then, it barely fits him now and they leave the row of tiny mother-of-pearl, buttons down the back open. It will not be seen.

"It was my mother's, and then mine. No one else will need it now," Victoria says.

A knock comes on the door. It is Reverend Moreau and Melchior. Behind them is Hector, one of the coffin maker's boys, with a small white washed wood box in his arms. There are so many child deaths, they always have a few made in advance. He carries it in and places it on the table.

Doffing his cap, he ducks his head and says, "Captain Sutherland ordered it sent, Ma'am," before he backs out of the door.

Next to arrive are two wives of English military officers, friends of Sutherland's who have accepted Victoria into their midst. Finally, a third young woman arrives with more food and a knitted baby shawl in which to properly wrap Victoria's son. She is a friend, mistress to another officer, and she rushes to Victoria with a flood of words and hugs, ignoring the pastor who is hovering over her. With things under control, Elisabeth takes her leave and promises to return.

Slipping through the woods, she taps on Anne Guidry's door, wanting to be the one to tell her of the tragic event. When Anne answers the door, Elisabeth can tell that she has already heard. The two embrace in consolation and exchange a few words before Elisabeth returns home. There is little they can say to soften their grief.

"Tell her that I sorrow for her and will pray for them both. Il est avec les anges, among the angels in Heaven. When I can, I will see her," says Anne.

"Merci," whispers Elisabeth. "Thank you."

She returns to Victoria's house to sit vigil with her through the night. Reverend Moreau returns at evenset to pray with them and tell Victoria that he has arranged the funeral as she has asked, at sunrise the following morning. Victoria tells her that Patrick came, but she sent him away, however, he will come in the morning.

"I feel guilty. Patrick and I were so happy last night. What if I failed to hear Tory call out because I was engrossed with Patrick?" she murmurs in a barely audible voice, made husky with shed and unshed tears. "Oh, Elisabeth, what if he cried out and I didn't hear him?"

"If he had cried out, you would have heard him," she answers firmly. "You would have heard him; I have no doubt about that. He crossed over peacefully, in his sleep, with no fear or pain." She strokes her hair gently, "You know that you made his life full of love and comfort, he wanted for nothing. Dearest Victoria, there is no blame in this, for you, or for Patrick."

"Why did Patrick choose last night to stay with me?"

"I do not know, only God knows these things. Don't blame Patrick either; it would have not changed things had he gone to his quarters. Sometimes there are no reasons for things. Thorold did not lack for care, or love." Elisabeth sighs and says, almost to herself, "There are no answers, sometimes all there is, is faith."

She persuades Victoria to sleep for a time then, when she wakes, Elisabeth lays down to rest. At one point she hears voices and opens her eyes. She can make out two figures huddled together at the table, murmuring to each other. Victoria holds something in her arms; the other woman is Anne. She does not wake herself up further, the conversation seems intensely intimate, not to be interrupted. There is no stress in Victoria's voice; she lets them be. Tonight she has no solace, even for a friend.

In her half sleep, she hears her father's voice, "There is no profit in raging at God; you must trust in Him and seek within yourself for healing and purpose."

She has shed her own tears and knows there is little relief except for that offered by time. She awakes before dawn and when Patrick and Melchior come to carry the coffin, they are ready. They stand quietly while Hector's boy nails the lid in place. It is still half light, the sun not clearing the eastern horizon. A small group of people have gathered and join the words of consolation and prayers offered by Reverend Moreau. By the time they walk to the cemetery on the northwest slope of the town, the sun has scattered the morning fog and is sending rays of golden hope through the tops of the tall evergreens and highlighting the green haze of spring spreading over the hillsides. Eventually a plain stone will read, "Calvert Thorold Downing, May 7, 1755, 8 mos. Beloved son of Victoria and Patrick."

The warming earth and long days of June bring a frenzy of planting and spring activities. Elisabeth takes time each day to visit Victoria and is heartened to find her engaged with daily activities, receiving a few friends and, although still pale and reserved, at least talking about plans for the summer. Patrick has assigned himself a small garden lot and given it over to Victoria. She has cleared some of it and planted barley seed. Her house is at the back of the property and the front has been cleared, so she has planted a small home garden of vegetables. Elisabeth admires the courage Victoria displays and marvels at her serenity.

"I admire your courage," she tells her. "I was much longer accepting the death of my babies many years ago. You are an inspiration. How do you do it?"

"I am not so calm at night," Victoria tells her. "Some nights Anne and I talk all night, she tells me the legends of her Acadian and Mi'kmaq ancestors, they calm me. I know he is dead, but somehow he is also still alive and I am not as alone as I was. "

"She is truly a healer," replies Elisabeth, "with much to teach me."

Immersed in the pressing work of spring planting, moving the animals to pasture, cleaning up the byre, planting the cleared farm land, planning improvements to their house, and attending a flurry of spring births, Elisabeth is feeling more optimistic and peaceful than she has for some time. There is little time to take stock of the momentous event looming on the horizon of Nova Scotia's history. Except for the death of Victoria's baby, life has been steadily improving. Winter ended well with government rations keeping them from real hunger, spring weather smiled upon them, they suffered no serious winter illness, and they have land and seed enough to plant a goodly crop for fall harvest. Still, events can turn, so she takes a moment to remind God that she is grateful for his blessings and begs his continued care.

"Holy Father, You have been good to us this winter and we thank You most heartily. As we endeavour to walk in your grace, take care of us and watch over us in the times ahead. Amen."

Sunday, June 22nd , is an ideal sunny day. After the mid-day meal, Elisabeth and Stoffel are joined by Margarete, Adam and Melchior for a rare afternoon's idle conversation and rest in the dappled sunlight of Elisabeth's herb garden. There are wood slab benches and stumps for the men to rest their feet upon. And her excellent spruce beer to enjoy, in moderation. After a random discussion of crops and weather and town gossip, Adam mentions an unfamiliar ship he saw loading soldiers from the barracks.

"You mean 'off-loading', don't you?" queries Stoffel.

"No, taking on board soldiers from here," Adam confirms. "I wonder where they are taking them. Perhaps it means that things are quieter, fewer Indian raids. Maybe I can go back to my farm land this summer."

Last summer he had worked it only for a few weeks because it is far from the town and open to attack. Melchior leans forward and clears his throat.

"I don't think so, Adam," he says. "I have unwelcome news that I was keeping back so as not to disturb such a pleasant afternoon."

There is a collective sigh.

"I knew it was too good to last," remarks Margarete. "It was kind of you to wait, but now we should return to serious matters. We must not hide from matters that affect us."

Elisabeth nods in agreement.

"What have you to tell us?" she asks Melchior.

"It will take a bit of telling," he warns.

"We already know rags and tags," says Elisabeth, "and rather we should know all."

"We will listen," assures Margarete.

Melchior takes a moment for thought and begins.

"Jean Deschamps, whom you know as Cloverwater, returned from Piziquid on the Minas Basin yesterday. The Minas Basin, at the head of the Bay of Fundy, is surrounded by fertile land and a number of Acadian farms are located there, especially at a place called Grand Pré. The English Fort Edward is hard by there, too."

"Wait a minute, I'll be right back," says Margarete who hurries into the house and returns with a thin shingle of slate and a piece of soft white rock they call powder rock. "Sketch us the map; I, for one, don't know these places, but I want to understand."

Melchior smiles at her. "How clever you are," he says. He quickly sketches a rough map of Nova Scotia and picks up his explanation.

"You remember, last year when the Acadians were forbidden to ship their grain out of the province, and were obliged to send it all to Halifax? Well, in retaliation, the Acadians around Piziquid refused to cut wood for Fort Edward and, as a result, one of their priests was arrested. Since then, relations between the Acadians and the English have gone from bad to worse."

"I can see why," says Adam, "I would not like to be forbidden to sell my grain where I chose."

"Yes. The Acadians are mostly farmers, like we are, and resent the English interfering in their lives. I have tried for three years to persuade the governor of Nova Scotia to recommend a lenient treatment towards the Acadians." He stops for a moment and then says, "I should back up a little and tell you truthfully why I came here. I am a friend of the governor of Carolina who is a friend of Governor Shirley of

Massachusetts. Governor Shirley is anxious that the attention of the French is kept on Canada and not on the colonies of New England."

"He'd rather there be a war here than there," interrupts Elisabeth.

"That is right," agrees Melchior. "Therefore, he will assist the Governor of Nova Scotia prevail over the French. And I," he says, pointing to himself, "am part of that assistance. My instructions are to make sure the governor, in this case, Governor Lawrence, has accurate information about French, including Acadian, and Indian intentions, also, of course, to keep Governor Shirley informed on the situation in Nova Scotia."

"A spy, as I suggested before and you denied," interrupts Elisabeth again.

"Spy is such a censorious word. I think of myself as an advisor, both Shirley and Lawrence are on the same side, neither want the French to win any war over control of North America."

He looks at Elisabeth, waiting for her rebuttal.

"A spy for our side then, no question of loyalty," she relents. "I, too, am most anxious that the English win any conflict, but, even so, I have some sympathy for the Acadians and the Indians whose home this is, too."

The others are in accord to varying degrees and utter sounds of agreement. Melchior continues.

"I have failed utterly to dissuade Governor Lawrence to a more moderate attitude over the Acadian question. He has always been first and last a soldier, and since he became Governor, he listens only to military advisors. It is clear to me that he sees the Acadians as a threat, almost certain rather than potential, enemies. I talk to Captain Sutherland, but I think the Governor ignores his opinion and confines him to securing the growth and safety of Lunenburg."

He removes his old leather hat and runs his hand over his greying hair.

"Jean Deschamps, Cloverwater, tells me his Indian relatives report that the English soldiers have confiscated all the Acadians' arms and boats, leaving them unable to hunt or fish for food. When they protested, the men who signed the letter of protest were arrested. So, I fear that both sides are hardening their positions. Also, unfortunately, the Acadians have refused once again to sign the Oath of Allegiance to the British crown."

"What is this Oath?" asks Margarete.

"To what does it bind them?" asks Elisabeth.

"It binds them to sworn loyalty to the English king," states Melchior. "The French are willing to swear to neutrality, but the English have no faith in their vows of neutrality. On the other hand, the Acadians will not swear to anything that might commit them to taking up arms against fellow Frenchmen."

"Ach, these kings and their ambitions," interrupts Stoffel still bitter over the effects of constant war on his Hessian homeland. "They are never content. Don't they understand that leaving their citizens alone to prosper is the surest way for them to prosper also?"

"In history it is always thus," Adam agrees. "Even here, it seems we have not left their greed behind. And, I think also, the churches have an interest; the French to make this country Catholic and the English to make it Protestant."

"I am sure you are right in that, Adam," agrees Stoffel.

"You are indeed right," Melchior tells them. "Already, pirates out of Louisbourg have attacked English ships," continues Melchior. "The American colonies share the same concerns about the French as the English ones which makes them open to requests for help from the governor of Nova Scotia. Of course, all the governors of American and English colonies know each other, and support each other."

"We seem so isolated here, I forget about the outside world," says Elisabeth. "What will Governor Lawrence do?"

"He has wanted for some time to simply throw all of the Acadians out of Nova Scotia, to put them on boats and disperse them up and down the eastern seaboard, even onto the sugar islands of the Caribbean. Governor Shirley of Massachusetts agrees with him."

"And?" says Elisabeth, recognizing the expression of sadness on Melchior's face.

"Two weeks ago Colonel Monckton sailed from Boston up the Bay of Fundy with orders to take the French forts along the coast. He captured the French forts of Beauséjour and Gaspereaux as well as some smaller blockhouses. And, there are ships from Maine arriving in Halifax and at English forts along the Bay of Fundy as we speak."

"What does this mean?" asks Elisabeth, afraid of her own conclusions.

Melchior shares his thinking. "Always remember that Governor Lawrence is a soldier. He truly believes that war between England and France will be declared soon and that the Acadians will actively fight for the French. His military duty is to secure Nova Scotia for the English."

He looks at them to see if they are following him before continuing.

"Lawrence believes that this can be done most easily by dispersing the Acadians instead of allowing them to live close to one another, and apart from the English, as they do here."

"You mean ordering them to leave their homes?" asks Elisabeth. "Will they go?"

"Would you leave willingly if you were asked to move thousands of miles away?" Melchior asks back.

"No, never," she answers.

"No. Neither will they; they have been here for ten generations. He will have to do it with force, at gunpoint. And he is willing to do it and has the soldiers to do it."

"What will it mean for us here in Lunenburg?" asks Margarete.

"For this summer, I don't know," answers Melchior.

"No Indian raids?" asks Adam again, anxious to work his land. He considers it lucky that his land is quite flat and easy to work, but unlucky that it is so far from the town, too far to walk out and back each day.

"Yes, Indian raids, sadly. They will fight to defend their Acadian allies," says Melchior.

"But what of the Acadians? They have been here for 150 years; surely there is room for us all. They have much to teach us," Elisabeth says, thinking of all she has already learned from Anne and from Melchior's friend, Noel.

Silence encompasses the little group for some minutes. Elisabeth is thinking that life contains so many events over which ordinary people have no domain; happenings that alter the very warp of lives that come out of some unfathomable place where destinies are born. Are even kings and princes so powerful that they may control their own fates? Or does a restless God test all His people? She wonders if the English will recruit civilian boys as they did for the Hessian Regiments; best not even to ask for fear of making a suggestion. Reluctantly, she accepts the unavoidable conclusion; if the English lose this war, they could lose their new home or, at the very least, find themselves living in a French-controlled French-speaking Roman Catholic colony. They would be back under the thumbs of the priests that they have been two centuries escaping. She wishes no harm to the Acadians, or the Indians, but this alternative is completely untenable. They need the English to win the war.

"Oh, dear," she utters, "it is all such an excessive turmoil, and so unnecessary."

Gradually, the talk returns to planting and town improvements, but the relaxed chatter is forced and they soon make their farewells with embraces and solemn handshakes.

That night Elisabeth's prayers are long, and solemn. She begins with gratitude for her blessings.

"Heavenly Father, it is Anna Elisabeth. You have been good to us. We are grateful for health and life, for our friends and our improving lot. We ask that this season be fruitful in the fields and in our animals."

In her mind, she compares Nova Scotia against the land they left. She can see that in this country, those who work hard have an opportunity to secure their futures and prosper from their own talents; what she desires is that God's wisdom and compassion fill the hearts of those who control the political and religious destiny of Nova Scotia. To have come this far and left so much behind; to have worked so hard and lose it all again would be unthinkable.

"Am I being selfish, God? Is it a sin to want the best for one's family and future? I can see nothing but misfortune for us if France gains control over Nova Scotia, our new homeland, the land of my hopes. In a war, Lord, only one side wins, and I pray for it to be our side, the English side. Yet, how can I wish the worst for people I respect and admire, people I call friends?"

Elisabeth's innate sense of justice makes it difficult for her to feel hatred against the Indians into whose homeland they have intruded unbidden, or the Acadians who have lived here in peace for 150 years. She feels it difficult to take sides. It was easier when she did not know the enemy, but knowing Anne, and the Labradors, meeting the unfortunate young Mi'kmaq girl and holding her newborn son made them real to her, talking with Noel Rousse about his Indian family—.

"These are good people, Lord, who only want the same as we, to live in peace, raise their children and become grandparents. Guide those who

decide our futures, O God, fill their hearts with compassion and reason, and their minds with wisdom and justice. Amen."

She rises from the bedside with an anxious conscience, but a clearer mind. Her duty is to her family. She will do what she can do; look after her family, deal justly with the people of her immediate world, continue to pray and strive to walk in God's grace.

11

A DARING GAMBLE

July, 1755–September, 1755

The settlers celebrate the second anniversary of their landing in Lunenburg on the first Monday of July, 1755. It is a happy occasion. People know they can survive, not only survive, but prosper; businesses are opening and farms are starting to produce a surplus harvest. The town is growing, more families are arriving and the population is increasing. It is still a frontier town with a rough waterfront and few amenities, but Lunenburg is fulfilling its promise.

The fog that moiled about the buildings and streets for most of the day finally drifts out with the tide. The late afternoon sunshine warms the wood planks of the wharf and releases the smell of tar and creosote from the rigging of the ships along the waterfront. Christof is restless. He will be seventeen years old in a month, three years into his majority, and what looms on his horizon appears to be the life of a farmer. Such a destiny has never been his intent. He doesn't mind hard work, but to spend his life knee deep in mud, breaking his back lifting stones, mucking out byres and slapping at flies is a depressing thought. He imagines a family of his own. There are a number of eligible young women in the town who throw him glances from under their bonnets. He smiles in return and occasionally takes a turn around the church block with one, but has no serious intentions toward any of them. He has a life to build first.

He sits on a bollard and looks back at the main waterfront. Several ships are tied up at the wharf, one listing over on its side now that the tide has ebbed; the others dry in their cradles. Crewmen smoke pipes and jaw, waiting for the water to rise again. Boys are rolling barrels from the sheds; others are pulling bundles on hand carts, making piles of goods to be shipped out with the tide. Sea gulls wheel overhead or pick at the detritus of the harbour, scavenging for fish bits or dead crab. The wharf is quiet now, resting before the next burst of activity generated by the flood tide. Then the harbour will be bustling with sailors and military men sorting their crew and cargoes, captains yelling at slothful dock boys, everyone eager to be gone with the wind and the full tide. In particular, he watches a man in well made clothes, white stockings and leather shoes stride out from King Street and walk confidently to a large stack of timber secured with ropes near the edge of the wharf, not far from where he is sitting. Waiting for the man is the captain of one of the ships anchored farther out in the harbour who had arrived by shallop, oared by a member of his crew, stepped out onto the rocky beach and picked his way ashore.

The timber merchant carries a measuring stick and some papers. With the captain in tow, he carefully measures and counts his pile of long straight tree trunks destined for ships' masts and a stack of squared logs which will be sawn into lumber. After a careful inspection, the captain and the merchant sign the papers and depart with their copies. The buyer, or his agent, will receive the cargo in Halifax at an agreed price. On his next voyage to Lunenburg, the captain will bring back his money, or perhaps the merchant himself will go to Halifax and collect it. Such a man does not pay a middleman. No, he deals directly with the timber buyers. That is what Christof aspires to, on a modest scale if that is all that he can manage.

He arranges it so that he and the timber merchant meet, as though by chance, along the wharf.

"Good day to you," he greets him.

"Good day, young man," responds the man pleasantly.

"A fine load of timber," he says, gesturing at the pile.

"Yes, a fine load. There are many fine trees hereabouts. Are you a lumberer? Have you wood to sell?" he asks Christof.

"I have fine trees on my land," he admits. "Are these bound for Halifax?" he asks.

"No, this load is for Boston. With this war looming, there is money to be made in both ports. If you have good timber for sale, come and see me," he tells Christof, handing him a blank invoice with his name on it. "Good day to you, lad." He touches the brim of his hat and walks briskly back up the hill.

Christof continues his stroll along the dock, thinking about what the man has said. He owns land covered in timber, some of it already cut and ready for limbing, but there is no road over which to haul it to the wharf; also, he has several acres of cleared land and a sizeable area of naturally farmable land which would grow potatoes and barley if he could get it to market. The breeze shifts and brings with it the stench of rotting fish and seaweed.

"Phew," he comments to himself in exasperation, "the stink of the ocean's offal."

He turns decisively and strides uphill to his home where his mother soon will have a meal ready. His mother is a good cook, serving up hot meals, even when there is little in her cupboard. Tonight she has prepared chicken, a gift from their new found Aunt Catherine in return for some favour, probably helping her with sewing for her husband's daughters. He wants his mother on his side when he makes his proposal to his father. The steamed pudding has strawberries in it, a favourite of everyone except Evie whose skin turns blotchy when she eats them.

"This is delicious, Mother, one of the best ever."

Alerted by his compliment, she wonders what he wants, but waits calmly for him to reveal what is on his mind. He clears his throat as the dishes are cleared away for the girls to wash in the outdoor bucket.

"I've been thinking," he starts.

His father is leaning against the doorway, gazing at the sky and planning tomorrow's work. He turns a questioning look on his son.

Christof starts, "I was down on the wharf today. There are a few more shops every month, and more ships loading and landing cargo. The merchants are trading with Halifax and also with Boston."

He leans forward to make his next point.

"Do you know who is making the money? Not the man digging the potatoes, not the man felling the trees. The man buying the lumber, or the harvest, from the farmer and selling it on to the merchants and businesses in Halifax or Boston, he is making the money."

His father continues to look at him without comment, but Elisabeth says, "What have you in mind?" Christof is not one to indulge in idle speculation or chatter.

"We have two farm lots with cut and uncut timber. We have several acres of cleared land and I have several more that only require removal of shrubs and brush, perfect for barley or potatoes. We are three men here, Peter is a good worker, and the girls can run the house and home garden. If Adam cannot go to his farm this year, maybe he could work with us. We have more land, timber and hands than many others. We should sell our harvest directly, that is where the profit is. If we do well, we can buy from other farmers and become local agents for Halifax and Boston merchants. We can make enough to restart the butchery full time, perhaps rent one farm to tenants, or acquire another—"

"Whoa. Slow down. One step at a time," admonishes his father.

"Sorry, Vater," says Christof, "I was running ahead of myself. What do you think of the idea? Basically. Could it work?"

"Ja," responds his father thoughtfully. "A good idea, but we have not enough seed for such a large planting and it is late already in the season."

"I thought of that. This year we sell our timber. Instead of increasing the planted crop, we take this summer to prepare timber to sell in September, when the prices are higher. By then, war may have been declared and prices will be good."

"Christof," exclaims his mother. "Surely, you do not wish for war."

"No, Mother, but it does bring opportunity in its wake. Everyone has timber this early in the summer; they have been cutting all winter. This summer they will be farming, so, this summer we cut timber and have it for sale when others do not. We can also prepare land for planting next year to surplus potatoes and barley and sell it to the English for their soldiers. Those crops need little work so we can also cut more timber for fall sale. Our problem is that we sell locally. We need to sell directly to Halifax or New England merchants."

"We have too few potatoes and too little barley to sell directly this year," interjects Elisabeth.

"Not if we buy up small surpluses locally and take them to Halifax ourselves when we deliver our timber," says Stoffel.

"Who will hoe and tend the potato fields while you are cutting timber?" asks Elisabeth, suspecting the answer.

Christof admits, "I was thinking that you and the girls could do the fields, maybe with the help of a couple of the younger boys of the village who would work for a small portion of the crop. Maybe Daniel who works for Catherine, Aunt Catherine. Just for this year because we'd have to work in the woods; next year, we will plan earlier and can tend the fields ourselves. What we need even more," her son says, looking at his father, "is a way to haul the timber to the wharf."

"And a merchant in Halifax to buy the timber or the potatoes that aren't planted yet," adds his father.

Christof pauses and then broaches the next part of his plan.

"I was thinking, I could go to Halifax and find us a buyer. We would have to promise him a goodly volume of timber and negotiate a price on its quality in the fall. I have some tall straight trees at the head of the bay that thrusts into my land, perfect for masts. We only have to get them to the wharf. You already have cut timber, it only needs squaring. Timber and potatoes, that is where the money is to be made. I have a tightly built *Hutt* on my land; I could rent it to a tenant who will pay us with a share of the potato harvest. Then we could all work the home farm and increase our harvest."

His enthusiasm makes his face flush in excitement. Elisabeth is thinking how like his father he looks, solid and strong, intense blue eyes, square hands moving on the table to emphasize his points. She looks at her husband and sees the growing interest in his face.

"There are some obstacles and a lot of 'ifs'," he says. "The only things we have are some cut timber of good, but not excellent quality and a couple acres of potatoes planted."

"It could be done with hard work and a little luck."

Stoffel sees the excitement in his son's face and remembers what it is like to be young and full of ideas. He understands that a farmer's life does not call to Christof; it had never called to him either; however, the prospect of a successful business deal; now that was different.

"You have made a good start, let us think about it for a couple of days, see what we can find out to solve some of the problems and talk again," he advises his son. Christof agrees. "Would you agree to Adam joining with us? We need more hands to make this succeed."

"Of course," agrees Christof. "Adam is a fine worker, and honest."

Later that night, Elisabeth finds Stoffel sitting on the chopping block at the end of the wood pile with his head bowed and his hands hanging between his knees.

"What are you thinking, husband?" she asks, putting her hand on his shoulder.

He sighs and pats her hand briefly.

"I am getting old," he says. "I had not realized it."

"You are not old, only forty-six," she says. "You are as strong as you were ten years ago, and are rarely sick."

"I mean old in my head," he answers. "I have been working and thinking like my grandfather, always the land, the crop, the weather. Except for selling a few sausages, I haven't thought like a tradesman since I left home. I am becoming a farmer; Christof has made me see that."

"There were many other things to be done, things that had to be done first. You have done everything for us, for the family. We are doing well, only a few more years and we will be better off than we have ever been," she reassures him. "We came to make a better life for our sons and we are doing it."

"Ja," he agrees. "This is a better year than last and, I hate to say it, but war makes prices rise. The English will want timber for their ships and food for their soldiers. Christof may have inherited his great grandfather's sense of business timing.

Several days later, Christof and Stoffel, Margarete and Adam sit with Elisabeth around her table. Peter is lounging on the doorstep, silent, but all ears.

They have been talking over Christof's idea and have met to share all their information. Christof begins.

"I spoke with Melchior Seiler. He is sailing to Halifax on the *Neptune* on Sunday. She sails with the turning tide before mid-day and returns on the following Sunday. He spoke with the Captain, a Mr. Abraham Welton, who agreed to take me as a deck hand, well, cargo hauler and labourer, in exchange for passage.

Adam Schauffner speaks next.

"Margarete and I have talked this over. I am a farmer, not a man of commerce, but I think you have the right of it and I will help you. I will need two weeks of labour on my land to keep open what I cleared last summer. I have already planted potatoes on enough land to harvest near forty barrels in the fall, God willing. If you help me from time to time to tend the potatoes and to clear the scrub that grows this year, I will help you for a fair portion of the proceeds. I helped you fell a number of those trees anyway." He smiles and groans as he rubs his shoulder in memory of the work.

"I have been thinking about getting the timber to the wharf," says Stoffel. "Eventually, we could have horses, but without horses, how to do it? I spent yesterday pacing it out. The path to our land on the North West Range is good enough for a wheeled cart. Philip Schmeltzer, Christian's mother's husband, and some of the others working farther away, have made a walking trail along the south edge of our land to that section of farms. It leads to the beach; if you can get your timber, the mast quality timber, to that beach in good shape, we can haul it by cart to the wharf."

"If we had the use of a shallop, could we float it down?" asks Adam.

"I have news, too," interrupts Peter who has waited as long as he can to be recognized and allowed to contribute to the excitement. "Monsieur Bizette and his family are moving to their farm for the summer, they have land planted and want to be near to tend it. He says that if I look after his garden here in town they will give me a quarter of the harvest from it. And," he shares his piece of important news, "he is leaving his shallop here for now."

"Moving away, into the woods?" asks Stoffel.

"Yes. They have a house there. They say it is very pretty there, not on the ocean, but by a long pond. I was thinking he might let us use his little boat; I know how to row it."

Ideas fly. They men talk until late into the night, bringing up obstacles and suggesting solutions. Margarete and Elisabeth leave them to it; it appears that they will be trying to sell their own produce and timber in Halifax.

Christof arrives in Halifax on a humid July afternoon. With his good clothes wrapped in a bundle, he walks along the waterfront with Melchior. They turn into a doorway and climb to the second floor where Melchior unlocks one of two doors. It is a single room with two narrow wood and rope beds with mattresses and quilts, a table and two chairs. On the table are a glass lamp and a tin wash basin.

"Welcome to my Halifax lodgings," Melchior says to Christof.

They leave their bundles and go outside. Melchior gives him a quick tour of the waterfront, pointing out places to buy something to eat and a fresh water trough to fill the wash basin. And the public privies. After a cup of watered rum and a hot plate of meat and vegetables, they return to the room. Christof falls asleep, exhausted.

In the morning, very early, Melchior tells Christof that he is leaving and will return in three days and expects to meet him here. With a parting handshake, he leaves Christof on his own.

Outside, Christof finds breakfast at an open stall and goes down to the edge of the wharf to eat it. There are several wharves, many boats tied up and tens more anchored off shore. The harbour is full of open shallops, bigger than he is accustomed to seeing at Lunenburg, being rowed back and forth to the ships. Many ships are flying English and colonial flags and their crews are naval men, not casual hired hands. In fact, there are many military uniforms about and the naval ships outnumber the private.

He paces the waterfront again, locating the likeliest of the businesses to approach; he's looking for a small to mid-sized provisioner, one whose needs might fit with what he hopes to supply. He tries to listen in to some of the conversations around him and is frustrated to hear only English. No familiar German. This is a problem he hadn't expected. He feels stupid for not anticipating this. Walking more slowly along the open doorways of the places that sell ships' stores, he starts to listen intently for someone who is speaking German.

The first day yields nothing except a great hunger which he has insufficient money to feed adequately and blistered feet. The second day he widens his circle; he remembers that some of the German settlers stayed in Halifax; surely some of them started businesses. The morning of the third day he follows a lesser trod path towards the far western end of the docks. Suddenly, he realizes that he can understand the conversation emanating from inside a workshop built out over the water. It is a woodwright's shop. The familiar words are coming from an older man sitting on an upturned barrel, smoking a pipe and telling a yarn. The story is obviously well known to the listeners as they josh with him and egg him on. Christof stops to listen. It has a familiar theme of strong men and beautiful women, this one about a ship at sea, a storm and a brave captain who, if course, is a close friend of the old man.

Christof smiles and compliments the storyteller when he is done.

"I'm Christof Baltzer, son of Christoffel Baltzer, from Lunenburg along the coast," he says gesturing westward with his arm. You speak

German," he comments. "I was beginning to think no one in Halifax spoke German."

"Most pleased to meet you, young Christof. I am Josef Beltzen, of Pennsylvania, more recently of Halifax. These are my sons, Karl, Gerhard and Heinrich," he introduces, pointing in turn at the three other men in the shop.

The men ask questions about his family and Lunenburg and tell him a little about themselves. It turns out their fathers and grandfathers came to America during the Palatinate immigrations in the early 1700's. They talk about their lives in Pennsylvania and he realizes it is much more advanced and comfortable than it is in Lunenburg; however, it had begun as Lunenburg had fifty years ago.

They were born in the New World and so speak English, but German remains the language of their homes. They are furniture builders whose customers include many English army officers. They had followed their customers when they moved first to Fortress Louisbourg and then to Halifax. They have a good trade in Halifax what with the increasing number of upper class families who want fine furniture with which to impress their neighbours. As well, they also build the row boats used as life craft and harbour transport by the navy. There is enough work to keep them busy.

"Where do you get your lumber?" he asks them, listening carefully to their answers.

It is the first of many questions which they answer with good humour.

After a time, Christof thanks them for their patience with his questions and wanders away to review what he has learned. They can use timber although maybe not spar timber, they are family working together which is reassuringly familiar; they have steady buyers from the military and civilian families, they have no use for potatoes, but know who does and, most revealing, they all speak English and, therefore, deal directly with the English and do not rely on translators. He feels comfortable with the men, they seem interested in his life in Lunenburg and in how the settlers are faring. For sure, they can use the timber he has to sell and they know the buyers in the English community.

True to his word, Melchior returns in the evening. He looks tired.

"Where have been? You look worn out. " Christof asks him.

"Thank you, that makes an old man feel better. I've been visiting friends here and about. We stayed up late, talking and reminiscing. I admit that I am not as young as I used to be. Now, tell me of your days."

Christof tells him about the Beltzens and their business, Beltzen & Sons, Woodwrights, and his intent to talk business with the men in the morning. Melchior pats his shoulder and nods his encouragement before retiring to his bed. Christof lies awake for a time, dreaming of his future and building his plans.

Melchior groans as he rises from his bed the next morning.

"Are you alright?" asks Christof.

"Yes, yes. A little stiff is all, I walked far, and I need my breakfast," he answers. "Come. Wash up and let's eat and go meet with your new friends.

The Beltzen men greet them with handshakes as they make formal introductions.

"We thought you might return," they tell Christof. "You asked a mighty lot of questions yesterday."

"I apologize if I was rude. It was such a relief to be able to speak to someone. However, I do have a proposal I would like to put to you," he admits.

Several hours later, they shake hands again. It is agreed, they will buy his timber direct, including the spar timbers. The arrangement seems fair and Christof is satisfied. Beltzen & Sons have become partners of Baltzer & Sons. While Christof talks with the older men, Melchior is deep in conversation with one of the younger men and as they share a cup of hot rum to seal the business arrangement, Melchior reveals the results of his conversations over the last few days, confirmed by what the young man has seen about the harbour.

"It is the only conclusion," he tells them, "Lawrence has decided to force the Acadians off their lands and disperse them from Nova Scotia to the Gulf of Mexico. England is going to war with France. When, is the only question."

"Who will win?" asks Christof.

"The outcome of a war is never certain until it's over, but, if the English can take the forts at Louisburg and Quebec, they will win. In Nova Scotia and Quebec, it will be fought from the sea and the English have superior sea power. But the French have awoken their colonial ambitions and they thirst for power both in Canada and in the American colonies. I do not know."

"The English soldiers tell me they won at Beauséjour several weeks ago," says one of the men. "The Acadians fled along with their priests and that Abbé Le Loutre who goes about stirring up the Indians. Apparently he dressed up as a peasant woman and ran away with the women. I suppose he's used to running in skirts," he adds with a joking laugh.

"So I heard," agrees Melchior.

"Also," begins another, "there are many ships from Massachusetts gathering in the harbour. The crews are busy scraping hulls and repairing canvas, but they are not loading cargo or taking aboard supplies. What are they for if not for taking people?" he asks.

"We have heard rumours for many months that Governor Lawrence wants to remove the French peasants from the area. They have lived here for ten-twelve generations. What harm can they do? They are farmers, not soldiers," says one.

Another voice jumps in, "They are all armed. They live near the English forts and have been delivering grain and potatoes there for years so they must know where the armaments are stored. They could be saboteurs. Better to kick them out before they have the chance."

"If the English win the war, they will lose their land anyway. I'd fight for my land if the French tried to take it away from me," says one nodding his head.

It is a thorny problem, they agree. To lose one's land after so many generations strikes a sympathetic chord in their hearts; however, their fortunes lie in an English victory.

Elisabeth greets their return to Lunenburg with relief. She had feared for Christof in Halifax where he might meet thieves or gangs looking for strong backs to work on the ships or fall ill or fall into the harbour or fall in with bad people, whatever her fertile mother's mind could imagine. To celebrate, she prepares a large meal of stew and vegetables with skillet potatoes and bread. She watches as he eats, relieved that his appetite is as hearty as ever. He relates his adventures with excitement and pride. Her older son has become a man.

His father approves his choice of buyer and talks of going to Halifax with the timber in the fall to meet them and further the business arrangement.

"Baltzer & Sons, partners of Beltzen & Sons. That sounds good. Beltzen is similar to Baltzer, I wonder if they are relations? You know how the English mash our names about."

"Oh, Papa, if we were related, it is too many generations ago to consider them so now," he tells his father. "Also, while I was walking about in Halifax, I made another decision. We must learn to speak English. If we are to do business with the English, it is the edge we need to succeed. We must not be dependent on a middle person."

They argue about it, but Christof is adamant; he, at least, is determined to learn as fast as he can.

"How are you going to learn?" asks Maria. "None of us can teach you.

He turns to his mother. "What about Victoria?" he asks. "Would she be willing? I would work hard. And Melchior, he might speak with me in English, too. We managed on the voyage and I already know some words.

"I have been learning French from Jacques," pipes up Peter. "He says that I'm quick. I could learn English, too.

"When are you going to do this, with all the work we have to do to meet the bargain you made in Halifax?" asks Stoffel.

"Sunday, after church for the lessons, and we can practice in the evening."

Within a few days the new plans are put in place. Elisabeth and Maria are tending the potatoes on the farmland, Peter and his younger sisters are tending the home garden lot and that of the Bizettes, Margarete is looking after the two youngest children and preparing meals. They work to limb the timber and tidy it up for hauling to the head of the trail to the wharf. Stoffel has a branding iron made with his mark to identify their logs. The men tie Christof's spar timber into rafts and row it down the coast, but it hard work and takes a lot of time.

"We need a wharf at Mahone Bay," Adam tells Christof. "It wouldn't have to be protected with a blockhouse, not if it is only used for loading lumber."

"A good idea. Who's going to approach Captain Sutherland with it?"

"You do have a connection there," Adam points out.

"You mean, ask my mother?"

"You could put the thought into her head."

Peter and Christof have persuaded Victoria to teach them English and they exchange elaborate greetings and farewells with each other, ask for more meat, or comment on the weather throughout the evenings. Amusing to them, it quickly becomes an annoyance to the others who by now know as much English as do the boys. As for Elisabeth, she is happy to have her friend showing an interest in life again and having a reason to visit more frequently.

One Sunday evening, near the end of July, Elisabeth walks home with Victoria after the English lesson. There is a shady glade behind Victoria's house which offers a cool place to rest. Surrounded by tall trees, it is also very secluded, a favourite place to have private conversations, or merely sit in contemplation. Anne finds them here, slipping silently into the glade, but remaining close to the shadows of the trees. "Good evening, Elisabeth, Victoria. I have been watching out for you. I wanted to see you."

"I am glad to see you," Elisabeth tells her. "How have you been?"

"In body, well, but in mind, full of sorrow. Nous sommes bien tristes à cause des evenements récents, au sujet des décisions du Gouverneur Lawrence concernant les Acadiens."

"Anne, dear Anne, what is the matter?" says Victoria. "Noel came to see us last night," she begins. "He has bad news. I don't think the English Captain Sutherland has heard yet. At Grand Pré, near Piziquid, the English took the rifles of the Acadians and arrested the men. If they do not declare loyalty to England, they must leave for French territory, or they will be taken away in boats, their land, animals and goods given to the English.

"Noel is here?" asks Elisabeth, eagerly remembering the intelligent man.

"No," replied Anne. "He did not stay. It is too dangerous for him. He just came to warn us that we should leave, go away from our homes, maybe to Quebec, or Île St. Jean. His family has already gone north, nearer to the Quebec border, and he follows today. He told us that his lands in the St. John River valley were lost when the English took Fort Gaspereaux."

"Go away?" repeats Victoria.

"Yes, it is becoming too dangerous for the Acadians and the Indians. Many of the Indians have already slipped away."

"We never got to know each other," laments Elisabeth. "There is much more I want to learn that you can teach me. I will miss you, miss knowing you are here. Perhaps it is a false alarm."

"I don't think so," says Victoria. "Patrick told me that Governor Lawrence has brought in ships from New England to take away the Acadians and is just waiting for enough to arrive before he gives the order."

Anne continues. "The Indians will move to other camping grounds until things are more settled. I think the Mi'kmaq begin to understand that it means the end of their way of life, but they still hope and will hide away and wait. Moi, I think there will be too many settlers from other places, settlers who will not want to be allies, but overlords. They want more land for farms and big homes; they will tear up the land and cut down the trees. There will be no more easy hunting; domestic animals will be brought in; the wild plants for food and medicines will disappear," she says with her eyes full of tears.

"The dispersion of the Acadians is beginning, and you are leaving before the English send you away," states Elisabeth, finally understanding what Anne is telling them.

"Yes," she confirms.

"When?' asks Victoria.

"Soon. Paul has his boat ready and we are putting stores aboard for a long voyage."

"Will Cloverwater go with you?" asks Victoria, "and the others who visit you?"

"They have already gone. Cloverwater left to take his family to safety. They are all at Grand Pré. If his wife refuses to slip away, he will stay and take his chances with the English."

"They choose to stay with the Acadians?" asks Elisabeth. "Why would they not go to safety with the Mi'kmaq?"

"We are both Acadian and Mi'kmaq by blood, but we are Acadian in our hearts. We are Acadian, and do not think of ourselves as Frenchmen meaning 'people of France'. We are Acadian and Catholic and speak French; the Indians are our allies, our friends, and in some families we intermarry freely, but, always we are Acadian."

She held up her hand to stop them from interrupting her.

"I tell you things so that you will understand and because," she pauses and then looks up, "I don't think we will see each other again."

The two women make sounds of protest and grief.

"It would never be possible for us to be friends openly, not in our lifetime. The French and English now want to settle our land with white people, not only a few, but with many of them. It doesn't matter whether English or French, the old way is gone, the Mi'kmaq way is ending, the Acadian way as well. People are angry. If I didn't know you, I would be angry as well. Now I am just sad."

There is little to say. The three women stand, embraced silently in each other's arms.

"I prayed that this moment would never come," says Elisabeth. "I guess God could not prevent it. Even his will cannot stand against the greed of man."

"I will never forget you," Victoria tells Anne. "You kept me from taking my life after Tory died; I am forever in your debt. I wish I could help you now."

"And I," adds Elisabeth.

"You can," she tells them. "Enlist Melchior's help, too. Keep Captain Sutherland from looking for us for a few days, until we are well away. I hate to ask, but it may mean our lives, if he remembers we are Acadian or receives orders to capture us."

"Yes, I will not tell Patrick," says Victoria.

"Melchior will do all he can to distract him," Elisabeth assures her. "Where will you go?"

"Our family is gathering on Île Royal. Beyond there are French islands, near Terreneuve, perhaps it will be safe there. I must go."

She turns back as she leaves, "I will remember you," she tells them.

"Adieu. Go with God," calls Victoria.

"May God bless you," says Elisabeth. "You will be in my prayers. I will think of you often."

They watch her slip silently into the trees and disappear from their sight.

"I can't believe it has come to this," says Victoria. "This blessed looming war has reached us even here. Oh, Elisabeth," she turns to her friend, "what if it takes Patrick from me?"

"Patrick has huge responsibilities here, I'm sure Lawrence will leave him here. Let us not worry over what we can't foresee."

The two women embrace, there is nothing to say, it is out of their hands. Elisabeth is honoured by Anne's trust and cherishes her act of friendship.

By mid-August, Stoffel and Christof have a stack of timber of a size to command a goodly profit if they can ship it to Halifax for a reasonable rate. The vegetable garden and the farm gardens are looking vigourous and productive. Peter has used the little shallop to set a fish trap in the rocky inlet which Bizette had showed him and they have a growing store of salted and drying fish. Elisabeth isn't certain she is grateful to the old man for so much fish, but Peter is happy to be contributing. Only on Sunday do they see their neighbours as they leisurely walk to church and stand about after service in pleasant conversation.

Maria spends a few minutes talking with her friend, Anna Wirth, whose husband has been away most of the summer leaving her to care for the two boys, his son and their young infant, and the garden lot. Maria tells her mother that she is not the same bubbling girl she was last year.

Elisabeth nods her head, "She made her bed now she must lie in it. Some people must learn from their own mistakes."

People know that war is coming between England and France. They have been told to stay near the town and the protection of the soldiers; there have been Indian raids and killings on outlying farms around the province, even armed soldiers have been attacked. Agents have been about, arranging to buy up crops and timber, putting together shiploads of cargo for Boston and Halifax. The harbour is busy with ships arriving and departing.

The morning of August 9th, Peter slips out early to check his fish trap and returns to breakfast with the information that the harbour is nearly empty of ships, only the three that regularly bring military supplies are at anchor. He finds his mother to give her the interesting information. She is sitting in the backyard with a basket of plants and flowers in her lap and looks as though she has been weeping. Alarmed, Peter fetches his sister, Maria.

"Is something wrong with mother?" he asks her.

"Yes, but it is private. Just leave her alone. Don't ask questions," he is told. "If she wants to tell us later, she will. Papa said to be quiet and leave her alone today."

Everyone else seems normal, but they are taking care not to bother their mother. Eventually, his father hands him a hot morning cup and sends him out to offer it to his mother. She accepts it, so he sits down on the earth at her feet.

After a time, she places a hand on his head and says, "Thank you, you're a fine young man, my son," before she stands up.

The others look at her when she enters the house to see if she wants to tell them what is on her mind.

She says, "I think it is beginning. I think Lawrence has ordered his soldiers to take the Acadians from Nova Scotia. I think that's where the ships have gone, Peter, to take them away at gunpoint."

Her voice chokes as she quickly covers her lips with her handkerchief.

"Where did you get the plants?" asks Evie.

"They are a gift from a dear friend," she says through her handkerchief. "They were outside the door this morning," She buries her face in them. "Along with a fine sturdy rocking chair that has a seat of bearskin. You may carry it in and put it by the hearth."

Evie can be persistent with her questions, so Maria diverts her with another toasted molasses pancake. She suspects the giver was Anne, the wife of the half-breed informant used by Sutherland. She is afraid her mother will find herself in trouble some day for her willingness to make friends with people outside the group of German families they know so well. The English are going to war with the French and the Acadians are French. Why would she stay friendly with the enemy, even one who is tolerated? She sighs at her mother's follies, as much angered by them as in awe of her courage.

Elisabeth smiles to herself; she knows the cause of Maria's sigh. It sounds like herself when she sighs at her daughter.

Several weeks later, a flotilla of ships sails past the mouth of Lunenburg Harbour bound for the Bay of Fundy and the Acadian lands of Grand Pré. The Acadian men have refused a final chance to sign an Oath of Allegiance. They will be put aboard ships; some are with their families, others are separated from their families, their wives and children put on other ships and sent after them. News of the affair drifts in with the arrival of ships from Halifax and Boston, with the movement of soldiers and with messages to Captain Sutherland.

Melchior, seeing his hopes for a different outcome fade, turns to hard work and introspection. He helps Adam and Stoffel with their timber, spends days with the women in the potato fields and occasionally tends his own small garden. He refuses to take Sunday service although he attends and passes the time with his head bowed in thought and prayer.

Christof views the military activity with distaste, but sees the opportunity it presents. The demand for produce has increased, the price of timber has crept up, shops are opening along the waterfront, and he even had an offer for his farm land which he refused. The commercial life of Lunenburg is burgeoning and his father and he are placed to take advantage of it. He is more determined than ever to master English, at least to speak it reasonably well. When he returns to Halifax with his timber and produce he plans to speak with the merchants in their own language.

At the end of September, Stoffel and Christof sail to Halifax with their timber. They sell their barrels of potatoes and extra barley to the military for a fair price and have a quantity of timber for Beltzen Woodwrights. Elisabeth watches the ship sail out past the headland and turn for Halifax. She knows it is superstition, but she grow nervous when life goes as planned. God has a way of keeping you humble if you became too prideful.

Despite the tragedy that has been wrought on the Acadians, for the first time life has been good to the settlers. Most of them make cash on their produce and can now afford improvements to their way of life; new shoes, warmer cloaks, mortar and bricks for fireplaces and root cellars, an iron stove to heat the church, and material for clothes.

Elisabeth sets down her basket of turnip and carrot tops. She is returning them to the garden where she will dig them into the earth. The air is colder and the nights are longer. No more long balmy summer evenings under the stars. The leaves have turned brilliant gold and red, showering to earth with every sudden breeze, a flash of glory before the white of winter. Tonight there will be an orange harvest moon against the ebony sky and the stars will twinkle like holiday candles.

She remembers Anne telling her that this means a week of cold days followed by two weeks of warmth, the last warmth until next spring, a time to finish preparations for the long winter.

"Where are you now, my friend," she wonders about Anne. "I will think of you as a friend, a sister healer, even though we saw little of each other. May God watch over you."

It has been over six weeks since the Labradors disappeared into the night. Sutherland had been angry at the loss of his informant, but relieved not to have to arrest him and send him to Halifax as a prisoner. He questioned Victoria and Elisabeth about the family, but neither, truthfully, knew where they had gone.

The last of the detritus of summer dug into the earth, she tamps the garden bed into rows that will drain off the floods of spring and shoulders her hoe.

Although she still hates the sea and rejects any suggestion that would put her on it again, she has grown to like the rolling restless waves. They have their own rhythm, an always changing mood and sound; a soothing lap followed by pebbles rolling in the retreating water, a booming comber echoing down the beach and quickly drawing breath for the next onslaught, or a quick succession of clattering waves that snatch at the beach and wear whitecaps in the harbour. The sun has an hour or so before it will dip into night, so she decides to walk along the peninsula and watch it turn from yellow to gold to crimson. It is not far, she can walk home in a quarter of an hour.

A hundred yards beyond the last garden lot, the bank has fallen in on itself and created a small gully which leads to the narrow beach. High tide covers most of the beach, but this nook is always dry. One can sit on a boulder in the protection of the gully banks and look back at the town and harbour. Some days the wind blows directly into your face, but today it is a breeze on an ebbing tide. Elisabeth removes her bonnet and loosens the pins that hold her braid tight to the top of her head. She needs her shawl about her shoulders, although the wind in her hair is pleasant.

The past weeks have been busy and she can't recall when she last had time to think about anything other than meals and work and laundry and work and church and work and more work. Before she begins to mull things over, she sends prayers heavenward for the safety of her men and for success on their venture. She thinks about Anne and Noel, and their families, about Azelie, and reminds God to watch over them.

Tales of hardship, of families broken up, of houses burned and farms destroyed have reached the town. Many Acadians had escaped into French territory, nevertheless, a lot were taken away on ships and forced to leave all their belongings behind. Elisabeth sorrows for them. She can't imagine how it will end for them.

It is difficult enough to be German and allied to the English. Acadians dropped into American colonies may not fare well. She has seen how some of the people, those close to the English, have received more favourable land, more tools and seed, more lumber; how they become appointed justices of the peace, stores keepers and aides. These positions mean a cash wage. However, there is no use in complaining, some things do not change.

She is sorry that Melchior has taken it all so personally. He is blaming himself for not influencing Lawrence at least to wait for instructions from the Board of Trade. If there were word, it arrived too late and she knows nothing about it.

A pebble falls at her feet, interrupting her wandering thoughts. She stares at it and then up to the top of the gully behind her. Melchior waves to her.

"May I join you?" he calls.

"Come down, it will be warm for a few more minutes."

Melchior climbs down and sits on a piece of drift wood, saying, "The sun is starting down; see how its colour is deepening."

"I have been watching," she says. "How did you find me here?" she asks.

"Actually, it was Peter who said if you were not in the garden, you would be here."

"Yes, it would be him. Or Evie. They are watchers."

"They are not content unless they know where you are, especially with Stoffel away in Halifax," Melchior comments.

"Then I must be off home," Elisabeth says. "Besides, it is becoming chilly."

"Let me walk with you. Maria invited me for supper, but I deemed that not to be seemly with both Stoffel and Christof away."

"You are ever thoughtful," she answers, "although you would be welcome."

"Thank you. What I really came for was to apologize for my behaviour these last weeks. It was patient of you and Stoffel to put up with my moods and silences."

"You worked hard, side by side with us, and it is much appreciated by us all. This summer may be a turning point in our life here. I am beginning to believe we made the right decision to move to this country."

Melchior laughs. "You should tell the English of your confidence in their ability to win the war."

"I pray for their success nightly, and in between. Selfishly, I admit, because their success is our success."

"Not selfish, practical."

Elisabeth puts her shawl over her head to hide her immodestly exposed braids. They walk back to her house in companionable silence.

12

THE SPAR TREE

December, 1755–February, 1756

Elisabeth and Margarete watch as the men swing their broad axes to smooth the joins and eliminate chinks where the winds and rain can enter and then lift the heavy lumber into place. Stoffel and Christof had a successful trip to Halifax. They put aside enough of the profits to grow their business, but they also bought materials to rebuild and enlarge the house, needed wash tubs, buckets, boots and shoes, warm wool cloth and mattress ticking. Even the animals would have a new byre. The women's work will begin when the squared logs are in place and ready to be filled with mortar and straw.

Margarete has a new hearth and mortar caulking instead of mud. Stoffel has torn his house down to the sills and is rebuilding it from the ground up. He plans another room above the first, creating a second floor sleeping area for the children, girls in one room and boys in the other. There is no staircase, only a wall ladder and a partition of canvas, but it will be snug and warm.

Elisabeth's joy is a new brick lined root cellar built into the slope of the land. It is already filled with potatoes, carrots, turnips, cabbages, salt fish and smoked meat. She has made two barrels of sauerkraut, dried some of the sour plums and wild apples from the trees scattered here and there, living reminders of the previous Acadian farms. Dry marsh grass coverings should keep them from freezing.

Neighbour women are helping them beat out the bedcovers and air them in the clear December sun. Snow is threatening and everyone is working as fast as possible. With everyone's help, it will be together by nightfall. Elisabeth and Margarete have a meal which everyone will share in celebration when the work is done. The Bizettes who have returned for the winter, the Bubechoffers and Kohls from next door, Christian Graff is there with his parents, even Tobias Wirth and Anna have joined in. A new house is a chance for a party as well as shared work.

When dark falls, the work is done and the furnishings are in place. Some of the young people clap and the boys dance, mostly to keep warm; the men have a cup of rum and hot water, the women serve out plates of food and there is harmony, and mutual congratulations for work well finished. The success of one is success for everyone.

In pleasure, Elisabeth stamps her foot on her new wood floor. No more mud. Extra earth is banked up around the sill to keep out some of the cold; it will be removed in the spring until needed again. There is even a small cold pantry built onto the back of the house to store rations and the boiling kettle she uses on the tripod over the outdoor fire pit. Stoffel and Peter built a special cupboard with a lock for her herbs and tonics, her medicine cups and birthing kit. Among her herbs she has spruce tips and balsam gum, juniper berries, heal all, raspberry leaves, yarrow, sweet flag and blue flag carefully identified, golden seal and squawroot from Anne, absinthe from Madame Bizette. In the food storage she has dried blueberries, some of the small strawberries and some blackberries, wild rose hips and water lily corms. She has a container of the boiled sap from the maple tree that Old Labrador showed her which she boils up every week to keep from spoiling.

There is joy in the town this Christmas. People come outdoors more often, take brisk walks along the waterfront and check the depth of the ice on the ponds and along Back Harbour. They call greetings to each other, men doff their hats and the ladies nod graciously. The hymns are sung more merrily and the amens are more heartfelt. There is not bounty, but there is enough and people are feeling the confidence of full bellies. Since the departure of the Acadians, there has been no word of retaliatory attacks by the Indians and life seems to be headed for a peaceful winter. There is much visiting from house to house, sharing of hot drinks and recipes for mulled toddies, and small tokens of friendship. Elisabeth and her family join in the festivities.

By January, 1756, their joy has turned to grief. Before Christmas, a few people had started falling ill with an influenza, now the town is suffering a full epidemic of winter illness. So far the Baltzers have been spared, so they celebrate Three Kings Day on Jan 6th by attending church and sharing a special meal with family and friends. Melchior joins them as does Victoria.

"You'd best watch out, Melchior," Victoria teases him, "the Widow Felton has been waving her gloved hand in your direction. She'll be bringing you little cakes next, or requests to help her carry in heavy hearth logs. Don't let her get you inside the house lest you be compromised," she teases. She had regained some of her gaiety lost when her son died.

Melchior flushes red, but retains his composure.

"I'll not be remarrying at my age. A few more years and I'll be retiring to my daughter's farm and her dutiful care. A warm corner and a comfortable rocker, that's all I'll need," he says.

"You're not ready for the hearthside yet, my friend," retorts Stoffel. "Find yourself a good German woman to warm your bed and fill your belly," he advises.

"Stoffel, such talk," admonishes Elisabeth. "Your daughters are listening."

"That's what I'm looking forward to, a warm bed, a full belly and a house full of grandchildren to entertain me in my old age. In another twenty years, I expect to be here, resting my bones, and listening to the chatter. A fitting reward for all my hard labour." Stoffel looks at his family with affection and pride. "Yes, a fitting end, God willing."

Maria gives her father a look and a smile. "Yes, Papa. Just remember, if you want grandchildren, then you must allow your daughters to marry."

"Don't be bold, young lady," he answers. "I know your plans. Johannes has started to talk to me several times, but lacked the gumption to finish. He has been faithful in his courtship of you, I must admit, but he was a rebel during the uprising in '53." He takes a sip of toddy. "A tailor," he continues, "how can he work the land? And there are no fine fellows to buy shirts and suits in this town."

"Papa, he has a business started. He has special scissors, two pairs, and measures, thread and needles, even pattern pieces cut from muslin. He has brought in material to take orders this winter. He works with his relatives in the spring and summer to have a share of the harvest and, then, for himself in the winter. He wants to have a proper house and then he will speak with you," Maria tells her father. "Soon," she adds.

"What is the building that they are putting up downhill from the saw pit? Have you heard?" asks Melchior.

"An ice house," says Peter. "I was talking to the men yesterday. They plan to cut ice blocks from the pond at the top of Back Harbour and keep them in sawdust. They said the ice will stay frozen until May, maybe longer."

"Who will buy ice? There will be ice everywhere in a few weeks," asks Stoffel.

"The large blocks last longer and stay cold in the sawdust. The ice house is colder than a root cellar they said," explains Peter.

"Tomorrow we should go out to the Mahone Bay farm," says Christof, his mind turning to the work of cutting enough timber to have a shipment for the woodwrights who now want a shipment both spring and fall. "The snow is not too deep yet. We should have another try at retrieving the spar tree which hung up today. It is near the beach. With that one ready to float down come spring, we can then put all our efforts into the trees on the home farm."

The near farm on the North West Range has become the "home farm."

"If you had a wharf at Mahone Bay," interrupts Elisabeth, "you could load your timber directly onto the ship instead of hauling it all the way back to Lunenburg."

Christof doesn't miss the opportunity, telling her, "That is a fine idea, Mother. Do you suppose Sutherland could be persuaded? The ships would not have to wait their turn like they do in Lunenburg, they could load faster. Much of the timber at Clearland is just lying on the ground because it is too far to haul it to the dock here in Lunenburg."

"Why not take the idea to him yourself? Try out some of the English you are learning. Captain Zouberbuhler will go with you, just ask him, Christof," his mother responds. "It is a practical idea; I think Captain Sutherland would agree. Go tomorrow."

"I still say we need to cut down the maple," says Stoffel, returning to the problem of the felled white pine; it is not a mistake they often make, but the pine had rolled off its stump and not fallen cleanly.

"We will look in the morning. It may only be a matter of some branches," says Christof. "Then I can approach Captain Zouberbuhler for his help."

"There's damp in the air, and the wind is from the southwest, we may have a storm tomorrow," cautions Melchior.

"Not until nightfall," predicts Elisabeth.

"Ah, speaks the weather witch," says Stoffel, smiling.

"You josh, but you will see," she replies. "It is still too cold."

"Cold is right, poor Lieblingsblume had a frost beard this morning," says Maria.

"Lieblingsblume?" asks Victoria, laughing. "Was ist das?" she asks, showing off some of her German.

"She is my friend, don't laugh at her," states Evie in a hurt voice.

Victoria quickly hugs her, "Oh, my dear, I was not laughing at her, or at you." She kisses the top of her blond head and Evie smiles at her, not knowing the English words, but understanding the tone.

"Lieblingsblume is our milch cow," explains Elisabeth, "who had a beard of frost this morning."

Victoria laughs at the picture that conjures up in her mind.

They are eating some of Stoffel's wonderful sausages. He has made them with a mixture of deer and pork meat. He has also taught Elisabeth how to chop the meat, prepare the intestine skins and fill them through a hand funnel, then twist them into links ready for smoking. Johann Eisenhauer who has built a small house nearby has a smoke house at the back of his lot. He has a knack with the fire, and keeps it smoking evenly, neither scorching nor charring the meat. During winter in the root cellar, sausages will keep for several months. Their neighbours have acquired a taste for these excellent sausages, and the demand has grown until they now have to decide how to meet the demand. Stoffel's mind turns to this problem.

"Wife," he starts. Elisabeth's eyebrows go up. "Elisabeth," he amends, "can you manage the sausage making if we turn our hands to lumbering this winter? I think we should have more timber ready for the first ships making the return trip in May. Then we can divert our energy to the land and the crops in June. What say you?"

Elisabeth and Victoria glance at each other. They have received an order for some woven woollen cloth and embroidered finery. One of them is for lace, and tatting takes a long time. Elisabeth raises an eyebrow and Victoria nods her head.

"What are you two talking about?" asks Melchior.

"Talking?" asks Stoffel. "We are waiting yet for her answer."

Melchior laughs, "Oh, Stoffel, my friend, you are in bliss, unaware of the language of women. A fortunate state."

Confused, Stoffel looks at his wife who smiles at him and answers, "Of course, I can manage the sausage making. It will be good to feel I am helping in the business. That's what we are becoming," she says, "a family business. And Adam and Margarete, our partners."

Elisabeth is thinking that she can do the embroidery and weaving in the daytime when there is light, and make the sausage later, when the daylight has gone. Maria, who has understood that she will be running the house, also nods at her mother.

A knock on the door announces Margarete and Adam, come to share a Yule cup in celebration of the day and to mark the end of the Christmas season. Tomorrow they will begin the winter's work, short hard days in the woods and evenings by the fire.

The group of friends crowds the room and fills it with laughter, chatter and happy talk. As they leave, Melchior turns and blesses the house for the coming year, saying, "Christus mansionem benedictat."

When their guests have gone, Elisabeth tidies away. In the quiet, listening to the even breathing and occasional snores of her husband, she sits in the rocking chair by the last of the embers flickering among the logs banked for the night. She wears Anne's moccasins on her feet. For the first time since deciding to leave her homeland, she dares to feel some contentment. For a few minutes she allows herself to relax and believe that the future holds more than promise. In the dim light she bows her head and prays the familiar words of thanksgiving.

"O most merciful Father, we humbly thank Thee for all thy gifts so freely bestowed upon us; for life and health and safety, for strength to work and leisure to rest, for all that is beautiful in creation and in mankind and, above all, for thy grace and love and the promise of life everlasting. Fill us with joy and peace; allow us to walk in your grace, through your son, Jesus Christ our Lord. Amen."

She crawls under the covers and curves into Stoffel's warm embrace. He murmurs in amourous comfort as she responds.

Wednesday, January 7th, breaks clear and cold with a wind from the northwest. Stoffel, Christof and Adam set off to retrieve the spar tree. Melchior joins them, feeling the need to be outdoors after the many meals and gatherings of Christmas. Elisabeth has kept Peter home, she needs his help today. They had avoided the subject yesterday, but many people in town are falling ill with an influenza that starts with a vomiting flux and then fills the lungs and drenches them with sweat. Many have died already. That is the reason for the icehouse; the ground is frozen and it's impossible to bury the bodies. She is glad the builders had not told Peter, although he will learn soon enough.

She has made a restorative broth and wants Peter to deliver it to several households where people lie sick. She gives him strict instructions not to enter the house or accept anything to eat from them. He is to pour the broth into their cup or bowl and leave. Peter nods his head in agreement; his mother is a believer in fresh air, good food and cleanliness. For one of her children to enter a house of illness would be unthinkable, she'd scrub him from head to toe in vinegar and water if she found out. He'd seen her scrub her hands raw and boil her coverall aprons when she had to enter homes during epidemics; his stomach turns when he sees the bloody cloths she boils after a birth.

After sending Peter off on his errands of mercy, Elisabeth airs the bed clothes and cleans up after the celebratory meal, making a pot of soup from bones and pan brownings and vegetable ends. She keeps enough for her own family and takes the extra to another family where illness has struck hard. Their youngest child has already died and the father is still very ill. She passes several houses with black ribbon on the door and automatically repeats a prayer for the dead. She takes a moment to stop at the Herman's and inquire after Catherine and the girls. Catherine answers the door and they stand in the hall. Catherine worriedly tells her that the youngest is ill. Elisabeth has little to add to what Catherine is already doing, not surprisingly she is turning out to be a competent housewife.

Returning home, she mixes some salt meat and bread puddings to keep wrapped in greased cloth and frozen near the door of the root cellar. They can be steamed when they are needed. She checks the vegetable store, and is pleased by their condition. No mould or mice nibbles yet.

She is setting the table for the supper meal when she hears men shouting outside. One is Tobias, another she does not recognize. The urgency in their voices can only spell trouble, so she takes her wrap and goes out to see what is happening.

"Mistress, you can do nothing, wait here. We will bring him back," one of them calls to her.

A paralyzing fist of fear slams into her chest, nearly throwing her to the ground; terrifying premonition blinds her.

"Has there been an accident?" she calls back, her shawl clenched in her fist.

"Yes. We've come to fetch something to carry him on," they call, hurrying past.

"You will need me," she answers. "I am coming. Where is he?"

"At the path to the North West Range.

Elisabeth grabs a blanket, her bundle of clean rags and straight sticks, and a bottle of rum. Nothing more will be needed until they bring the victim back. She has strapped many limbs needing stitching or removal, or bandaged hands nearly severed with axes. The calmness that precedes dealing with an accident scene comes over her; all her thoughts concentrate on what might be needed.

She has on a pair of Stoffel's old pants under her long skirt for warmth while working in the root cellar. Long skirts would hold her back in the snow so she recklessly tucks them into the trousers and sets out after the men who are hurrying along the path toward the head of Back Harbour.

"Go back, Mistress, you cannot help," one of the men, Tobias she thinks, again urges her.

She does not listen. Four men, maybe more, whom she cares about are out here. One of them may be the injured one.

"Who is injured?" she calls.

"Go back, Mistress, we will bring him to you."

Their refusal to answer makes her heart thud in fear, dread falls over her like an enveloping grey blanket, sucking the breath from her lungs and the strength from her knees. She focuses on her footsteps, one after the other as fast as she can move through the snow. It would not do to fall and become another injury to look after.

The small group hurries along the path trodden between the snow banks along the ridge and down the hill to where all the paths to and from the town meet. On the flat, where the paths to the common land and the North West Range meet the trail from the town, there is a small huddle of men. A lone figure lies on the ground, not moving. Hands try to hold her back, but she drops to her knees and lifts the edge of the jacket covering the head. It is Stoffel. His eyes are closed and his face is the colour of old lard. As the breath leaves her body, she puts her face and ear close to his mouth and listens. He breathes.

"He is breathing," she cries. "Where is he injured?" she demands.

It is Adam who answers her. "He was crushed, under a falling tree." He says quietly. "There is nothing we can do here. We'd best take him home, Elisabeth."

Tobias has brought a two-man hod, the kind used for carrying animal carcasses. The men lift Stoffel onto the hod, cover him in the blanket and start the long trek back to the house. Christof carries one end, refusing to share his load with another. Finally, he allows Adam to take one handle.

Melchior takes Elisabeth by the arm and helps her stumble along the path to her house. She directs them to place him on the table where she can tend his injuries. As she tenderly removes the blankets and jackets the men have placed around him, Christof and Peter build up the fire to warm the house and the girls huddle together on the bed. No one makes a sound, even Bettina is quiet, awed into silence by the tension in the room.

Though Elisabeth examines him thoroughly, there is no mark on him save for the spreading bruise that covers his chest. He feels cold to her touch, so she warms blankets and wraps him in them, adding warmed stones at his feet as she has the men move him to the bed. He is unmoving. In the silence his breath sounds harsh, labourious, each measured intake a struggle. Elisabeth keeps him warm; it is all she can do. The men leave to make more room in the house.

"What happened?" she softly asks Christof.

"It was that blessed spar timber. As we were securing it to the tree before taking off the branches that were holding it, one snapped and the tree twisted away, onto Father." Christof's voice cracks in emotion before he continues. "It fell right on top of him, crushing him into the ground. At first he seemed fine, only pinned down. None of the branches hit him and he was in a bit of a hollow under the trunk."

Elisabeth moans at the picture. When Christof stops, she tells him to continue. "It is best we know," she says. The girls were softly crying. Peter crouches by his father's head, his hand clutching the blanket.

"We braced the timber and pulled him out. That's when he groaned and fell unconscious. We hauled him back on the small timber skid to where you saw us. Everyone who saw us stopped their work to help.

Then Tobias came for his hod, it seemed a gentler way to carry him. I should have left that cursed spar," he finishes in anguish.

"It was an accident," whispers Elisabeth. "It was an accident."

Christof abruptly grabs his jacket, "I need some air," he says rushing out of the door. Peter makes to go after him, but his mother shakes her head.

"Leave him be. He blames himself."

Stoffel's breathing is increasingly strangled and bits of bloody foam appear at his lips. Elisabeth tenderly wipes them away. She gathers her children at the bedside and leads them in prayer. When anxiety steals her voice, they each take turns. At some point both Adam and Melchior come into the house and stand silent watch over their friend. Christof returns and takes his place with the other children standing with their arms around each other.

No one dares to ask the dread question, "Is he dying?" They know the answer and don't want it confirmed. This limp bloodless person shrouded in blankets is not the strong energetic man who dominated their lives. They rarely thought of their parents separately. Mother and father form a single unit, protecting them and guiding them. The thought of one without the other is inconceivable.

"Mother," dares Maria, "is there something you can do?"

Elisabeth tries to hide a shuddering cry. "I don't know of anything to do. He is unconscious and cannot swallow. He has no wound to bind. His chest is crushed." Her control falters and she falls silent. "He is in God's care," she manages to whisper.

They keep the fire burning and sit their desperate vigil through the night. Toward dawn, his breathing changes, becomes faster, lighter. Anxiously, Elisabeth leans over him and is startled to see his eyes flutter open and look at her. She draws a breath of joy that changes to a cry of pure grief as the life flickers out of them.

"Stoffel," she cries. "Nein, gesegneter Gott, no!"

Behind her the children start to wail, even Bettina who doesn't understand that her life just changed forever. Elisabeth doesn't hear them. For the first time in her life she is unaware of her surroundings; she cannot think or move, her world spins around her, she fades in and out of a miasma of pain and emptiness. The unthinkable, the unimaginable has crashed around her. She is adrift with nothing to cling to, nothing to anchor her to life. She reaches for the comfort of her faith and finds it vanished. Even God's love has deserted her. A sudden anger fills her heart; this cannot be the will of a just God.

Gradually, Elisabeth becomes aware of hands pulling at her arms, attempting to raise her from the floor, to move her to the chair, but she is limp and slips through their hands like a rag doll. A frightened cry from Evie, "Mama, are you dead, too?"shocks her and she lets people help her to a seat by the hearth. Someone folds her hands around a hot drink, mostly rum she realizes as she takes a sip. She is reluctant to return, her present state of semi-awareness is comforting; she is numb to the appalling reality that lies on her bed toward which her eyes refuse to turn.

Victoria has arrived, Melchior must have gone for her; Margarete takes the younger children to her house, Gertrud, Evie and Bettina, putting them in the charge of the men who leave the women to lay out the body. Elisabeth beckons Maria to her; not sending her with the other girls is tacit acknowledgement that she is a woman in her mother's eyes. "Would you go and fetch Catherine? She has a right to be here," she asks her.

Maria pulls on her boots and cloak and leaves on her sad errand. Elisabeth, Margarete and Victoria sit quietly until they return. Then they begin their duties, their last homage to the man who was their friend, relative and husband.

Many from the town attend the funeral; the little hutt is crowded and people move out into the back yard. A number of the men come forward to offer their respect with a short speech or a story of his kindness and honesty. Elisabeth is gratified at the respect with which he is remembered; she hadn't realized how many people knew him and liked him. She looks at her older son, a man by age, but, at eighteen, still young to be responsible for his mother and five siblings. He is doing well, she thinks, solemn, but composed, making all the arrangements and notifying the English authorities. She is proud of him. Her eyes turn to Peter, her little boy, not so little now at thirteen and sprouting like new corn. He is still shocked and hollow eyed, pale and silent by his brother's side, but accepting the condolences of the men calmly. Whatever dreams they held in their hearts have been dashed by their father's death along with the rest of their boyhood.

"Do they know it yet?" she wonders.

The girls are still weepy and sad, but their lives are not as affected. Maria will marry her Johannes as soon as it is respectable; she is sixteen, seventeen in May, as ready as she will ever be to start her own family. The other girls are twelve, eight, and two years old, still children. Gertrud is quiet and efficient, she is old enough to help with the house and garden, but Evie needs supervision and Bettina is a baby.

The service comes to its end; the pastor intones the final prayer. Her heart is still angry at God for his malicious sense of fate that could be so callous to his faithful servant. Today she doubts there is a heaven. It, too, could be a cruel deception. She feels deserted and betrayed and in no mood for the platitudes of the pastor. Her Stoffel had believed; she waits patiently through the service for his sake.

There is no interment; the ground is frozen so the body will not be buried until spring. People depart with words of sympathy and offers of help; the family follows the pine board coffin to the ice house where Stoffel is laid beside those who have died of the epidemic, waiting for warmer weather. The box is taken back to the coffin maker's shop; it will be used for the next needy corpse. Stoffel lies wrapped in a linen shroud and tied with cord, like an infant in its swaddling clothes.

Life in a frontier town has scarce time for grieving when there are children to feed, a house to maintain, animals to look after, and a living to earn by the labour of one's hands and back. Elisabeth takes Bettina back into her bed to remind herself of why she must continue to live. Slowly, neighbours dare to ask her for sausages and help, life returns to its routine. Peter joins Christof in the woods along with Adam, Melchior helps out when he can, Maria orders the house and her mother lets her.

Elisabeth takes over the sausage making. When she minces and stuffs the sausages, she can hear her husband's voice chiding and instructing her to be more gentle, to fill them evenly or they will burn when they are cooked. She spends most of her time at Victoria's house, or visiting Catherine, or with Margarete. She finds the weaving a balm to her spirit, the wool soothing to the touch and the clack of the treadle a reminder of a happy childhood. The embroidery can be done wherever she sits whether at home or with her friends. She knows she is hiding, refusing to face the future, but she has done nothing except work and strive for years; the devastation of Stoffel's death has killed her as well.

Unfortunately, she continues to breath, eat, sleep and think. She doesn't want to think.

She goes to church because it upsets her children if she doesn't, but she lets her mind wander, remembering other churches, other Sundays. She doesn't know what to say to God so she closes her heart to him, knowing that if she admits her need, it will overwhelm her, expose her frailty, her lack of faith. Today, Victoria and Melchior are coming to mid-day meal. She suspects that they know she is only going through the motions of living.

Maria has made a splendid meal, salt beef and chicken, skillet potatoes and turnip, carrots and lots of gravy over the soaked hard bread. Buckwheat pancakes and rum sauce for afters with Labrador tea. She thinks of Anne as she takes a sip.

"Don't desert her as well," she says angrily to God.

When the meal is finished, Maria stays on her feet and faces them all. "I have something to say," she announces. "With all of you here, I want to say that Johannes is coming over here this afternoon to visit me. Christof, he wanted to speak to father, but now it is you he would talk with. He wishes to pay court to me officially, so that we can be wed in the spring."

Christof glowers at her slightly, he is not happy being put on the spot. How like Maria he thinks. Johannes is his friend, and older than he. How can he take his father's place?

"It is your duty," says his mother, "to your sister and your father." She turns to Maria, "He will be welcome. It is not as though this is a sudden development; he has been courting you for three years."

Victoria and Melchior leave to allow the family some privacy for this meeting.

On the way out, Melchior takes Elisabeth's hand and holds it briefly, "If you need anything, anything at all, ask me. I am here to help you, Elisabeth. Don't shut yourself away from us," he tells her in a low voice.

She nods in acknowledgement that she heard him, but says nothing.

Johannes arrives and asks to talk formally with Christof. They go out for a look at the animals and a private conversation. Christof grants permission for his friend to officially court his sister and announce their intentions to wed in the spring. Elisabeth realizes that the daughter on whom she relies will be leaving, perhaps in a few months. She feels like a bridge whose foundations are eroding.

In early February, there is an unusually sunny warm day. Maria and Elisabeth open the door to the house and the shutter to the window; bedding is thrown over tables and benches to air. Unexpectedly, Melchior turns up and suggests they go for a walk.

"Would it be too unseemly?" he asks her, knowing this is like a lure to a hungry trout.

Maria waves them away, "Go, she hasn't been out in a week. I can manage here. Go while the sun is warm."

Elisabeth accepts the sudden invitation. They take the path to the eastern blockhouse and down to the waterfront. There are few ships at anchor although the ice along the shore has broken up and started to float into the bay. They rest on two upturned barrels in a sheltered corner by the general store and the chandlery, faces turned to the sun. A few men pass them, touching their hats to Elisabeth and waving at Melchior.

"Actually, Victoria is expecting us for the mid-day meal," he admits. "She is concerned about you."

"I know," she answers. "I thank her. I am less strong in her presence so I have been avoiding her. I am afraid if I start to weep, I will never stop," she confesses.

They walk uphill towards Victoria's house. On the way, Melchior tells her that he has been staying in the Labrador house and has let his little home to another man. "I seem to move from house to house, just visiting," he jokes.

"You seem such a part of Lunenburg, I forget that you have a home elsewhere," Elisabeth admits.

"I feel at home here; I have acquired many attachments here," he answers, his voice lowering as he looks at her.

Elisabeth avoids acknowledging his implication.

Before he knocks on Victoria's door, he stops Elisabeth and faces her, holding both of her hands. "I want to tell you how saddened I am about Stoffel's death. I didn't know him for long, but he was a dear friend, a man I trusted and respected. He was a gentleman and you were the centre of his life. I can't imagine how you feel, but I, too, have lost people I love and know you think the grief will never pass. It will lessen, believe me, Elisabeth, it will lessen and you will go on living. With God's help."

At the mention of God's name, Elisabeth, who had been near weeping, lifts her head in sudden anger and, through lips white with passion, fiercely tells him, "Speak not to me of God. He has betrayed me, deserted me when I needed Him most. He is not a God of love; He is cruel and unjust. Why should I put my faith in Him? He will not help me."

Her anger startles him; of all the feelings he had thought she was concealing, it had not occurred to him that she was burning with rage against her God. It should have occurred to him, she is forever full of questions. The sudden burst of anger has shattered her calm and she begins to weep as Victoria opens the door and sweeps them inside. Once again things are taken out of her control; someone removes her cloak and boots, seats her beside the hearth and presses a hot drink into her hands. She holds it to her chest, trying to warm the coldness living there. Her two friends pull chairs to her side and put their arms around her, Victoria's light and tender, Melchior's strong and warm. They utter words of comfort and share her tears, waiting out her need to pour out her grief.

As her tears slow and her weeping quiets, Melchior hands her a clean white linen handkerchief. She laughs in surprise and explains, "It has been years since I have seen a man's handkerchief, let alone a white linen one. I am honoured."

"It is my pleasure," he answers. "It is yours as long as you need; however, I would do more than give you a handkerchief."

Elisabeth is not unaware of Melchior's fondness for her, but she is not ready to deal with it. Sensing this, Victoria interrupts and insists they have a taste of the meal she has prepared. Elisabeth remains silent; the now damp handkerchief clutched in her hand.

With a look of apology at Victoria for continuing a serious conversation at the meal, Melchior puts his hand over Elisabeth's and says, "God has not deserted you. You have hardened your heart so that you could endure the pain, now that you have loosened it a little, open a small crack to God's love, He will enter. He will not question or chastise you; He knows you did not truly abandon Him. Ask for what you need, you will find it, either in God or in yourself."

"Amen," murmurs Victoria. "It is difficult to regain the will to live in the face of death. I thought my heart had stopped beating when Tory died; but yet I live and sometimes laugh. You are not alone; we will walk with you through the valley of shadows."

Elisabeth feels the lifting of an unendurable burden and a resurgence of her inner strength. She accepts that she can and will go on. The three friends eat their meal in harmony, relishing the release of tension and the restoration of hope. On the way home, she allows Melchior to take her elbow, even when the way is not slippery.

That night she is able to pray and her sleep has only one dream. In her mind's eye she sees Stoffel as clearly as though he were in the same room. He is smiling at her, his face peaceful and unworried, happy. His mind speaks to hers saying, "I am fine, do not grieve." For a moment she feels his hands on her shoulders then he smiles again and turns away. Elisabeth wakes up briefly, but not in terror, calmness fills her heart and she sleeps for the first time since he died.

Her children sense the difference in the morning and chatter away as usual, planning their day's work and telling stories. It has been a long five weeks. Christof tells her his plans for the day as his father used to do; the girls go about their chores and Peter passes behind her chair so he can put a hand on her shoulder as his father did each morning before leaving. She pats it. It will never be the same, but they will continue.

Several times a week she visits Victoria, ostensibly to fulfill her weaving orders, but also to pass an hour in happy talk and tales of people they have known. If the talk is serious, that is alright, too, during the three years they have been friends, a lifetime has passed. Melchior often turns up in time for a cup and to walk Elisabeth home. They take different routes, admiring the widening of the streets, the improvements to the houses, the growing waterfront and, when the weather is willing, they take the longer trail to the garden lots and calculate number of days until it is time to dig the earth. Their conversation is easy.

Elisabeth doesn't feel the necessity to guard her tongue lest she offend. Melchior's mind wanders along many pathways and twists and turns and asks questions as does hers. When she reveals her vision of Stoffel he answers that, of course, Stoffel would never leave her without a final farewell and reassurance. He doesn't find her questioning of God's purpose shocking or blasphemous. He finds beauty in nature, and peace of mind, and restoration of purpose, as she does. On days when he does not turn up, she feels let down, as though an expected promise has not been kept.

In the mornings, she and Maria do the housework, idly chatting. One morning when they have their mid-morning cup of spruce tea, Maria tells her mother they she and Johannes will marry in May and asks her mother if she can help her sew a new dress for her wedding.

"By May, it will be four months after Papa's funeral and time to do the planting. After that, there will be no time for weddings until the harvest is finished in the fall. I don't want to wait that long."

"I am happy for you," her mother says, giving her daughter an embrace and kissing her cheek. "You have my blessing, and I know your father would have given his, too."

"About a new dress?" Maria persists.

Her mother chuckles to herself, this daughter never lost sight of her objectives. Did Johannes understand that?

"Yes, I will see how it can be done. It will have to be grey or another dark colour, it would be disrespectful to have a bright colour. Maybe a blue one. I will talk with Catherine, she is good at these things. Yes?"

Maria kisses her mother's cheek, "That will be fine. Thank you."

That afternoon Elisabeth visits Catherine and tells her that Maria is to marry Johannes Bauer, probably in May. Catherine is happy to be consulted on the wedding dress, offering immediately to give Maria the dress as a wedding gift.

"After all, I am almost an aunt, ja? New material," she says, "a wedding dress deserves new material. Oh, how wonderful. Thank you for asking me."

Elisabeth refuses the offer of a bonnet, knowing that Victoria will want to create the bonnet. The afternoon passes pleasantly and Elisabeth walks home more peacefully than she has for weeks. She decides to spend a few minutes with Margarete, sharing the news of Maria's wedding and discussing the happy plans. When she knocks, Adam meets her at the door with a sombre face.

"I can't let you in," he tells her, "Margarete has started this stomach flux that swept the town this winter. I thought the epidemic had abated, that we were over the worst for this year, but she fell ill at mid-day. I sent Ferdi over to Maria, I hope that is alright."

"Of course. I have some dried summer berries still, I will crush some into a paste. Add hot water and feed it to her a little at a time. It will keep her strength up. I am very sorry, Adam. It has been a terrible winter."

Elisabeth's heart sinks; if Adam is this worried, her friend is very ill. Adam won't allow her to enter for fear of spreading the contagion, but agrees to follow her instructions faithfully.

For two weeks, Margarete lies in her bed while Adam tends her. He takes his meals with the Baltzers, but Elisabeth makes him wash thoroughly before he enters the house.

When he teases her she shakes her head at him. "Don't scoff," she retorts. "My dear mother taught me so, and we have escaped illness, even on the voyage. During times of sickness, boil all water drinks; wash your hands before table and bathe yourself weekly; keep a clean house and privy and spend as much time out of doors as possible."

Despite their efforts, the illness settles into Margarete's lungs which fill up with phlegm and send her into coughing fits that shake her tiny frame. Elisabeth brews a tea of white pine bark for her; it helps for a short while, but the congestion does not abate. Ferdi stays with the Baltzers.

There is only sorrow, not surprise, when Adam comes to the door one morning with the news that his wife has died. They lay her in the ice house next to Stoffel on, February 27, 1756, the day after Ferdi's first birthday. Elisabeth is devastated, this is another blow. She has known Margarete well, although they had been parted for a time before their reunion in Halifax. Stoffel and Adam had been together constantly since they came to Nova Scotia, working in tandem, sharing their lives and planning their futures. The two deaths so close together shatter the dreams of both families.

Death in a family creates a week of hard work, but then life slows down, friends return to their lives, relatives go home and one is left alone. It happens to Elisabeth a few days after Margarete's funeral. Her family are about their business, the house is clean, no pressing task awaits her immediate attention. She has prayed herself into silence and, anyway, her future is in her hands, not God's. It is time to consider it.

She is not content to be the Widow Baltzer for the rest of her life, spending her years with one child or another. Christof will do what is dutiful, and not resent it overmuch, but he is young, too young to be burdened with his mother to house and feed for years to come. What if he marries? How will his wife treat her? Or Peter, when the time comes. Living with Maria is out of the question, they would never be able to share responsibility. Her other girls are young, and will need her care for years yet. The land will revert to Christof, one lot being held for Peter until his majority, in fact, the very home she lives in now belongs to her older son and she lives here on his sufferance. Even if she could inherit land, she could not work it, nor afford to hire men to work it for her. That is now Christof's to control. She is entitled to a widow's mite, one third of her husband's wealth until she dies. Stoffel died with only the dreams in his head and a few coins needed for seed and passage to Halifax to sell the timber. Her mite is a mite indeed.

"Stoffel," she murmurs to the memory of her husband, "it is a man's world; how can I care for our children alone? I am not a lady with jewels and even rich women have to marry. I cannot become a nun in the Catholic way. If I am honest, I must think of another marriage. You were a good man and I loved you, but I have our children to raise."

The idea of another man in her life, sharing her bed, perhaps even having his children, disturbs her. Her Stoffel had been a friend as well as a husband, a rare coupling if other women were telling the truth. Elisabeth enjoyed the independence Stoffel had allowed her; she had always been careful not to abuse it, her house was well run, their children well raised and his needs well met. Few husbands she knew allow their wives the extent of freedom she has taken for granted.

She takes inventory of her assets and faults. She is forty-three, not young, but still able to bear children, her four week cycle regular and plentiful; she is not a beauty, being on the stout side, but her skin is clear, her sight and hearing acute; her body is firm and strong. Her hair is beginning to streak with grey, but it is long and lustrous still; she has her own teeth, all of them, not many can say that. She smiles at her vain thoughts. Her forthright manner might not be to everyman's taste, but she is respected in the community and held in esteem by all manner of people. She is not a charity case. For some time she ponders carefully her chances of continuing the rest of her life as a widow, then sighs in acceptance of her situation.

"I shall have to marry, but not a drunk, nor a wastrel, and, especially, not a fool." She draws a deep breath and quotes her Stoffel's words, "The sun will rise tomorrow; I will be ready."

13

WHEN NEEDS MUST

March, 1756–June, 1756

"March is the worst month of the year," mutters Elisabeth, scraping the mud off the bottom of her wooden Schuhe and leaving them at the door to dry. "It is too cold to plant new crops, last year's harvest is eaten or rotting; it is impossible to get warm. The only good thing is that the lambs are due and Lieblingsblume is ready to calve again."

Last year's surprise calf had grown into a strong heifer. Next year, she could be bred. If Lieblingsblume produced another little female this year, they could count on another cow each year and maybe a steer to slaughter.

"What are you grumbling about?" a voice asks.

"Melchior! When did you arrive?" She gives a startled reply and looks up to see the figure in the chair by the hearth. "Where is everyone?" she asks, meaning the girls and Ferdi whom Adam brought over each morning before he went to the farm with Christof and Peter.

"Victoria invited them all for the mid-day meal."

"All of them, including Ferdi?"

"Including Ferdi," he answers.

"And how do you know this?" she asks.

"Because I asked her to," he says. "She was delighted to help."

"I smell a conspiracy," she replies with an uncertain smile. "Help with what?"

"You are full of questions," he says. "I asked her because I want a chance to be with you without one or several of your adoring children listening to every word and watching me like a hawk. I love your children, but it is you that I want to see today."

Elisabeth's breathing deepens. Over the past weeks she has been aware of Melchior's growing feelings for her; even so, she is reluctant to have him bring them into the open. He had been their friend, hers and Stoffel's, but, admittedly, her friend first and foremost. Without intention, he has become an integral part of her life, their talks something she relies on and anticipates with happiness. She turns to him for reassurance, for answers, for comfort, a person whose guidance she accepts and whom she expects to be there for her. She has deliberately ignored her growing feelings for him, not wanting the complications they would cause. In her inner heart, she knows she has been completely selfish, accepting his friendship and company and using it for her own comfort, yet keeping her own heart shuttered and unyielding.

"Here, sit in the chair by the fire, I will sit on the bench," he says, standing up. "Let me make you a hot cup. Sit. I know where things are, nearly as well as in my own house."

He efficiently prepares her a drink of water, rum and molasses. "Soon it will be time to make spruce beer, a change from the winter's molasses," he says, handing her the cup and sitting down on the bench.

She takes a sip; he has a good touch with the mix, not too sweet or strong.

"Elisabeth," he starts. He hesitates and then repeats, "My dearest Anna Elisabeth." He reaches out and takes her hand, raises it and presses his lips to it. "I would be more than your friend, but if friend is all I can ever be, I must know."

When she doesn't say anything, he continues. "I liked and admired Stoffel and respect his memory, will respect it all my life; however; life moves along, and faster as one grows older. There has been an exceptional friendship between us, a rare harmony of spirit. Do you not agree?"

"Yes," she murmurs, "I agree. I have felt it, perhaps more than was seemly. I feel a peace in your company and pleasure when I see you coming."

"You cannot be in ignorance of the way I feel about you," he says. "You are more to me than a friend, much more."

Elisabeth blushes deeply.

"You do not take me completely by surprise," she manages to say. "You want to know how I feel about you and I do not know what to answer you. You are dear to me, a source of comfort that I treasure;

however, I have not thought beyond that, deliberately. My dearest Melchior, it would be easy to love you, perhaps I already do."

He slips to his knees and places his hands on her arms. "That is where we differ; I already know that I love you."

Elisabeth tilts his head forward with her hands and rests her brow on his.

"What will people think?" she asks.

He gives a snort, "You know you don't care what they think. It is not as though you were a maid with a strict papa to appease. You are your own woman; you can decide these things for yourself. If you say I may court you, I will tell Christof myself. He thinks of you as his mother, not as a woman, so he will be distressed at first. But he is a man now and will understand after he thinks about it. The children all know me; they will adjust in their own time. What say you?"

Elisabeth's mind is in disorder. To distract him, she points out, "You stopped coming to eat with us, I wondered if you were distancing yourself?"

"Being the generous person you are, you opened your home to Adam and his son when his wife died. I felt he might not approve; I did not want to put you in the awkward situation of having to ask me not to come. Adam needed your steadiness which you offered without hesitation or thought. He is a good man and an old friend of your husband's."

"Yes, I can see it could have been awkward; you are very considerate and patient," she admits. She retrieves her hand from Melchior's grip. "It has been a long time since I have been a girl; I am not practised in these matters and know of no other way except to speak the truth," she says.

"I doubt you would do otherwise, practised or nor," Melchior half jokes. "It is one of your more frightening aspects."

She looks at him to see what he means, but he is smiling.

"I should not have said 'frightening'; I meant unexpected, unexpected in a woman and rare even in men," he explains.

"I suppose honesty can be awkward," she admits. "Often it's better to say nothing; however, I must speak frankly on what is between us." She looks at him directly. "I've never asked myself if I love you, if I want to be your wife which, although you did not say directly, is what I think you are asking me. That may have been deliberate on my part, a reluctance to awaken any more disturbing emotions. I can't imagine being without you, without your steadiness and wisdom. I am never happier than when I am with you and I would not have survived these past two months without you in my life."

She pauses to take a breath and order the thoughts that she had never before allowed herself to consider. She holds up her hand to prevent him from speaking.

"I am another person when I am with you, I am not mother, wife, teacher and guardian. Perhaps I am more truly myself, less conventional, as I would be if I were not those other things to other people; nevertheless, I am those things to other people, and a mother still, and for some years to come."

"Do you not see a way to be both yourself and what others need you to be?" he asks.

"I don't know, at this moment I do not know. I have considered my future, and there is no recourse except to remarry, but I don't want to marry out of desperation and fear for the future. I need time to look within myself for the answer. Will you give it to me?"

"Yes, I can wait, but not forever," he replies. "I will come on a day, in a week or so, when we can go for a walk and hear your answer then. I do understand that what might have been simple has become more complicated with Margarete's death."

Elisabeth nods her head slightly; she already realizes the burden of family responsibility that the death of her husband and her friend has created, and the obligations it has imposed on her. Always so many things to consider, and weigh, when choosing a path.

At the door he asks, "May I kiss you, once at least?"

Elisabeth feels awkward, but he holds her quietly in an unyielding embrace until she relaxes and curves into his arms and raises her face. She doesn't open her eyes until she hears the door close.

April is the month that restores faith in the ever turning cycle of seasons. Winter's icy grip loosens with increasing tempo, melt water erodes away the choking ice and opens a path to the sea, birds chirp more merrily and under its cover of snow the earth stirs with returning life. Elisabeth feels her soul stirring like a sleeping creature stretching in its den, scenting the coming season of warmth and growth, preparing to awake and leave the shadowy safe darkness behind. There is little time for reflection with two households to run. Adam takes his evening meal with them, collecting his son and a skillet of food to heat for breakfast. After breakfast he brings Ferdi back and leaves with Christof and Peter for one of the farm lots. He is careful to check with Christof on the plans for each day; after all it is his land they are working. Soon they will have to talk about the future, but not yet; this is the son not the father, and he must not presume.

Adam is a quiet man, older than Elisabeth by ten years. He is tall and strong with grey eyes and greying blond hair, not unlike Stoffel in looks, but more thoughtful and serious in demeanour, slenderer. He has lost three of his children and now his wife, his sorrow is revealed in his reluctance to join conversations and his slowness of movement. Elisabeth has just been through that trial and does not allow the others to bother him nor pester him with questions. He needs time yet, time to heal.

Elisabeth does the chores at Adam's house while Maria orders their own place. Afterwards, one of them takes the older girls to the garden to continue readying it for the first of the seeding. During the afternoons, she and Maria work on the contents of Maria's dowry chest.

Christof talked the chandler out of a solid wooden box and Peter turned it into a carved hope chest. Into it she and Maria put embroidered bed linens, her Sunday clothes and best petticoats, extra shoes and sleeping gown, lace edged kerchiefs and her few pieces of personal adornment. Elisabeth adds a carved bone hairpin and some handkerchiefs from home. There are not many things from which to make a dowry. Her own gift to her oldest daughter is a woman's pocket, tightly sewn and lined with heavy linen with a stout woven sash to secure it around her waist. The front is embroidered with symbols of happiness and wealth, flowers and rondels, herbs of fertility and long life. Into the back, between extra pieces of cloth is sewn her gold dowry coin, unstitched from its hiding place in Elisabeth's own special pocket and passed to its new guardian.

"Oh, Mama, thank you. How did you keep it all these years? I shall never spend it."

"I pray you never need to, my daughter."

Maria and Johannes have set their nuptials for May 18th, she is sixteen and he is twenty-three. Elisabeth, Maria and Catherine, spend many hours cutting and sewing and trying on her new skirt and jacket.

It is the deep blue of an October sea with tucks and pleats to fit the jacket to her figure and bands of black around the bottom edge of the skirt, both sober to respect mourning for her father and joy in her womanhood. Her apron is the one her mother wore at her own wedding, preserved wrapped in silk and linen, with hand spans of fine lace and blue embroidery. The bonnet which Victoria made for her is black with long heavy ribbons to tie it in the wind or to flutter at her back on fine Sundays. It has rows of ruching and tiny bows around the high crown which cover the braid that will be pinned on the top of her head. Victoria also gives her a fine kerchief of cotton lawn to put about her neck and pin into the neckline of her jacket. It is lying on the bed, carefully drying, when Adam comes in for his meal.

"What is this beautiful kerchief I see here?" he asks. Happy to see him able to tease again, Elisabeth answers, "It is for Maria on her wedding day. A gift from Victoria."

Adam replies, "I had forgotten that it was coming so soon. When is the day?"

"In three weeks, on the 18th of next month."

"May already, nearly. It is only four weeks since my Margarete died, it seems like an eternity," he says. "It is hard to believe."

The next morning Adam has a small cloth wrapped package in his hand when he arrives with Ferdi. He looks at Christof, "With your permission, I would like to give Maria a small gift for her marriage," he says, holding out his hand. "May I?"

"Of course, Adam," answers Christof, looking startled that Adam would ask his permission for anything; another reminder that he is now the head of the house.

Adam offers the packet to Maria who accepts it with red cheeks and happy smiles.

"It is for the neck kerchief, for your wedding jacket, to hold it in place," he stammers, not sure of women's clothing and whether it is polite to speak of it. He has never spoken of these things except with his wife.

It is an oval brooch of black hard stone with a white cameo, a delicately carved silhouette of a woman encircled with a narrow band of half pearls in gold filigree.

"It was Margarete's, from her own mother. I know she would be happy to have you keep it."

Maria clutches it to her bosom in delight, "Mr. Schauffner, it is beautiful. I will always treasure it. Are you sure? I recall Margarete wearing it."

"Yes, I am sure. Your father was my dearest friend. And, please, it is time to stop with the Mr. Schauffner. I think Adam will do within the family. You are grown up and we have known each other for many years."

"Adam, this is very generous of you, and very thoughtful. Thank you," Elisabeth tells him.

"You and Margarete were friends, Stoffel was my friend and you have been a good friend to me," he tells her. "It gives me pleasure give Maria a gift for her wedding."

The first Sunday of May bursts forth with the promise of summer. By Monday everyone who can be spared is on the land. The gamblers start to plant their cabbage and turnip beds, the others wait another fourteen days. Potatoes risk rot in wet cold ground and seedlings may damp off; Elisabeth waits the fourteen days. Sure enough, an overnight frost sends the early planters out during the night to cover their fields with what brush and dried grass they can find. A number of plants are nipped and a few patches have to be replanted.

On the Friday before Maria's marriage, Melchior finds Elisabeth at work in the garden seeding rows of vegetables and lightly covering them with stems of last year's marsh grass, her remedy for another early frost. She is bent over, her hands dirty with the earth and her shirts kilted up to keep them out of the dirt. Around the perimeter of the plot she has driven alder branches side by side.

"What are you doing?" he calls out.

She straightens and shakes out her skirts, covering her bare shins. "Making my plot look less attractive to the rabbits than the next one," she answers.

"You live in hope," he replies. "As I do," he tells her softly as he nears. He drops his coat to the ground and says, "Give me those seeds; I will help you finish this last row."

It is quickly planted and covered.

"Come, we will gather some of the bulrush pods that are ready for eating," he tells her, donning his coat.

She smiles at the old long riding coat with its split back, a reminder of days when he lived elsewhere and rode his horse instead of wearing out his boots. He has brought an alder basket and his hunting knife, prepared for gathering the pods, tasty enough boiled and flavoured with salt meat. And they are fresh and not preserved, a treat this time of year. He leads the way. He allows her to divert the conversation until the basket is full, enough for everyone to share, then he turns her to face him.

"Tell me your decision. You have avoided it, and me, and I am afraid that indicates you are going to reject my suit."

She puts a hand on his breast, her fingers gently gripping one of the brass buttons on his coat, and looks at him miserably.

"Yes. I must. It is the only decision I can make—"

He turns away from her abruptly, leaving the button in her fingers, and stares off to the horizon with his head unmoving. He turns back and asks, "Would more time make any difference?"

"No," she says softly with a catch in her voice, her hands clenched.

"Is it Adam?" he asks.

"No, not in the way you mean," she replies. "Adam has said nothing to me. May I explain?"

"My wife used to say that when she had something disagreeable to tell me," he says through tight lips.

"You are free to marry whom you choose, your children are grown, you are outside this community and you are a man. I, on the other hand, have young children, must live within this community as I will not leave it as long as I have children here and, it makes a difference that I am a woman. I am not as free to choose, to follow my preferences," she tells him. "Do you agree that I am right?"

"So far, I don't understand what difference that makes," he replies. "I am not asking you to leave either your community or your children."

He starts back along the trail to the town. Elisabeth is forced to follow.

"Melchior, please, slow down and listen to me."

He slows, but doesn't stop.

"I am part of the town, with ties and obligations. Stop. I will not say these things to your back. Stop and hear me," she insists, her voice shaking with regret and anger. Regret at the choice she must make, anger that she has to make it at all.

He stops, but refuses to look at her; too much shows on his face.

"Melchior, I am a middle-aged woman, not a carefree girl. I have responsibilities, conflicting duties that take priority over my personal wants. If I let myself love you, it would be with a passion that overcomes my other loves and that I cannot do. Eventually, despite my efforts, my love for you would make me into someone other than what I am. My feet are set on a path that I have followed faithfully for twenty-six years today; I can find no justification for stepping off except personal indulgence," she says to his back. "That would be a failing in myself that I could not excuse. It would destroy our love."

"What are you afraid of?" he demands over his shoulder.

"I am forty-four years old, not a carefree maid innocent of the turns life can take. I am past the years for adventure; I need serenity and harmony, and my own hearth. You have the power to take not only my heart, but my mind, I will not allow that. It would shatter the integrity of my being. You offer me a life I could not imagine a year ago, but I am too old to start a new adventure."

"Now we come to it," he says angrily, "you will not give up control, you will not trust yourself to me, trust me to look after you and your children. You must be in charge always."

"Oh, Melchior, that is unfair," she cries. "It is a question of what is most right—for everyone."

He stops and looks back at her. "You are afraid of passion because sometimes it cannot be controlled; afraid to throw yourself into the arms of an unknown destiny, to risk all for a love that surpasses such concepts as duty and reason. That's the way I would love you, with passion and tenderness, with all my being for all eternity. Are you afraid of that, my dearest Elisabeth?"

He drops the basket and steps toward her, putting his arms around her and holding her to his breast and body.

"You have a passionate soul. Can you spend the rest of your life hiding it under your ironed apron? You revealed yourself to me. I have seen you defy God until you force life into a baby's lungs; rail at injustice and cry for an unknown Indian girl; question the meaning of God's teachings. Why are you so afraid to trust yourself to me?"

"I am not afraid," she says. "It is a question of what is most right." She pauses and then continues, "Adam has said nothing to me, but he will; it is only commonsense to merge our two families. And when he does, I must say 'yes'."

"Why?" cries Melchior in a taut voice.

"Because he needs me more than you do; because he belongs to my past; because he belongs here as I do. You have a restless nature; after a time, you would feel confined and become discontent here; you would want to leave and I cannot leave."

And because loving Adam will be safer than loving Melchior. Adam will never challenge her the way Melchior would, never make her think new thoughts, never make her question the teachings that guide her life. He will never demand to be let into the core of her being, past the inner gates of her heart where vulnerability hides. Melchior would charge those gates and breach her defences, leave her open to the pains of life. She has had enough pain and uncertainty.

Melchior picks up the basket and a few fallen pods and walks the path in silence. Elisabeth follows. He stops where the path divides and hands her the basket.

"You are wrong, Elisabeth, no one will ever need you more than I. No one will ever love you more than I. No one will ever understand you more than I."

He lifts her face in his hands and holds it close to his. His eyes are the grey of storm clouds and the lines of his cheeks are deep with unhappiness and anger. His arms crush her until she is pressed along his body and their hearts beat in unison. She feels his shape through her garments as his lips nuzzle angrily into the tender skin behind her ear and his breath blows hotly against her neck. Time ceases. Thought stops. When he pulls abruptly away, his sudden release makes her stagger.

In a passionless voice he tells her, "I will leave you here; it is safe back to the town. There is no response to what you have said; I must accept what you say as final even though I don't agree with it. Good bye, my dearest Anna Elisabeth."

Maybe she cries out his name, but she isn't sure. She watches him out of sight, watching, but not seeing through the tears in her eyes. She feels icy where his heat had inflamed her skin. What has she thrown away?

"Good afternoon, Elisabeth;" calls Victoria, "I have been looking for you and here you are, in your garden."

"And here I be, knee deep in dirt; I seem to spend my life here these days." She wipes her face on her apron and invites Victoria to sit under the shady elm tree.

After some minutes, Victoria tells Elisabeth, "I came to tell you that Melchior left Lunenburg this morning; he is returning to Carolina. He came to see me last evening and bid farewell. I am sorry."

Elisabeth drops her head to her knees to hide her face. Only Victoria, and perhaps Maria, guessed at her feelings for Melchior, but they never spoke of it.

She raises her head and says, "I knew in my heart that he would leave."

"He is returning to where his children live. He said that he will not be back. I am going to miss him terribly," commiserates Victoria."

When she can speak calmly, Elisabeth agrees, "Yes, he will be sorely missed."

"He left me a few of the things he had acquired here, mostly household things. Is there anything that you would like to have?" asks Victoria in a soft voice.

"No, no. There is nothing which I need," she replies quickly, knowing that the break must be complete, final. Then she begins to laugh quietly to herself.

"Why are you laughing?"

"I must laugh, or cry," explains Elisabeth. "I was remembering how many times news has come to me while I am sitting under this old tree. Do you remember? It was here, on this very spot, that you helped me give birth to Bettina, the first day we were in Lunenburg. It seems a lifetime ago. We met Melchior while we were standing here and many times we sat under this tree and talked; he came to me here on the last day we spoke. Now we sit here and you tell me that he is gone."

Victoria lays her hand on her friend's. "I don't know what happened, but he said that you would understand why he cannot stay. He asked me to tell you that he understands your decision and that his anger is not with you. He said, 'She cannot change; the call of those who need her is stronger than of those who love her.' He put his clenched fist to his heart and said, 'Tell her she will always be here, and that I pray for her happiness'."

"And I for his," she whispers. "And he in mine."

Their conversation turns to safer topics for a few minutes before Victoria leaves.

During April, just as soon as the ground is soft enough, the men of the church dig graves for those who died during the winter; they remove their bodies from the icehouse and, putting them on hand carts, move them to the newly dug graves. The weather is warming and the ice is melting.

Reverend Moreau gathers the families at the burial ground for a service. Peter has carved his father's name on a wooden slat and Christof hammers it into the ground where it marks his resting place. Next they go with Adam and Ferdi to erect a cross where Margarete is to be buried.

There are no flowers and the only music is the cry of the gulls.

The day of Maria's marriage is enveloped in a morning fog that burns away with the rising sun. The ceremony will take place in the early afternoon; the men have gone to the fields with strict instructions to return in time to bathe and dress.

"Remember, you are responsible for Ferdi today," she admonishes them. "He climbs on everything; don't take your eyes off him."

Catherine and Victoria will arrive nearer to mid-day.

"Do you think they will get along?" asks Maria, referring to the tentative friendship developing between the two woman.

"Oh, yes," her mother assures her. "Today is your day, they will rejoice for you. Besides, they are coming to respect each other."

She hangs up a blanket in front of the hearth, letting the fire blaze up a little, the mornings are still chilly and they both will take a full bath in the laundry tub on the floor in front of the fire today. The luxury of a warm bath and a warm fire is allowed on such a special day. She washes Maria's hair and rinses it with a little vinegar in the water to make it shine. The fire will dry it in a few hours. Today it will be plaited into a tight braid and pinned to the top of her head, in the style of a woman; outside her own home, it will not hang free again. Her mother gives her the last of her instruction for marriage, on her duties as a wife. Her three sisters are banished to the loft to play with their dolls. Victoria and Catherine will dress the younger children when the time comes. Still, they speak in low tones; there is time yet before her sisters come to their womanhood. "We must talk of your wifely duties," begins Elisabeth. "Some parts of married life may be a surprise to you."

Maria covers her head with her drying cloth. "I know most of it," she says, "we live in a small house and I have seen the animals in the fields. I love Johannes and I am not afraid."

"Johannes may not know as much as he says he does, or thinks he does, Maria." Her mother tells her. "Men think they know about married life, about how to bed a woman and make babies, but they know less than they think. Sometimes men can become inflamed and impatient, wanting to complete the act for their own release and, through ignorance, be hurtful and rough."

"Johannes would not hurt me," she protests.

"He will not mean to," agrees Elisabeth, "and even though it may hurt at first, and you may bleed, it will not always hurt. Bleeding is natural, do not fear. After he falls asleep, get up and wash yourself carefully. Here," she puts a small pot of ointment into her hand, "this is rendered sheep tallow mixed with golden thread. Rub a little into yourself, it will help."

She takes her daughter into an embrace and holds her a moment. "May God watch over you and Johannes, I will pray for your happiness. A good marriage is a blessing and a joy."

The other women arrive and the extended toilette begins. "There are two days in a woman's life when she is coddled" thinks Elisabeth, "the day she marries and the day she gives birth to her first child." Not something to tell a young bride, however, who, on this day at least, anticipates being loved and coddled forever.

Maria and Johannes are married in her father's house with their friends gathered to celebrate and wish them well. After rounds of congratulations and celebratory drinks, Maria's brothers pick up her hope chest and lead the couple back to the house Johannes has built a few blocks away. Their friends follow in procession. Another round of well wishes and they leave the young couple alone.

It seems natural that Adam joins Elisabeth and her family on the walk back home, and natural that he comes in to wait until the meal is ready. Most of them were too busy or too nervous to eat much at mid-day, so they are eager for their evening meal.

That evening after they finish eating, Adam asks Elisabeth if she would care for a walk before the sun sets. Surprised, but always ready to put off washing dishes, she agrees. Adam has her shawl ready and slips it around her, his hands lingering a second on her shoulders. They walk in silence for a time. At the top of the western end of the ridge they stop to look at the setting sun.

"It is beautiful don't you think? The setting sun," comments Adam.

"Yes. The blaze of colour before the dark, a brilliant show to end the day, and a foretaste of the morrow to come," says Elisabeth.

"I like to watch the setting sun at the end of a hard day's work, sort of a reward," says Adam.

"I'd never thought of that," admits Elisabeth who prefers the promise and renewed hope heralded by the golden glow of a rising sun.

Adam clears his throat and turns to her, "It is time that Christof and I discuss how we are going to continue, whether we share as Stoffel and I did, or if he wants to go it alone."

As Elisabeth starts to speak he stops her. "I want to say all my thoughts first then you will know how to answer. I am not much for speeches, but I want you to know what I have been thinking over."

He walks a few steps away and comes back. "Elisabeth, I don't want to be presumptuous, or offend you, but it seems to me that we should wed. Our families get along well; I love your children as my own. I admire and respect you and would swear to be a good and faithful husband. Stoffel was my finest friend and you were my wife's friend. I think they would approve."

It's a moment that she knew would come and she is ready. Elisabeth holds out her hand and Adam takes it in his as she answers him, "Yes, they would approve. I know you for a good man and I am agreed. I will wed you.

Adam heaves a sigh of relief and tucks her hand into the crook of his arm. "Now, now I must speak with Christof."

She laughs out loud. "He will fall over in shock if you ask his permission to marry his mother," she teases. "However, he surely does not expect me to spend the rest of my life sleeping in a cold bed."

"I mean about the land, about the most profitable way to work our land. You, only you will decide if we marry, not Christof."

"I have decided, Adam. I will marry you. About the business, you will find Christof agreeable, if somewhat opinionated about matters of commerce," she warns him. "But he seems to have a nose for it."

As it turns out, Christof is ahead of everyone and has only been waiting for Adam and his mother to reach the same conclusion.

"Mother, I have no disagreement with this decision." He gives her a brief embrace, and reaches to shake Adam's hand. "Adam, I'm happy for you; this is the best ending for all of us in this situation. It restores some measure of security; perhaps everything we've worked for isn't lost."

As the two shake hands, Adam assures him, "I've no intention of taking your father's place. His lands have fallen to you and they are yours to look after; however, I was his friend and partner and I'm willing to be yours, if you want it so."

"I welcome your offer and accept. It seems our fortunes have been linked and will continue to be. We've decisions to make, and soon, for the summer is upon us."

"Tomorrow we will talk." Adam turns to Elisabeth, saying, "Tonight, Elisabeth will want to talk to her children." He gathers his son into his arms and bids them good night. "Elisabeth, I want to tell you in front of your family, I promise to take care of you, and them, for the rest of my life. I will treat your children as my own and have no intention of trying to take Stoffel's place. He was my best friend; I think he would be content with this solution."

She goes to stand beside him, "Yes," she replies, "I think so, too."

He leaves to a chorus of "Good night, Adam." "Good night, Herr Schauffner."

She gathers her children around the table and tells them, "He is right; your Papa would be happy for Adam and me to marry. It is best for all of us. Papa is gone, Margarete is gone, Maria has her own house now, but we are still together and we will be fine, you will see. This is the best way."

"Are we moving to Adam's house?" asks Gertrud looking unhappily around their cosy home. "Where will we sleep? He has only one room."

"No, you will all stay here except for Bettina. She and I and Ferdi will live with Adam, you can stay here. It will be like one family, but two houses."

"I can't call him 'Papa'," Peter tells her in a strained voice. His face is white with anxiety and tension. "I can't call him 'Papa'," he repeats, looking at his mother.

"You don't have to, he does not expect it. You have always called him 'Adam' and can continue to do so. The girls can call him 'Papa Adam'."

On the night before her marriage to Adam, she performs one last act. Secreted under her pillow and hidden from prying eyes, she has kept Stoffel's nightshirt, the one he was wearing before he died. His other clothes have been given to his sons, or his friends. It still smells of him and she has been unable to put it into the wash. Tonight it must be put away. Removing it from its hiding place, she holds it to her face as she tiptoes silently to the little pantry room and shoves it between the boys' shirts that are waiting for the morning's wash.

The only things she moves to Adam's house are her few clothes, the rocking chair Anne left her, her medicine chest and the trunk that came from Germany.

Elisabeth has birthed eight children and buried two; left her homeland knowing she will never see it again; buried her husband of twenty-five years; has five children still to raise and half a lifetime left to live. Three days short of her forty-fourth birthday, she marries Adam Schauffner and begins again.

Adam's house is nearly as familiar to her as her own. She helped Margarete here many times, with cleaning or cooking, with tending sick children or preserving the harvest. Her friend's clothes and mementoes still lie in the leather trunk at the head of the bed, now she is to get into that bed with her friend's husband. Adam has given her time to prepare for bed, spending far longer at the privy than is necessary, inspecting the little garden and stamping his feet clean at the door. Bettina and Ferdi are asleep in their cot at the end of the bed.

When Adam comes in, she is on her side of the bed, the side away from the wall; she doesn't know which side Adam sleeps on. She listens to him prepare for bed, blow out the lantern and set it on the table. She gasps in surprise as he nearly sits on her and then laughs as he leaps up; obviously she is on his side of the bed.

"I'm sorry," she whispers, "but if I'm on the outside I can be up to start breakfast without waking you. Do you mind?"

"No, no," he protests, "it is fine, I was just surprised." Carefully, he makes his way gingerly over the end of the bed and struggles to slide under the covers without hiking his nightshirt up around his chest. Eventually he turns to her and says her name, "Elisabeth?"

Without turning to face him, she answers, "Yes?"

"We have been friends for a long time. I never expected to be your husband, but I'm very happy. Thank you. " He pauses to seek the right words, "After a time it will not seem so strange." He curves around her back, careful not to touch her. "Some things can wait. I will be patient until you are ready."

Elisabeth doesn't answer, but relaxes slightly into a more comfortable position. In these few minutes, she realizes that this is a very different man than she had expected. This is a gentle, considerate man; a man of thought and action, but few words, his perceptiveness hidden by a layer of quiet reserve, a man it will take time to understand. She remembers the years during which he cared tenderly for Margarete, the understanding and patience with which he treated her, and realizes that she should not be surprised. Wrapped up in her own affairs, she had not seen him as a man, but as her husband's friend. He is right, it feels very strange, but she is no longer anxious about the outcome.

"I forgot to pray," she whispers.

"Hold my hand, we will pray together," he answers.

She feels the calluses and scars on his fingers as he enfolds her hand between his.

"Lord, bless us and our children; guide us and protect us through our years together and take us to your home when our life here is over. Amen," Adam says into the warm darkness of the room.

"Amen," she repeats. Yes, a man of few words, but the right words.

14

THE CATTLE DRIVE

July, 1756–January, 1757

News of the impending cattle drive spreads through the town. People have been waiting weeks for the distribution of additional livestock and are disconcerted with the news that, instead of receiving livestock, they are going to walk across Nova Scotia to the vacated Acadian lands, retrieve the cattle which have been roaming free and drive them back to Lunenburg. To the English it is a sensible idea and would cost a fraction of buying livestock in New England; to the settlers who have crops to tend and months of work to do, it seems folly.

The plan is announced on July 4th, during the third Landing Commemoration Day service. Agitated whispers swirl around the church. Captain Sutherland rises and strides to the front of the congregation.

He explains.

"There are at least a thousand head of cattle, free but for the taking since last year if we can capture them. Not all of you need go; some will go and others will take care of your crops. The cattle will be equally divided. Here is the plan for those of you who want to participate. You will divide yourselves into groups of six who have farms near to each other. One of you will go on the cattle drive; the other five will care for your land. The cattle will be divided equally among the groups of six, and then the six of you will divide the livestock among yourselves."

Captain Zouberbuhler translates.

Sutherland continues, "If you wish to take part, gather on the green outside after the service concludes and the lists will be made. Afterwards it will be posted on the church door. Captain Zouberbuhler will answer your questions." He steps down and returns to his seat.

"Why does he always have to sound so pompous?" wonders Elisabeth to herself. Her feelings for him have moderated somewhat, but she will never be comfortable with him. Wisely, Reverend Moreau hurriedly ends the service and the people surge on to the green.

The preparing of the lists takes most of the afternoon. When Adam returns home, he announces that he will be going. He is both excited and apprehensive about the trek. He is not a young man, but he has experience with cattle and oxen, even horses.

"We talked, Christof and I, I will go. He joined with his neighbours in Mahone Bay, but will stay here while one of them goes. My farm neighbours will look after my land at Clearland while I am away. That way, we will have shares in two groups. Fifty or so of us are going with some soldiers for protection. We are to leave before the end of the month," he explains to her.

Christof, who has come in with Adam, nods in agreement. "I can be of more help here," he says. "There is no need for both of us to be away, it is better for me to produce the best harvest I can, and then we can share in the livestock. Christian is going, too, and Nicholas Berghaus, and Bernhard Herman, they will help each other. They will return in a few weeks, well before harvest time. We will have the produce from three farms this year; we should make a goodly profit. As well as the timber for the Beltzens in Halifax."

It will mean a hard summer, harder with Adam away for weeks. They have three farms under planting plus timber to cut, the vegetable garden and the livestock now increased by the spring lambs and an additional heifer. All of them will have to work from dawn to dark.

That night when Adam struggles up over the end of the bed, Elisabeth says, "Let me get up and let you in, there is no need for you to creep up onto the bed as though I am going to heave you out. From now on, I will retire last as is my usual habit."

"Thank goodness," answers Adam in relief, "I was afraid to mention it. I am not built for sneaking into bed."

Elisabeth stifles a giggle at his exaggerated huffing and puffing and slips out of bed to let him retire with more dignity.

As he settles into place, Elisabeth remains facing him. She can feel him looking at her in question, his hand tentatively touches her arm. It is time. She is ready and nestles into his strong arms. Stoffel had been a vigourous man and Elisabeth had enjoyed his lovemaking to an unladylike degree. It crosses her mind that probably Margarete had been a lady in all things, including matters of the bed. Alert to any resistance, she senses a hint of surprise at her enthusiastic response, but no reluctance. Adam is as gentle as he can be, careful of hurting her; however, he turns out to be a man with unexpected depths of passion and she is well satisfied, content to relax wholly in his embrace. The needs in each other are well met.

"I am happy to find that life holds pleasant surprises yet," he whispers in her ear to which she offers only a contented murmur of agreement.

The morning of the July 30th is set for the trek to Grand Pré and the cattle round up. The men, about fifty of them, and fifty soldiers, gather at the western end of the town and start out along the cleared trail which quickly dwindles into a path and then into an unmarked trail leading first to the head of Mahone Bay, there turning inland through the hills and swamp spruce to the Basin of Minas. Victoria has begged a sketch of a map from Patrick and Peter makes a copy for Adam on the back of a piece of scrape leather. The men are not taking a regular trail such as leads from Halifax to Piziquid and, thence, to Annapolis Royal which is protected by the English. This route will be unprotected for most of the way. Many of the Indians took to the woods after the Acadians were taken away and attack unarmed men.

Catherine and Elisabeth walk along Lawrence Street to the departure point and wave to the men as they walk off. Their husbands will be gone a month or two, depending on the vagaries of weather, the cooperation of the cattle and the cargo space available in Halifax to bring the animals back to Lunenburg. Neither of them is looking forward to the intervening time; they are aware of the dangers the men face in the dark woods. More than half of the settlers are armed, but that provides small comfort to the women remaining in Lunenburg.

When Christof returns that evening, he asks his mother why Peter had not come to help him today.

"I thought he was with you," she responds. "I haven't seen him all day."

"Let me check with the neighbours," says Christof. "Now that Bizette is in town again, he may be there."

Elisabeth is a little worried, it's not like Peter to be late for his meals, but, at almost fourteen, he follows his own mind and should not come to any harm.

Christof is soon back, but not alone. With him is Maria and both of them have apprehensive looks on their faces.

"What is it? Where is Peter?" demands Elisabeth.

Maria faces her mother across the table. "He has gone with the men on the cattle drive," she tells her. "He told me this morning before he left."

Elisabeth collapses into a chair. Gone with the men. He didn't tell her. Of all her children, Peter is the one who takes the most care not to upset her, or confront her. He prefers to talk around a subject and ease her into understanding his decisions before announcing them. Not that he ever changes his mind once it is made up. She doesn't know if she is most upset at the danger he has put himself into or his sneaking off and not telling her about it.

"Mama," says Maria, "I saw him just before he left. He was prepared with his boots and clothes and a bedroll. He is smart; he will come to no harm."

Elisabeth has a question. "Did Adam know?" That would be intolerable.

"No. He plans to stay out of Adam's sight until it is too late to send him back. Then he will seek him out. Adam will take care of him, you know that. They are both safe, Mama," says Maria.

"Why didn't you tell me?" Elisabeth asks her daughter.

"It would have done no good. He spoke to me just as they left and ran after them to catch up. There are a hundred men; it is easy to sneak into the crowd. He knows the woods as well as anyone, almost as well as you," she says. "He begged me not to tell you until tonight. I was on my way to you when I met Christof."

Maria finally sits at the table.

"Listen, Mama, I must tell you this. Peter is still very angry that you married Adam, angry at you not Adam. He adores Adam, but you are his mother, and Stoffel was his wonderful Papa. He doesn't know how to talk to you about how he feels, so he ran away for awhile." Maria looks her mother in the eye, "I decided it was best to let him go. He'll have worked it out by the time he returns. Don't be angry with him. Or me."

"I'm not angry; it's my fault," says Elisabeth. "I should have noticed he was too quiet."

She shoos her two older children out of the house, "Go away now, I must look after Bettina and Ferdi. I have work to do."

That night she lies in the darkness and tries to imagine what kind of night her Adam and her Peter are spending. Are they warm enough? Are they frightened? She hopes Adam has had a thought for her and that he has found Peter. She grows unhappy as she thinks of her younger son.

"Heavenly Father, I failed to see my son's unhappiness and now he has run away. Take care of him, and Adam. Help him to understand why I married Adam; that it doesn't mean I no longer love his Papa. I should have made him understand."

Her relationship with God is still on shaky ground since the death of Stoffel and Margarete, but the habit of praying is deeply ingrained and comforting. She uses Adam's brief, but all encompassing words.

"Lord, bless us and our children; guide us and protect us through our years together and extend us your grace when our life here is over. Amen."

There is little time for reflection. Day runs into day. Christof works the two farms single-handedly, the younger girls do as best they can and Elisabeth shares her time between them all. Elisabeth sees Catherine on her way to the garden lots, but they rarely have time to stop for pleasantries except on Sunday while walking home after church. She is grateful, too, for Victoria who helps the girls when she can. The English lessons continue, but there is little time for practice.

She is weeding a shaded patch of mint at the back of the house when she sees Adam Kohl, whose house abuts hers at the back and calls out to him, "Good day, how come you are not at your farm?"

Adam and Rosina spend most of the warm weather out at their farm at La Havre.

"I am embarrassed to admit this, but I was clumsy and fell over a haying rake. I injured my shoulder. Rosina insisted we come back here to rest for awhile. According to her, if I stayed at the farm I could not resist working. So here we are, taking care of this little garden."

"Do you want me to look at your shoulder?" she asks.

"No, I am sure it is healing. Why don't you come and sit for while, have a cold drink with us. Tell us what's been happening in the town. You're always rushing past, take a moment with us."

He ushers her into the tidy side yard under the maple tree where his wife has a pitcher of cold sweet cordial waiting. Elisabeth is familiar with Frau Kohl's cordial, strong and potent, made from the wild red strawberries.

She accepts a cup and sips. Delicious. They congratulate Elisabeth on her remarriage, telling her that Adam is a fine man and that she has acted with courage and good sense.

"It will work out well," Rosina says, "after all, it has worked for us." Rosina lost her husband and three children on the voyage across the ocean and understands very well the necessity of being sensible.

Elisabeth tells them of the cattle drive, about Peter's going with the men and the gossip of the town. Little to tell really, people have been busy this summer.

Finally, Adam puts his cup down and says, "I have a story to tell you, if you will be wise about whom you pass it along to."

"For shame, Adam," says Rosina, "you know Elisabeth is most discreet."

Adam flaps his hand in apology and begins.

"It was about two weeks ago now. You may know that our land is the farthest away, at the very end of the lots given out at La Havre which is why we either have to move out there or, at least, live there for the summer. Anyhow, we decided to walk the outside of the entire lot, to explore just what we had been given. It is nice land, sloping away down to the river, near the head of the long harbour entrance to the river. Did I tell you that I have been talking to old Bizette about how to build a boat and set fish traps?"

"Adam," reprimands Rosina, "don't get side tracked or I shall have to tell it."

"Yes, well, as we followed the top of the highest ridge at the back of the farm, we heard voices. At first we were afraid so we hid ourselves in the trees and were very quiet. Nothing. Just as I began to think it was only the wind, I heard them again. Very quiet. We didn't move, but we could hear them passing by, just below the ridge, going toward the narrow part of the river before it widens below our farm. When we could no longer hear them, we went along the same route, but above them. We caught up with them when they stopped to camp for the night, so we crept past and stopped farther away, following the boundary of our farm."

Adam stops to take another sip of cordial. Elisabeth is intent on his tale.

"I could hear them speaking, I'm sure they were speaking French. It was not English or German and I don't think they were Indians. If they were, we would not have heard them before they scalped us."

"We think they were Acadians," interrupted Rosina eagerly, "Perhaps some of the ones who escaped the soldiers and fled into the forest. They must be looking for another place to live."

Elisabeth says, "I wonder where they spent last winter? With some of the Indians?"

"That is possible. We think they have met up, some of the families or groups, and are moving to another place, away from the English," repeats Rosina. "But where can they go? To be truthful we, I, was a little frightened. What if they attack the farms at La Havre?"

Adam breaks in, "They will not do that, it is too close to Lunenburg and the English soldiers. They know they would be caught and imprisoned or taken away. If I were them, I would go overland, all the way to Louisbourg and the rest of the French settlements. What I don't understand is why they are here."

"How many were there?" asks Elisabeth.

"I don't know, we didn't dare get too close," admits Adam. "By the sounds, a dozen or eighteen, some children and woman, I only heard one man speak."

"Who has the farm next to you?" questions Elisabeth, thinking that a Montbéliard family very likely could be helping them.

"One of the French from Switzerland, I don't know him very well," replies Adam. "Do you think he is helping them to escape?"

"I don't know," says Elisabeth.

"They are all French, it would be hard to refuse them aid," says Rosina. "Should we do anything?" she asks.

They look at Adam. It will, of course, be his decision. It's his farm they are using.

"I have been wondering about that," he tells them. "It's one of the reasons I agreed so readily to come back to town. I don't like the thought of them destroying my crops; equally, I don't want to be responsible for the poor people being imprisoned. I just want to live in peace, these machinations of kings and governors are too much for me to understand."

They sit considering the implications of telling or not telling.

Elisabeth tells them, "If they are just passing through, on the way to a more distant and safer village, I don't think they are any danger to us. The only trouble would come if we actively aided them."

"I agree with your assessment on that," replies Adam. "I have decided," he states finally. "We will have to start harvesting in two weeks. We will stay here for five more days, until after Sunday; then we will go back. If there are no more sightings, and no damage to my crops, we will speak of it no more."

And so they leave it.

Christof has welcome news that evening. He heard from one of sailors that the men from the cattle drive are in Halifax with the cattle awaiting transport to Lunenburg. They should all be back in a few days.

"I imagine Peter will have some grand tales to tell," he says to his mother.

"I imagine, too," she replies.

"Wait 'til I get my hands on him for leaving me with all the work this summer," he comments. "I'll give him what for."

"You will do no such thing," remonstrates Elisabeth. "I, too, have worked without rest in the fields and made up for all he missed. His sisters helped, too. We'll welcome him home and say nothing about his behaviour until he does," she states firmly. "You, too, have done foolish things in your day," she reminds Christof.

"All right, I'll leave him to you," he agrees.

The two ships with the men and the cattle sail into the bay two days later. Most of the townspeople go down to the dock, even those whose husbands were not on the cattle drive, to see how many cattle had been rounded up and share in the general festivities. Elisabeth is among them, with the two youngest children in tow. She keeps a hand firmly on them, Ferdi is impetuous and as apt to climb over the edge of the wharf as put a half eaten crab shell into his mouth. She can't see Adam or Peter among the group of men lining the ships' rails.

"Don't look to be many cattle," comments the woman next to her. "Not much to show for five weeks away from their farms."

"Is your man among them?" asks Elisabeth.

"Certainly not. He's more sense than to go gallivanting off on a wild goose chase, or a wild cattle chase." She laughs hoarsely at her own joke.

Elisabeth moves along the wharf. Three men have landed on the shore from a shallop and are talking to Captain Sutherland. They are gesticulating and shaking their heads. She edges closer. Catherine Herman has found a spot near the slipway where the men will come ashore. The tide is a few hours from high, but it will soon be deep enough for them to tie up at the wharf. They see Sebastian Zouberbuhler turn away from the Captain and climb on an upturned barrel and raise his arms for silence.

"Everyone has returned," he announces. A cheer goes up, their worst fear is allayed. "They will wait on board until we are ready to unload the livestock. The animals have turned quite wild and will be led off one by one by two men who have tied a rope around their heads. When they start, please, stay away from the road to the common land," he explains. "First, the soldiers have to strengthen the fences. You can be of assistance by helping with the fences."

A number of men and boys and a few women move up the hill toward the common land. Elisabeth and Catherine stay with the children, but move farther up the hill, out of any danger. They stare at the ships, trying to locate the men they know. It takes a time, but eventually the ships are nudged to the wharf and a plank gangway tied into place. The cattle are lowing and tossing their heads against the ropes. The people move back and fall silent; most of those not waiting for someone have gone home. The first of the cattle are led off; as soon as they touch land they try to run, but are held fast and taken off at a trot to their new pasture. A number of the men have tied their shirts around the eyes of the beasts and this seems to be helping.

At last, Elisabeth spies Adam, grasping tightly to the rope around the horns of a huge beast. On the other side is Peter, dwarfed by the size of the animal.

"Look," she says to Catherine, "they have brought back some oxen, too."

"Yes, I see them now," she replies. "My grandfather had a pair, I remember seeing them. They are huge."

Then Catherine spies Bernhard at the head of a long horned cow. She waves, but he is focused on the animal that seems docile enough at the moment.

"Come, let's go along to the common, that's where they will be able to leave the animals and greet us. What a relief to see them again. Here they come, let's hurry," she urges and sets off up the hill.

"Coming," Elisabeth says, picking up Ferdi and handing Bettina to Catherine. "If you carry her, we can go faster."

The two women reach the common just as the men herd the oxen into a hastily erected pen. There are six of the beasts, beige or red and white with long horns that need bobbing. The commons is a confusion of animals, the new ones spooked and tossing their heads, the few older ones gathered in a defensive circle on the far side. There are no sheep or horses, but there are cows and a bull or two, plus the oxen.

She sees Peter and, before he has time to think too much about his reception, gives him a welcoming hug.

"You are back; I'm so glad to see you safely returned. What an adventure you must have had," she tells him.

"Hello, Mama. I'm fine and I'm sorry."

She plants a kiss on his cheek and only lets him go when Christof hurries up and grabs him in a bear hug.

The oxen secured, Adam comes over and opens his arms. Elisabeth gladly feels them close around her.

"This old man is happy to be home," he says.

They collect Bettina from Catherine who is with Bernhard and go home.

The whole family gathers for breakfast the next morning, eager to hear about the trek to Grand Pré and the capture of the cattle. Maria arrives as well, wanting to hear their adventures.

"Well, the trek overland was not so easy," admits Adam. "It's a single file trail, hardly marked at all, sometimes I think the soldiers were lost and just going in the general direction."

"It is an Indian trail," Peter adds. "They always walk in single file and keep quiet so they can hear any animals or enemies. They leave markers that only those who know what to look for can find. I found a way tree that pointed us in the right direction."

"Oh, and how do you know these things," asks Maria.

"Melchior taught me."

"What is a way tree? I don't know this tree," asks Elisabeth, moving the conversation away from Melchior. It is the first time she has heard his name since he left in the spring and it unsettles her.

"It's not a kind of tree. It's a tree with a branch that the Indians bend when it is a sapling and tie in place as it grows, so the branch points the way to go," Peter explains, holding his arm up to demonstrate. "When it grows hard, it keeps the bend."

Christof breaks in, "Tell us about the Acadian lands, I've heard they are rich and fertile and spread for miles without a hill."

Adam laughs, "Not for miles and there are hills, but they are lush and protected from the harsh winter winds, more like your old village of Rosenthal. I think it is warmer there than here. Most of the fields have grown up with weeds and bush already. No houses remain; they were all burned to the ground and everything taken. If there were farm tools, they were all destroyed. " He shakes his head in disgust at the waste and continues his story.

"The cattle had been running wild for a year. Most of them were hiding in the edges of the woods, they broke down their fences and scattered everywhere. I think they were half wild to begin with, every time we'd get close, they would run off. What trouble we had, getting them roped and fenced in. Some were too wild to bother with, especially the grown bulls. Some were sick or injured. We did well to come back with sixty, but the oxen are healthy. Four of them seem to be trained as pairs, they naturally stay together; two others are young and untrained."

"Adam was the only man who could catch the oxen," says Peter, looking with pride at him. "They are bulls who have been castrated and allowed to grow old instead of being slaughtered. Well, you can still eat them, but they are tough."

Recalling the look of satisfaction of Adam's face as he led one the creatures off the ship, she says, "Tell us more about these oxen."

"Yes," agrees Christof. "I want to hear about them, too."

"We used them back home. They are slow, but very strong, stronger than horses; they eat many different types of hay and are easy to manage if they are properly trained. We use them in pairs to haul heavy wagons long distances, or in the fields to plough, or to pull stumps. They are very useful." He stops and looks at Christof.

"I've been wondering if it would be wise to acquire the oxen instead of another cow. We have a cow and two heifers. Now that there are two more bulls, they will produce a calf every year which is enough for our own use. The thing with oxen is, other people want to use them, but don't want the bother of owning them. If we had a pair; people would hire them from us. I think we could earn good money on a regular basis. The oxen can haul the logs out of the woods all winter, pull stumps and plough the fields in spring, haul barrels of potatoes in the fall, for us and for others."

Adam's enthusiasm shows on his face.

"You really like these animals don't you, Adam?" says Christof.

"Oh, yes. They are wonderful creatures," replies Adam. "I've known them for many years and have missed working with them."

"Can we get a pair? It seems one is not much use," asks Elisabeth. "Won't others see their worth?"

"I think I have a good chance. Not everyone will want to take on two oxen. They have to be fed, sheltered and cared for; they produce no milk and meat only after they are old. Not everyone is comfortable with them. Unlike many others, we already have a cow, plus the two heifers that will be ready to mate this coming spring, thanks to Evie." He smiles at her and she dips her head in embarrassment and pleasure. "Maybe not many will want them."

"Also," he continues, "our little group brought back two of them and two cows. Besides, Peter is now fourteen and entitled to his share and he helped to bring them back. So we count as three men, me and Christof and Peter, all entitled to a share of the spoils." He pauses for a moment and then shares his thinking. "There are not many cattle, far too few to go around. Many will be disappointed." He looks at Christof as he says, "If Christof drops out of his group, they will be happy not to have to share; maybe we can, between us three, have two oxen." He beams at everyone. "All together, yes? One big family."

He smiles around the table. Peter is bursting with pride. Elisabeth has never seen Adam so exuberant; it occurs to her that he likes being the head of a big family and loves all these children. God has been good.

Adam looks at Christof and tells him, "You think it over Christof, and then we can talk about it on the way to see how the oxen have fared overnight. I don't want to lose out for being late; the other men will be gathering to share the livestock."

Two hours later, they have possession of a pair of oxen. They appear to be about five years old, young as oxen go, but well trained if a bit rambunctious after a year's freedom.

"Now," points out Christof, "all we need is a plough and a wagon."

Adam laughs happily, "Only a plough, we don't have any roads yet for a wagon. So, first we will haul out the stumps and make a road."

The weather gradually becomes colder, the leaves drop to the ground, the harvest is put down for winter and the surplus sold. Adam, Christof and Peter have erected a strong barn on the farm and fenced in a paddock for the animals, six pregnant sheep, two pregnant cows, one sow that will farrow in the spring and the oxen. They realize how fortunate it is to have drawn a farm so close to the town; they can tend the animals through the winter and continue to live in their town homes.

Christof has given his mother and Adam use of the home farm, the one on the North West Range that she and Stoffel had worked; he has kept the Mahone Bay land for himself and Adam has given use of the Clearland farm to Peter. The redistribution means little for they run the farms together, deciding on the use of the land and the selling of the timber and produce together as a family.

Thanks to Catherine's insistence and Bernhard's connections, they have acquired a housekeeper, Frau Wilhelmina Getz, Minna. She is a widow of some thirty-five years of age who was working in Halifax for an English family. When they returned to Pennsylvania, she was persuaded to remain and move to Lunenburg. Like most second generation Palatinate Germans, she speaks both English and German.

"I'm an honest woman," she tells Elisabeth, "and I tell you bluntly that I'm looking for a home that will want me to stay with them, even when I get old. I'm tired of moving here and there, I want a home to call my own. I work hard and I'll care for yours as I would my own. If that suits you, I'll stay. "

It suits.

She has one of the loft bedrooms in the Baltzer house while Gertrud and Evie share the other. Christof and Peter sleep in the main room.

Minna is as industrious as she is talkative and soon has them organized. Elisabeth cares for her own house and prepares lunch; Minna takes care of the other house and prepares dinner for everyone.

Now that she has time to receive them, Catherine and Victoria call on Elisabeth in the afternoon. Occasionally, they arrive on the same afternoon which produces some awkward moments. Catherine is still apprehensive about associating with someone's mistress, even Captain Sutherland's. Victoria's curly red hair does not help her image. Unless ruthlessly anchored under her bonnet, it sends out curly red wisps that frame her heart shaped face in a most unladylike way. And she smiles readily, and she laughs a lot, and she attracts men's eyes, but she is Elisabeth's friend.

Victoria on the other hand, considers Catherine to be prickly and judgmental; altogether too ready to tell others how to live their lives, and she has a habit of smirking when she is right. Victoria has had her fill of prudes and narrow mindedness, but she is Elisabeth's friend.

Elisabeth admires the fine qualities in both of them. They are not unalike, both have chosen difficult lives and dote on difficult men, neither has any family and neither find it easy to make friends. She admires their tenacity and loyalty, their determination to live life their own way and their capacity to be strong in a crisis. And they are both loyal friends.

This afternoon they arrive together. Elisabeth is at her hearth, alone with her embroidery frame in hand, completing a floral edging on a baby's gown. The younger children are napping under the eagle eye of Minna and all the others are out.

"Bonjour. Willkommen," she greets them.

It is a complicated three-sided conversation when they are together.

When the pleasantries are done, Catherine puts down her cup and says, "I have some wonderful news to share. I'm expecting a baby, Bernhard and I are going to have a child next year."

"Catherine," exclaims Elisabeth, "that is indeed wonderful news. Congratulations."

By their happy faces and gestures, Victoria understands the gist of the conversation. She smiles and says, "I'm so happy for you. That is happy tidings to hear."

Catherine is blushing and looks happy, her face has lost its pinched look and her posture is relaxed.

"I have been waiting for so long for this to happen. Bernhard was pleased when I told him. Now that Catherine Elisabeth is married and poor Henrietta dead of the influenza and Mary Elisabeth planning her wedding, the house would be so quiet with no family in it. Bernhard is either out or reading in his little room, this will be good for him."

"He must be proud to be a father again, to have a young family about the table to dote on," Victoria tells her.

"I am very happy for you both," repeats Elisabeth. "Is everything going well?" she asks out of habit and concern. Catherine is only twenty, but she is thin and has worked hard all her life.

"Oh, yes, I feel wonderful, better than I ever have," she answers. "It has been no problem at all. All I want is for Bernhard to be proud of me, to be pleased with me. I don't think he would like somebody being sick all the time."

"Surely he is proud of you already," says Elisabeth. "You keep his house in fine order and have cared for his daughters as though you were their mother. You are the best of wives."

Victoria tells her, "I know what you mean about feeling sick though, Patrick didn't like it either. He doesn't much care for sick people, especially women. Fortunately, I rarely felt sick. Men can be so particular. How do they think babies get born?"

"They want them, but don't want the bother until they are properly grown up," Catherine replies. They smile at each other.

"They can be so particular about things, about the way things are done," Victoria comments with an indulgent smile.

"Oh, yes, I know just what you mean. They must have their chair, their cup and the water must be just right for their drinks," agrees Catherine.

They have found something in common. Meanwhile, Elisabeth thinks, "Why would a man not want to see his children growing up, hear them learn to talk, walk and become part of the family?"

Thoughts of Stoffel and Adam cross her mind, to her knowledge neither of them ever said an angry word about children in the house nor at the table, as long as they were well behaved. Without thinking she rests her hand on her stomach. Her friends stay a while longer and depart, together as they had arrived, but this time arm in arm. Elisabeth thinks about her friends as she sets the table.

Victoria has recovered, at least on the outside, from the death of her infant son and her life with Patrick has settled into a routine. He comes in time for supper and spends the evening with her. She never speaks of marriage. Thorold's cradle still sits beside her bed with his blankets folded in it.

Catherine has never looked so radiant and confident. Bernhard is more than thirty years older than her and set in his ways. He is an indifferent father to his daughters, taking care of their material needs, but wasting little affection on them. He is accustomed to a well run adult household. Will he welcome the intrusion of an infant?

Adam returns home, tired, but pleased with himself. His team of young oxen have successfully hauled their training logs in tandem for a mile without breaking form. He declares them ready for use.

"I have the first team that is ready to work; that is good. People will know our name when they need the oxen. Anyhow, there will soon be more than enough work for two, maybe three, teams. Tomorrow I will take them to the farm and put them to the test," he announces with satisfaction, "and show them off to my friends."

"You are not the only one with an announcement," she tells him. "I, too, have news.

He looks at her to hear what it is.

She puts a hand on his arm, "You are to be a father again, my husband, next March sometime if I have it right," she says.

"You are expecting a child?" he asks just to be sure he has heard correctly. "I mean, we are going to have a baby? Our baby."

"Yes, that is what I mean; I am going to have our baby, husband."

His face shows bewilderment, astonishment and then happiness.

"This is welcome news. I just had never thought of it. Of course, we can have another baby, we can have many babies. We can have a big family, babies and grandchildren together in our house." He grabs her in a huge hug and plants a noisy kiss on top of her head. "We are going to have a baby." She smiles into his shoulder; this is an easy man to please, *"Thank you, Lord."*

As she falls asleep, she realizes that she, too, is beginning to feel the inner comfort of happiness again. Then she remembers the last time she dared to feel happiness and the disasters that followed.

"*Dear God,*" she prays, "*it is not wrong to be happy, do not punish me anymore, I've paid enough. For whatever I have done, forgive me. Let me again walk in your grace and feel the comfort of your love. Watch over my children and keep them from harm. Bless this tiny life within my body that it will be strong and healthy and ready for this world. Amen.*"

To her surprise, Catherine pays her another visit the next afternoon.

"I have come for only a moment," she says. "I didn't want to mention it yesterday. It is about Anna," she points in the direction of the Wirth house. "I visit her from time to time, just to see how she is doing."

Elisabeth remembers Catherine's concern for the young girl at the time her son was born and at her marriage. The town has a long memory and probably let's her know they remember her indiscretion in subtle, and not so subtle, ways. With Maria married, she does not see Anna often although they are neighbours.

"I remember your concern for her," she says. "Is anything wrong?"

"I think so, but I am not sure. She is not happy, I am sure of that. Tobias spends most of his time out on his farm where he has built another house. He is out at La Havre. She told me she refuses to move out there, so she is here with the two boys."

Elisabeth recalls the boys, Tobias' son Georg about seven or eight years now and little Isaac Alexander two years old. Georg could be a hand full, energetic and adventurous. Many times Anna has asked Peter to go in search of him.

Catherine continues, "I visited her yesterday before I came here. She had been crying. The house was not clean and she was still in her night clothes. Isaac Alexander was hungry and had not been bathed or changed. She told me that Tobias had been here last Sunday and had taken his own son back to La Havre with him. She doesn't think he is coming back."

Elisabeth stares at her in consternation. "What are you saying? What is Tobias doing?"

"She thinks Tobias has left her, walked out on her. I don't know, but it can't continue," she answers. "What can we do?"

"Did you tell Bernhard?"

"He said to stay out of it, but I can't. Her family, the other Herman's, still do not like Tobias and will never forgive her for having a child out of wedlock."

"This is not good news. Do you want me to go and see her?" she asks Catherine. "I have been too busy to be a good neighbour these past months. I knew she was alone, but she has family here after all. Maria sees her, but has said nothing."

"Thank you, Elisabeth. I would like your assessment of this matter. Anna is a good girl, just young and full of fun. She had no mother to advise her wisely."

Elisabeth visits Anna that afternoon and then goes to talk to Maria.

"I think she's right; he may not be back. He told me he has a well built house at La Havre," says Maria. "Anna likes to live in town, but there are people living out at their farms now, moving out of town. He is happy there and more settled, not so wild. Anna should go with him."

This is not exactly the story she heard from Anna, but it rings of the truth.

"She may have no choice," comments her mother, thinking to herself, women never seem to have many choices in this life.

As it happens, Tobias turns up and takes matters into his own hands by hiring Adam and his oxen to move all his belongings to La Havre. Anna is moving to the farm. There is no road, but there is a trail and the men load everything onto the two wheeled cart they use for logs. By the time Adam returns, he has an announcement for Elisabeth.

"We are moving, too," he says.

"What are you saying?" she exclaims in dismay.

"We should move, this house is too small, I never fixed it properly like Stoffel did his. So we should move."

"What are you talking about?" Elisabeth demands.

Adam has his chuckle. "Don't look so alarmed, wife, next door, we will move into Tobias' house which has a larger lot and more sun. Here we are practically in a stream during the spring. It is a small house, but we can make it bigger. We will need a larger house now, yes?" he teases, patting his belly. "Don't worry; your children will still be next door," he assures her. "Do you think I would take you from your family?"

"You would have trouble doing that," she tells him. "What will we do with this house?"

"Hush, leave all of that to me. Go and look at Tobias' house and think about what you would like your new house to be. I know a man who might buy this one, or trade for it. He has just come from Halifax."

Left with no options, Elisabeth takes the children and walks through her back yard to Anna's little house. She goes inside and opens up the window shutter, the doors of the dry sink and corner cabinet. There is only the one room, but there is a solid wooden floor and she sees no chinks in the walls or roof. The hearth is hugely out of proportion to the size of the room; Tobias must have planned to make it larger at some time. It draws well though, she remembers from her visits. The sleeping shelf is large and built next to the chimney for warmth. She feels it is a sad little house, one that has never been filled with joy.

She shakes her head to clear out the fantasies and announces to herself, "We will change that. This will be a house of happiness now, filled with laughter and good times. You will protect us during the storms both of weather and life. Hear that, house? Hear that, God? We will make this a house of blessings. I have had enough sorrow."

She laughs at herself and hopes no one is within hearing distance.

"Yes," she affirms to herself, "I am going to dare to be happy again."

Three Kings' Day is both happy and sombre this year of our Lord, 1757, happy within the love of those present and sombre with memories of the loved ones who are absent.

The family gathers with Elisabeth and Adam in their refurbished house. It is a day to bless the house and those who live within by paying homage to the Christ child as did the three kings of old, Caspar, Melchior and Balthasar. Over the door Adam has painted C+M+B in white wash in the old country style. Inside, they exchange gifts and wish each other blessings for the year ahead. Elisabeth has embroidered in blue thread "Christus mansionem benedictat" on a square of newly woven linen which Peter framed for her and placed over the bed. Melchior had taught her that phrase, and for a moment she remembers things past. The story of the Three Wise Kings is retold by Adam as they listen intently. She looks at the faces of Bettina and Ferdi who are now old enough to sit still and listen. Their eyes never leave Adam's face as he describes the visit of the magi to the baby Jesus.

When he finishes, he looks at them and smiles. "We have much to remember, and much to celebrate. I am very grateful that we are together and wish each of you the best for the year to come. *God bless all of you,*" he says.

"*Amen,*" repeats Elisabeth. "*God bless all of us, and all of those whom we love, both here and absent.*"

15

FULL CIRCLE

Elisabeth sits in the rocking chair with the bear skin seat in front of the burning hearth, colourful beads decorate the shoes she wears. In front of her is an open trunk, it is empty and the contents are laid carefully on the bed. In her lap rests a small wooden box decorated in intricately painted designs. The oak has blackened with age and the painted flowers have faded. Its leather hinges are brittle and worn. The lock has an elaborate metal escutcheon, and in her hand she holds a small intricately worked key. She is alone in the house except for her baby daughter, Catherine Elisabeth, two months old, asleep in a wooden cradle beside her.

Five years ago today, she and Stoffel had boarded the *Sally* and left all they knew forever. Looking around her, at the furniture Adam and Peter have made, at the new bedcover and cushions her friends have given her, at her new daughter, she knows that this place and these people have become her home. It is time to put the past away.

She unlocks the box and from it she carefully removes the items, putting them on her lap. She holds each one gently, looking at them and remembering, before she places them gently back in the box.

There is a pair of green ribbons which Stoffel had bought for her at the fair in Bracht when they were courting. She smiles as she remembers how clumsy he had been as he tried to tie them to the ends of her long braids. A roll of vellum tied with a white ribbon is her marriage certificate. Inside it is the posy of dried edelweiss which she had carried in her hand on her wedding day.

303

She unrolls two little bundles of linen, each with a long curl inside, a blond one from Christof when he had his first hair cut and a dark brown one from Peter. Christof had been stoic, she remembered him sitting with eyes squeezed shut and his lips in a grim pout; Peter had wiggled, trying to see what she was doing, she had been afraid she would nip him with the scissors. She puts them back in the box. Yellow, red and blue ribbons from the sashes of the dresses worn by her daughters on their first birthday follow. Wrapped in soft wool are an inexpensive child's locket and a toy whistle, treasures belonging to her two first children, dead of the scarlet fever long ago.

There is also an oval brooch of her mother's, a black and white cameo in a silver setting with the clasp broken off in a long ago mishap, and a frame with a mourning flower made of her mother's hair twisted and tied with purple ribbon. The worn piece of stag horn had belonged to her father's cane; it had snapped one day and she had begged the piece. Dressed in the bright *tract* of her homeland is a carved wooden pocket doll her father had given her over forty years ago. She returns them to their place in the box.

She takes from the pile on her lap, a man's handkerchief with "JCB" embroidered in the corner, delicately done so that it appears the same on both sides, a gift to Stoffel from his mother. A man's leather pocket and waist thong remain. It is worn smooth and stained with sweat; Stoffel had worn it every day after she gave it to him as a betrothal gift. She had removed it when she washed him for his burial. She adds this to the items in the box and closes it. Around it she wraps a black ribbon which she ties in a neat knot. She holds it to her breast for a moment before she lays it in the bottom of the trunk. This is the past, the memories of an earlier life.

From the table beside her, she picks up a new wooden box with delicate carving on the lid. It is a hand span wide and deep and two long, decorated with delicate carving, another piece of Peter's handiwork. A small pile of things are gathered on the table beside it.

From it she takes a lace edged handkerchief with the initials "MVD" and tiny flowers embroidered in one corner. It is Victoria's, loaned during the birth of Bettina and kept in memory of their meeting and that dramatic day.

A baby's bonnet pieced together from an old petticoat belonged to Bettina.

There is another baby's bonnet, a delicate one that has never been worn. Elisabeth made it for Catherine's baby, but it wasn't to be. The tiny premature girl had been stillborn two days after Three Kings' Day, on the first anniversary of Stoffel's death. That had been a terrible day. It had been Victoria who held Catherine for hours as she wept and hovered between life and death during the ordeal. Here in this very room, but it had brought the two women together; grief shared. She can't bear to give it to another baby; it goes into the box.

The scrap of bodice lace is left over from the edging on the one Maria wore on her marriage day. How beautiful and happy she had been. And seems to be, thanks be to God.

Another packet encloses a baby curl of Ferdi's. Ferdi is her responsibility now and she will care for it with her own things. She had found it in Margarete's trunk along with a ring and a brooch. The jewellery she has wrapped in one of her friend's handkerchiefs and will give it to Ferdi when he comes to adulthood. Until then, they can stay in the box.

There is a dried bouquet of spring mayflowers in a roll of birch bark from a bouquet Anne left at her doorstep in the spring of '54. Elisabeth looks up. There are other reminders of Anne everywhere, in her dried herb containers, in her herb garden, and in the woods of Lunenburg, of Merlegueche. At Azelie's spring. She strokes the smooth arm of the rocking chair and stretches her toes inside the moccasins, yes, Anne is everywhere. It is as though she has been left with a legacy, not only an obligation to remember the past and what Anne has taught her, but to care for the knowledge, and make sure the memory of Merlegueche is not forgotten.

A button remains in her lap. It is brass with an eagle embossed on it. It could be anybody's, her father's, an uncle's. A piece of leather thong is threaded through it and tied into a knot. She holds it in her hand. It had come off in her hand, off the great coat Melchior wore in rain and snow, on the day they parted. She had meant to sew it back on, but she had not had the chance. She wonders if the coat is still missing a button; if he thinks of her when he notices its absence. She could have made another choice. Why hadn't she?

He would have stayed here, settled down as a Lunenburger and been a wise and respected man, good to her children and faithful to her. There would have been time for their talks and long walks, mornings to watch the rising sun and evenings to savour the glorious sunsets. Melchior would have told her of America, of the Indians and Acadians, they would have explored the woods and learned its secrets. She sighed, not in regret for her choice, but for lost dreams. "Man proposes, God disposes." Another of her father's wisdom sayings.

Elisabeth believes there is always one choice more right than another. For her, the right choice is the one most defensible before God when she comes to the end of her days on earth. She has spent her life following her God and her conscience; she cannot change now. God sends his faithful temptation and opportunity, sorrow and joy, death and birth. The test of courage and faith is in how a person reacts to these circumstances, and how much one learns from them. Such things are sent for a purpose, one must seek the purpose.

Marrying Melchior would, for her, have been the selfish choice, the one based on her own desires. In the end, her guilt over that would have destroyed their love.

"May God keep you safe and grant you grace, dear heart."

There is a handkerchief in her pocket, a man's fine linen handkerchief. She removes it. It is carefully washed and ironed. Tenderly, she folds it around the button and places it in the box which she closes, but does not tie. There will be more memories to add in the years ahead.

She gathers the box to her breast, kneels before the trunk and gently puts it beside the other before refilling it with the clothes and covers she stores on top. She closes the lid, but keeps her hands on the trunk and bows her head.

"Himmlischer Vater, Heavenly Father, this is Anna Elisabeth. I have lived so much happiness and so much sorrow, yet it can be put away in two small boxes. More has happened in these past five years than in the rest of my lifetime. Please, dear Lord, may this remain so until the end of my days. I am ready for peace. Take care of those I love, bring quietness to their minds and favour them with your grace. Amen."

She stands, returns the keys to their pockets and tenderly lifts her newest baby into her embrace. Walking out into the sunshine, she amends a line from Psalms to suit her thoughts.

"This is the life which the Lord hath given me; I shall rejoice and be glad in it."

* * *

Author's After Words

The story of Anna Elisabeth is true in all its historical facts. The personal story is created from the possibilities between the facts. To weave the facts together, two major fictional characters are added: Victoria Downing and Melchior Seiler; the other Lunenburg people are from the historical records with the exception of Noel Rousse and Azelie.

Anna Elisabeth is one of my paternal ancestors. She was born, Anna Elisabeth Weber, in 1712 in Rosenthal, Hesse, the Germanies. At the age of 18, she married Johannes Christoffel Baltzer, age 19, who had moved from Bracht, a nearby village, to Rosenthal. He was a butcher, first in Rosenthal and later in Marburg where, as recently as 1995, there was still a Baltzer butcher shop; however, by 1997 it had been sold. In the days of Johannes Christoffel, butchers were middle to upper middle class people, so they were likely a modestly wealthy family. Almost assuredly they were German Lutheran in faith.

They had eight children, two of whom died, probably of a childhood illness, during the summer of 1738. This means that Anna Elisabeth lost two of her three children that summer, her 7 year old daughter and her four year old son. She also had a baby, a year old son, Heinrich Christoffel, the Christof who came to Nova Scotia. At this point they moved to Marburg where she had four more children. She was a middle-aged woman of 40 years with five children under fifteen years of age when she left her German homeland in 1752 for the unknown colony of Nova Scotia where she lived another thirty years, was widowed and remarried, and bore five more children.

The Baltzers arrived aboard the *Sally* on September 6ᵗʰ, 1752, which was the last of the Protestant Settler ships. By this time, the English realized that this grand scheme to defend territory, establish dominion and make a profit was not feasible.

The *Sally* was a standard ship for the time, but unspeakably rough by today's standards. The migrants were carried between decks where the average headspace was just over five feet and a floor area six feet by six feet was allotted for four adults. Children under 15 were considered half an adult, children under four received no space allotment. It is likely that the Baltzers were allotted a six by six foot space for all seven of them as the record shows that Stoffel was charged for 3 ½ adults. A shelf would have been built over their platform as sleeping space for the younger children giving them headroom of less than three feet.

Ships rations were scanty and the water often spoiled. Worms and maggots in the provisions and slimy green algae in the water would have been common by the end of the voyage. Rations consisted mostly of boiled beef, salt pork and salt cod, rice, barley, groats and dried peas, ship's biscuits, treacle, beer and rum or gin—as long as it lasted. Any washing down of quarters would have been done with water and vinegar.

Medical care was non-existent although a ship's surgeon was shown as having passage on the boat. The mortality rate was higher on the *Sally* than on any other ship of the emigration; 15.5% of the passengers died, including the Captain. They spent fourteen weeks aboard the *Sally*, plus three weeks in ship board quarantine upon arrival, a total of seventeen weeks; it was the longest of all the trans-Atlantic voyages for this settler program.

During their voyage, the Reformed Gregorian calendar was adopted by England and her overseas colonies, thus September was adjusted by the elimination of eleven days; 2ⁿᵈ September 1752 was followed by 14ᵗʰ September 1752. So when we read that the *Sally* departed Rotterdam on 30ᵗʰ May and arrived Halifax on 6ᵗʰ September, it is a date that did not exist in that year, it would have been already September 17ᵗʰ. Allowing for these eleven days but adding the three weeks aboard a river raft to reach Rotterdam, it is possible that the Baltzers had been en route 119 days in conditions of filth, hunger and crowded squalor before landing in Nova Scotia. They all survived; thirty-nine others did not.

During the last two hundred and fifty years, the children of Anna Elisabeth Baltzer-Schaffner settled throughout the Annapolis Valley of Nova Scotia, clearing land and developing farms, opening up the wilderness and helping to establish the network of roads that connect the villages of the Valley with those along the Bay of Fundy shore.

Elisabeth, Stoffel and their children were on the last ship of the short-lived Protestant Settler Movement, a movement conceived to provide a loyal bulwark against the French Acadians, crops to feed the British military, timber for their war ships and a Protestant counterpart to the Catholic French. What the London recruiters did not realize, or refused to acknowledge, was that Nova Scotia was a colony in its infancy, mostly a military foothold to protect British interests in the emerging conflict between France and England for commercial domination of the New World. Despite the promises of the recruitment handbill, when they arrived in Nova Scotia, there were no homesteads for them, no cleared farmland, no preparations even to feed or house them through the approaching winter. In fact, on the grounds that they had already been recruited, the five ships carrying 401 families arriving in Halifax during the summer of 1752 did so after the Governor of Nova Scotia requested that no more be sent because he had neither accommodation nor rations for them.

The plan to insert them into existing Acadian villages was not workable—they would have been killed—and no other land was ready for homesteading. The British lived mainly in the garrison at Piziquid, now Windsor, Annapolis Royal and in the newly founded garrison city of Halifax. The south shore of Nova Scotia, where the British decided to locate the settlers, was not farm land. It was mainly bog, rock and forest, unsuitable for farming. The best farm land was the Annapolis Valley which was already inhabited by the Acadians. Any other inland areas would have left the settlers at risk from Indian attack.

The Annapolis Valley is a 150 kilometre stretch of old marine bed running east-west from the Annapolis Basin in the west to the Minas Basin in the east, present day Annapolis Royal to Grand Pré, protected north and south by a low ridge of mountains. In the time of the Baltzers' arrival, it was heavily forested with a scattering of land cleared for mixed farming connected to each other and to Halifax by a rutted seasonal road, muddy in the spring and fall, frozen in winter and often impassable. Settlement was clustered mainly around Annapolis Royal and Grand Pré.

The expulsion of the Acadians between 1755–64 from British lands in Nova Scotia, changed the commercial opportunities of the newly arrived German settlers. While the area around Lunenburg continued to fell timber, clear the shallow rocky soil for farmland, develop a fishing industry and build its economic base, the fertile land already cleared by the Acadians along the Annapolis Valley became available to Protestant settlers. The German settlers were not given the same incentives in land and money that the New Englanders or demobbed soldiers were offered, but opportunities for commerce were better there than on the south shore.

The Baltzers were not farmers, and certainly not fishermen; they were trades people with a bent for commerce rather than agriculture. In Stoffel's case, he was a butcher which made him a respected middle class merchant. Why would a successful tradesman immigrate to a primitive colony? Interesting and pointless speculation, but a fascinating exercise.

The Hessian region of the Germanies had been in turmoil for decades: the War of the Spanish Succession, the War of the Austrian Succession, the Three Years' War between Hesse and Hanover, continuous demands for taxes and men to pay for the war efforts; agitation between the Roman Catholic and Protestant movements; constant interference by the state in the affairs of the common people; the formation of the Hessian mercenary regiments that recruited young men and boys to fill the royal coffers and the opening up of opportunities in the New World. Many Baltzer families had migrated to the Americas in the great Palatine emigrations of the early eighteenth century. On the more speculative side, perhaps Johannes Christoffel's expectations were not as personally optimistic as he had hoped; although he was the oldest recorded son perhaps he was not the owner of the butchery but merely family labour; perhaps he had had enough government interference and wanted to try a new life; perhaps the idea of clean air and open spaces seemed better than the crowed urban chaos of Marburg. For certain, they both must have viewed it as an opportunity for their children.

Christof and Peter Baltzer did not remain in Lunenburg. In 1764, with their mother remarried and settled, Christof, 27, and Peter, 22, along with their unmarried sisters, Gertrud and Evie, moved to the Annapolis Royal area. Elisabeth (Bettina) remained with her mother and Adam in Lunenburg. About this time, the spelling of their names changed; Baltzer became Balsor, Schauffner, Shaffner. Other variations often occurred among the illiterate church and community record keepers, and government census takers.

Six years later, Anna Elisabeth and Adam and their four children followed. They settled on a point of land which became, and still is, Shaffner's Point, a few kilometers west along the Annapolis River from Granville Ferry. This habit of selling land for profit and moving to a better location was one that persisted throughout the years. Records of land transactions are frequent throughout the historic record. My father, six generations later, did the same thing to survive the Great Depression of 1929. Anna Elisabeth and Adam Schauffner lived here another twelve years, until their deaths in 1782. They died five months apart, aged 70 and 79 respectively. Today the place is marked by an electric lighthouse near the edge of the water. There are no remains of their homestead nor, indeed, of the family cemetery where they were probably buried.

In the summer of 2003, I searched without luck for their grave stones, although one person said that he thought there was an old family cemetery back in the woods behind what would have been their property. Too, I found no marker of Stoffel's burial site in Lunenburg. Did he die of an accident or of the epidemic that invaded the town site in 1755? Anna Elisabeth kept all of her children alive on the voyage across the Atlantic, through the harsh winter in Halifax, successfully birthed a baby sometime that spring and winter and lost none of her subsequent children. I do not think he died of illness. It was a hard life of physical labour and he was a man in his mid-forties; hence, a medical event or an accident are also reasonable options. The only information in his death record is the fact of his death.

Family lore hints that Stoffel Baltzer and Adam Schauffner knew each other back in the old country. It also tells that Adam was very good to Stoffel's children. Certainly, the historic record shows that they remained in contact and continued to live in the same area of the Valley.

In 1775, Heinrich Christoffel Baltzer (Christof), from whom I am descended, married Lydia Woodbury, the eldest daughter of Dr.

Jonathon Woodbury who moved from Massachusetts to Nova Scotia during the Planter migrations of 1760–70. By now he is 38 years old and calling himself Christopher Balsor; Lydia was 15 years old. They had 11 children. Peter had married Hannah Zeiglar three years earlier. Some twenty years later, Christof and Peter moved eastward to the Wilmot area where they remained for the rest of their lives.

A year later, 1766, Anna Catharine Gertrud Balsor (Gertrude/Carey/Garey) married Hans George Heinrich Schenkel (Henry Shankle) in Granville Township. Henry Shankle and Garey (Baltzer) had four children according to the Granville Township register.

It is not known what happened to Ana Eva Baltzer or Elisabeth Baltzer/Schaffner.

The prototype for Anna Elisabeth is my Grandmother Balsor, herself a descendent of a family who arrived on the Protestant Settler ships. My father was her eldest son and he, like Christof, married a daughter of one of the Planter families from New England. Like Elisabeth, Grandmother Balsor married young, raised a large family, was widowed and remarried. Never wealthy but equally never poor, she believed in hard work, self reliance, kindness and generosity to ones' neighbours, a benevolent God and doing one's duty. She lived by the Golden Rule and expected others to do the same. If there were trouble in a family, they could depend on her to turn up with a home remedy and a pot of stew.

These German families did not scatter quickly nor far from their Nova Scotia communities. Their names, memories and bloodlines permeate the Annapolis Valley, colour their language and lore, flavor their recipes and bind them to each other as surely as they did 250 years ago.